Christian

Christian Tyler is a former staff writer of the *Financial Times* of London. He
has reported on industry, politics and international trade, and has travelled
widely in China. He is married to the actress Ciaran Madden, has three
children and a stepchild, and lives in Dorset.
This is his first book.

WILD WEST CHINA

The Untold Story of a Frontier Land

Christian Tyler

JOHN MURRAY

The illustrations that appear on pp. iii, vi, 1 and 127
are by Ciaran Madden

First published in Great Britain in **2003**
by John Murray (Publishers)
A division of Hodder Headline

Paperback edition **2004**

2 4 6 8 10 9 7 5 3

Copyright © **2003** by **Christian Tyler**

A CIP catalogue record for this title is available from the British Library

ISBN 0-7195-6341 0

Typeset in Monotype Bembo
by Servis Filmsetting Ltd, Manchester

Printed and bound in Great Britain by
Clays Ltd, St Ives plc

John Murray (Publishers)
338 Euston Road
London
NW1 3BH

This book is dedicated to the memory of my mother, who had been looking forward to it, and to my father, who has lived to see it.

Contents

Illustrations

The author and publisher would like to thank the following for permission to reproduce photographs: Plate 1, © Mark Kitto; 2, from Fang Zhao and Zhi Yongyu, *The Legend of the Desert King* (China National Silk Road Museum and the Xinjiang Institute of Archaeology); 3, © Jeffrey Newbury/Corbis Sygma; 4, The Metropolitan Museum of Art, Gift of the Dillon Fund, 1973 (1973.120.3). Photograph © 1994 The Metropolitan Museum of Art; 6, 7, 8 and 9, from Sven Hedin, *Big Horse's Flight* (London, Methuen, 1926); 10, © Ian Cumming/Corbis; 11, © Reza/Corbis Sygma; 12, © Ellis Richard/Corbis Sygma; 14, © Bohemian Nomad Picturemakers/Corbis; and 16, © Travelpictures.co.uk. Plates 5, 13 and 15 are from the author's collection.

Foreword

IF THE TITLE of this book sounds a little paradoxical, perhaps I ought to explain it. The Chinese have always regarded their far west with a mixture of fascination and fear. Europeans used to fantasize about the 'mysterious Orient', even while losing sleep over the Yellow Peril. America's pioneers shuddered at the cruelty of the Red Indians, noble savages who murdered and scalped white women. In the same way the Chinese have romanticized, even while they have tried to suppress, the 'barbarians' of Xinjiang.

This Chinese variant of orientalism was neatly illustrated for me in the film *Crouching Tiger, Hidden Dragon*, which came out while I was researching the book. At one point in the film the camera cuts to a wagon-train of horse-drawn carriages and pack-camels lumbering along a rocky corridor between high bluffs in China's western desert. Inside the leading carriage, toying with a jade comb, sits the heroine, the pretty 18-year-old daughter of the Governor of Xinjiang who is returning to Beijing with her family.

Suddenly, and invisible to the travellers below, a band of mounted and turbaned horsemen appears behind an outcrop. At a signal from their dashing young leader, the bandits draw their sabres and go whooping down the hill. Like Red Indians ambushing the Wells Fargo stagecoach, they race round the wagon-train, cutting down the escort and seizing the baggage.

In spite of her mother's pleas, our heroine cannot resist taking a peek out of the carriage window. The bandit leader catches sight of her and, lying forward on his horse's neck, gallops alongside the swaying carriage and looks in, his swarthy face only inches from hers. With a wink and a grin he snatches the comb from her hand.

The girl's curiosity turns to fury. Leaping from the carriage, she pulls down a passing bandit, jumps on to his horse and gives chase. Far out in the desert, she overtakes the comb-snatcher. The young couple tussle in the sand, and love blooms.

The bandit leader's *nom de guerre*, we later discover, is Dark Cloud, recalling the names of those Apache and Sioux warriors who, having been massacred by the rifles of the pioneers, were reconstituted as heroes by the camera lenses of Hollywood. *Crouching Tiger* was taken from a series of novels by Wang Du Lu (1909–77) who was writing Chinese 'Westerns' in the 1930s, at a time when Xinjiang had once again slipped from China's grasp.

Although this book is a history of Xinjiang, Chinese orientalism is in a sense its real theme. Compared with the Russians' conquest of Siberia or the Americans' trek to the Pacific, the colonization of Xinjiang has been late and difficult. Not until the Communists took power in 1949 was the province really developed – as a source of food, raw materials and living space for a starving and overpopulated country, but also as a penal colony for criminals and dissidents, a buffer against foreign invasion, and a nuclear testing-ground.

Xinjiang is more and more in the news, and this book is an attempt to explain the background to the present troubles in a region seen by Beijing as one of its biggest political headaches. For what China regards as its rightful property, the native Muslim people – like the Tibetans to the south of them – regard as theft by an alien occupier. Tension has led to violence, and to savage reprisals. Since the terrorist atrocities in the US, Beijing has cracked down more severely still.

My excuse for attempting a history of Xinjiang is that none has yet been written for the general reader. But I also wanted to convey something of the beauty of this wild and intimidating place, which I first saw in 1995 when I took part in a hundred-mile trek across the dunes of the Taklamakan desert. Then I was struck, as was the Chinese mandarin Aitchen Wu in the 1930s, by the people's ability to survive in a wilderness of 'great plains, and great mountains; smooth sands, and rocks so jagged that the stoutest leather seems to tear like paper at their touch; winds laden with knife-edged particles of ice, and blasts of air so hot that the lungs feel singed as they pass; peril by snow and storm, torture by thirst . . .'*

Later, I discovered the secret of their endurance. The native Uighurs show great stoicism and dignity. They conceal passionate natures beneath a social etiquette and an old-fashioned courtesy which seem quaint to us in the West. By our standards, too, their hospitality is extravagantly formal, but it is also warm-hearted and unaffected. Their way of life, in the tranquillity of the oases, cannot survive modern habits and seems doomed to disappear except in the remotest areas.

My notice was drawn to the ugly politics of Xinjiang by something quite trivial: the bullying behaviour of Han Chinese drivers towards the Uighurs who were walking or riding in their donkey-carts along the quiet oasis roads. I later discovered that Uighur drivers could be just as aggressive. But the contemptuous attitude of the Han colonists in general reminded me uncomfortably of some of Britain's own empire-builders: men like my great-great-grandfather who, appointed as a young ADC to the new Viceroy of India, Lord Canning, wrote home describing a pariah dog hunt: 'We crashed through everything scattering cows & niggers & their bamboo fences as if they were nothing.' Such callow insensitivity to alien cultures is still with us: I think of the American business-men I used to see in Beijing hotel lobbies, drunk, red-faced and roaring, losing face on a grand scale and making all us 'big noses' look like barbarians.

Although I describe China's treatment of Xinjiang as colonial, I have not set out to write a polemic. My preference is to let readers seek truth from facts, as the Chinese say. Besides, I agree with Peter Fleming that 'to read a propagandist, a man with vested intellectual interests, is as dull as dining with a vegetarian'. *News from Tartary*, Fleming's account of his journey in 1935 through southern Xinjiang with Ella Maillart *en route* from Beijing to Kashmir, was one of my favourite books as a boy. Fleming had reported on the Japanese occupation of China for *The Times* and professed a liking for Japanese people; but he had plenty of harsh

---

* Wu, *Turkistan Tumult*, p. 254.

things to say about their leaders. That is exactly my feeling about the Chinese and *their* leaders. Most Chinese I have met on their home ground have been delightful company; it is their bureaucrats and policies in Xinjiang which I find objectionable.

A series of coincidences occurred while I was preparing for my first visit to Xinjiang. I learned of the Taklamakan desert trip by chance while confined to bed with a bad back, and determined to sign up for it. When I rang a friend at the British Library for advice on reading matter, I discovered not only that she was cataloguing the archaeologist Aurel Stein's haul of manuscripts from Dunhuang but that she and the entire Oriental and India Office collection were temporarily housed a short walk from my office. Fate seemed to be on my side.

Then I wanted to learn to speak some Uighur. Uighurs were a rare commodity in Britain eight years ago, but I found one who happened to be living half a mile from my house in London. This was a great stroke of luck, for he became crucial to the entire venture. Things were being made oddly easy. Next, the British agent for the Taklamakan expedition agreed to meet me at his flat in South Kensington: it turned out to be a few doors down from the house where I was born. Again by chance, Charles Blackmore's book describing his crossing of the Taklamakan landed on my desk for review. Lastly, a few days before leaving, I was being given lunch by a friend at the Athenaeum when I saw Wilfred Thesiger, the doyen of desert explorers, lunching at the next table. Having interviewed him some time before, I felt able to go over and tell him that his books were partly to blame for my desire to visit the fearsome Taklamakan. 'In that case,' he replied, with a lugubrious smile, 'you can give me part of the credit – if you come back.'

I did come back, determined to help put Xinjiang on the map and to counteract some of the official propaganda about the disloyal and sinister motives of the Uighurs. I was further encouraged to discover I was not the only one taking an interest. In October 2000, I read that a three-year 'Xinjiang Project' involving leading scholars and promising to be 'the most comprehensive, authoritative writing project on the Xinjiang region ever undertaken' was being launched at Johns Hopkins University in the United States.

My more modest hope for this book is that those who know a little about Xinjiang will learn a lot more, and that those who know a lot may learn a little.

The book falls into two parts. The four chapters of Part I cover the history of the region up to the founding of the People's Republic of China in 1949. The first four chapters of Part II deal with events and policies under Communist rule, and the last two with the present situation of the Uighurs inside and outside their country. Readers who are mainly interested in current affairs may wish to skip the first part. In the postscript I ask whether the Uighurs' apparent desire for real autonomy has any chance whatever of being satisfied.

Although in writing this history I have used contemporary accounts as much as possible, it will be obvious that I owe a great debt to the small (but growing) band of present-day scholars who take an interest in Xinjiang. In particular I would like to mention the work of Christoph Baumer, Andrew Forbes, Ho-Dong Kim, Fu-Hsiang Lee, Colin Mackerras, James Millward and Denis Sinor.

Special thanks are due to Susan Whitfield, an historian of China, for her encouragement, introductions and help with useful monographs – not to mention her own book on the early history of the Silk Road. She was kind enough to read this book in proof. My friend Andro Linklater acted as writer's counsellor. Enver Tohti Bugda, who became a friend, brought me invaluable material and contacts. Other Uighurs to whom I owe thanks are General Riza Bekin and Enver Can. There are many more, living inside Xinjiang, who must for their own safety remain anonymous.

Nicolas Becquelin sent me his excellent analysis of the Western Development Plan; Hakan Walquist, keeper of the Sven Hedin Foundation in Stockholm, told me the story of the wandering village. To Dru Gladney I owe a number of acute observations and my thanks for reading Chapter 9. Among the many people whose expertise I profited from I would like to mention my camelophile fellow-traveller John Rabinowitz, and Deniz Cole. I am grateful to researchers at Amnesty International and the Tibet Information

Network, to Merilyn Hywel-Jones, of the Royal Society for Asian Affairs who dug out papers for me, and to Caroline Westmore at John Murray who helped find the photographs.

Gail Pirkis, my editor, forced me to give the material proper shape. Without her enthusiasm for the subject, her knowledge of China, her patience, persistence and skill, I doubt I should have got to the end. The book owes a lot to her: its remaining faults are mine. My grateful thanks go also to Kathleen Hopkirk for reading the book in draft and to Frances Wood for converting the historical Chinese names to pinyin.

Finally, I want to thank the two people without whom I probably would not have even begun the project. One is Mamti: to him – to his guidance, wisdom, tact and endless good humour – I owe more than I can say. The story would have been very much poorer without him. The other is Ciaran, my wife, who not only shared with me the hardships of travel in Xinjiang – the Siberian blasts, choking dust-storms, cold water and bumpy roads – but also produced some beautiful drawings out of it. The book has been hard work for her, too, and without her loving support I could not have done it.

Maps

EARLY
CENTRAL ASIA

← To Rome
Constantinople

Black Sea

ASIA MINOR

Caspian Sea

Western Turks

Aral Sea

R. Jaxartes (Syr Darya)

R. Talas

TRANS-OXIANA

Khiva •

Tashkent •

ARAB CALIPHATE

• FERGHANA

• Samarkand

SOGDIANA

R. Oxus (Amu Darya)

PARTHIA

HINDU

GAND-HARA

• Jerusalem

BACTRIA

• Mecca

ARABIA

MC

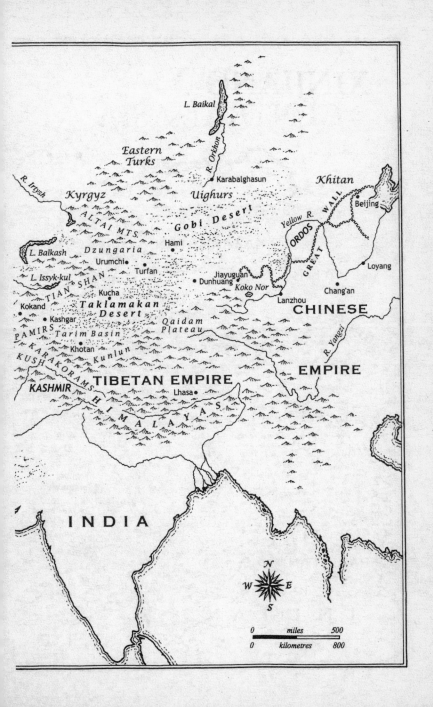

XINJIANG

Chuguchak

L. Balkash

KAZAKHSTAN

R. Ili

Gulja

Ili
Valley

L. Issyk-kul

T I A N   S H A N

Kucha

UZBEKI-
STAN

Andijan

KYRGYZSTAN

Uch
Turfan

Aksu

R. Tarim

Tarim

P A M I R S

Maralbashi

TAKLAM
DESER

Opal   Kashgar
Baren

R. Yarkand

R. Khotan

Merket

Karadong
Tongguzbasti

TAJIKISTAN

Yangi
Hissar

AFGHAN-
ISTAN

Tashkurgan

Yarkand

Dandan-
Oilik

Yawatongguz
Endere

R. Keriya

Kargalik

Khotan

Niya

K A R A K O R A M S

Keriya

ALT

PAKISTAN

KASHMIR

K U N L U N   M T S.

I N D I A

Srinagar

Leh

T I B

Part I
Beyond the Wall

I

In the Wilderness

WHAT THE SATELLITE sees as it hovers over the planet at night is a pattern of pinpricks of light, the phosphorescent trail of human habitation which every year grows more dense. From its aerial perch 100 miles high, the satellite's eye records not only the places where humans are so busily congregating but also the dark expanses where they are scarce or absent.[1]

One of the largest black holes in the Asian landmass is an egg-shaped void 300 miles wide and 700 miles long at the very centre of the continent. To its north, beyond a high mountain chain, is a smaller area, roughly triangular in shape. Together these two basins, the Tarim and Dzungaria, cover an area nearly as large as western Europe; they are a zone of desert, mountain and steppe separating the high plateau of Tibet from the endless forests of Siberia. Although constituting a sixth of the territory of China, this wilderness contains barely a sixtieth of China's population. The Chinese call it Xinjiang (literally, 'new frontier') or, more officially, the Xinjiang Uighur Autonomous Region, to acknowledge the presence of its indigenous people, the 8 million or more Uighurs. The Uighurs, however, call their land Eastern Turkestan.*

Separating the two basins is a long extension of the Heavenly Mountains (Tangri Tagh in Turkic, Tian Shan in Chinese) whose celestial name predates both Uighur and Han Chinese occupiers. To cross these mountains is to travel from one country to another, so different are their climates. The upper basin, Dzungaria, is an

---

* Xinjiang has had other names, used by different people at different times: Chinese Tartary, High Tartary, East Chagatay, Mugholistan, Chinese Turkestan, Kashgaria, Altishahr ('the six cities' of the Tarim), Little Bokhara and Serindia.

area of semi-desert, steppe and saline marshland bounded on the north-east by the Altai mountains and Mongolia, on the north-west by Kazakhstan and a 30-mile slice of Russia. An extension of the Gobi desert formerly populated by Mongols and now by the remnants of the Chinese Kazakhs, it is a cold, bleak place, damper and therefore marginally more hospitable than the desert to the south of the Tian Shan. Its name is said to be a corruption of 'Jinghiz' (Genghis) Khan, the Mongol warlord who ruled Asia in the thirteenth century. But some Hungarian scholars, following an ancient tradition, prefer to think it refers to the place from which their own people originated. Objects and writing unearthed in a graveyard first discovered a hundred years ago by the Hungarian-born archaeologist Aurel Stein near Urumchi, capital of Xinjiang, show strong affinities; and the songs of the local people, the 'Ugars', are said to fit the pentatonic scale of Hungarian folk music.

The lower basin, the Tarim, comprises the great sand sea of the Taklamakan desert, second in size only to the Rub al Khali, or Empty Quarter, of Arabia. Around its narrow shores, squeezed between mountains of sand and mountains of rock, are the oasis villages and towns that have defined the history of Xinjiang: on the southern rim Charklik, Cherchen, Niya, Keriya, Khotan, Kargalik and Yarkand, Yangi Hissar and Kashgar; on the northern rim Maralbashi, Aksu, Kucha, Korla and Turfan, with Hami flung out on its own to the east. In these tranquil places of mudbrick houses, trotting donkeys, whispering poplars and spreading fields, life is kept going by networks of irrigation channels laid down over centuries to capture the seasonal flood from glaciers thousands of feet above. On its eastern side the Tarim is defined by the pebble and rock of the Gobi desert, but elsewhere it is enclosed in a horseshoe of mountain ranges – in order clockwise from the south, the Kunlun, marking the northern edge of the Tibetan plateau, the Karakoram, the Hindu Kush, the Pamirs and the Tian Shan.

In addition to the Tarim and Dzungarian basins, two sub-regions are important to the story of Xinjiang. The first is the Ili valley to the west. Shaped like the head of an arrow pointing east-wards, it lies in the crook of the Tian Shan where two arms open out to the vast Kazakhstan steppe. The Ili valley is the most fertile part of Xinjiang, its steep alpine pastures reminiscent of

Switzerland. Where the two arms of the Tian Shan come together in a jumble of peaks south of Urumchi, a monument marks what is claimed to be the dead centre of Eurasia, equidistant from three oceans and the furthest point from any sea.

A second sub-region, one of Xinjiang's many geographical oddities, is the Turfan depression. It is one of the deepest inhabited places in the world. Lying beneath the southern slopes of the Tian Shan, halfway along their eastward extension, it falls to 300 feet below sea level and is rocked by occasional earthquakes. In summer, when the temperature climbs to 40 degrees centigrade or more, Turfan's inhabitants used to retreat to underground shelters during the day. Orchards and vineyards are irrigated from subterranean channels dug centuries ago to capture the precious snowmelt as it seeps through the desert. Early Western visitors were even more impressed by Turfan's vermin: the German explorer and archaeologist Albert von Le Coq recorded not only humble scorpions and fleas but also giant cockroaches with red eyes which sat on the sleeper's nose, and jumping spiders with great hairy bodies the size of pigeons' eggs whose jaws made an audible crunch.[2]

No one was alive to hear the great crunch that occurred when India rammed into the Eurasian landmass about a hundred million years ago to create the extreme geology seen today. Like the prow of a fighting ship, the northern edge of India embedded itself a hundred miles deep in the hull of Tibet. It threw up the Himalayan range and squeezed the rock of the Tibetan plateau like a concertina, doubling the thickness of its crust. Although knocked northwards by the blow, the Tarim basin seems to have withstood the force of the collision – which has been going on for millions of years – and transmitted the shockwave onwards where it pushed up the 20,000-foot peaks of the Tian Shan range, more than a thousand miles away from the point of impact.

Before the clash of continents, the Tarim basin and Tibet were under water, but all that now remains of the immense Tethys Sea, which covered the area to a depth of several thousand feet, are the fossils of marine creatures. As the water retreated, the basin was carpeted with a temperate, broadleaved forest interlaced by rivers. In one version of the story of Noah's Ark, it was not the Mesopotamian flood plain but the Tarim basin that God chose for the great inundation. No doubt the old mythmakers were impressed – as any visitor today must be – by the way in which this raw landscape, one of the driest on earth, is so clearly formed, moulded and scoured by water.

Beneath the Altun Tagh mountains, part of the southern Kunlun range that fringes the Tarim basin, the rough desert track is cut every hundred yards or so by the zigzag of a watercourse whose sandy bed is for most of the year as dry and cracked as an old snakeskin. In early summer the water comes blindly rushing through these channels, only to be swallowed by the pebble and sand of the wilderness. Out on the plain, growling dust devils whirl about like miniature waterspouts. From the rocky lintel of the Altun Tagh, the Taklamakan desert resembles a sea whose fury has been baffled by the great ribs of rock that reach into it like the groynes from a beach. The red and yellow ochre mountains themselves are being worn down by the action of water. Gullies run down their smooth shoulders, branching out at the base to form knuckles in the shape of lions' paws upon which the hills seem to rest like ancient colossi. Behind them, ramparts of grey-black denticulate rock rear like breaking waves suddenly arrested. Crazily paved mountain corridors run away to distant lakes which shimmer seductively in the heat but which, close to, mutate into dry expanses of salt. These false oases are ringed by xerophytic grasses whose desiccated fronds rattle in the ceaseless wind. Salt lies in every rut and crevice. It is as if a once lush landscape had been blasted dry in a nuclear explosion.

Yet what is left of the winter snows still runs beneath the earth; and autumn produces eruptions of colour in the apparently waterless river beds. Hardy tamarisk bushes show off flowers of pink or russet. Tufted pampas grasses wave dark gold plumes against the sun. A carpet of crimson sedum is spread below them as neatly as if it had been laid by a municipal gardener. Where the water succeeds in bubbling to the surface, the rare animals of the central Asian highlands congregate. Herds of the Tibetan wild ass (*Equus hemionus*, or *kiang*) gather in the mountain gorges. Belying their asinine name, they are shy and delicate creatures with reddish-brown backs and white bellies. When disturbed, their long, elegant legs carry them smartly up the steep sides of the ravines, their hooves leaving a smoke-trail of dust behind them.

When I was travelling through the Altun Tagh one autumn our party followed a herd of these beautiful creatures for a mile or two. We also surprised half a dozen black-and-white vultures, fat as turkeys, in the middle of a banquet. They were paddling about in the carcass of a big ram which had apparently toppled off an over-hanging ledge and now lay bloodily dismembered on the stream bed. His muzzle and huge ribbed horns lay propped on the ground like a hunting trophy. One of his eyes was out, his ribs and stomach were exposed and their contents strewn about the corpse; a foreleg had been torn off and dragged a short distance away. Caught red-handed by human intruders, the vultures tried to fly. But they had not enough room for take-off, or were too gorged to get airborne. So they hopped and waddled up the mountainside as fast as their legs would carry them, stopping occasionally to look back crossly at the creatures who had interrupted their feast.

The big-horned wild sheep which lay on the track is called *mouflon* in French, *argali* in Mongolian, and *Ovis ammon* in the zoological taxonomy. It is another rarity of the region. In the mid-nineteenth century the Russian explorer Nikolai Prejevalsky shot one in the Yulduz valley of the Tian Shan whose horns – so he said – measured 4ft 8in round the outside of the curve, were 1ft 6in thick at the base and weighed 36lb each. Prejevalsky may have been a braggart, but there is no reason to suppose this was sporting hyperbole: the animal on the mountain track in front of me was almost as large, and an even bigger *argali* skull hangs over the man-telpiece of the library of the Royal Society for Asian Affairs in Belgrave Square, London. Presented in 1945 by Lord Wavell, Viceroy of India, who got it from the British political agent at Gilgit, the horns of this specimen of *Ovis poli* (named after Marco Polo) are a fraction over six feet long.*

Once there were wild yaks in the Kunlun, and the Chinese claim that thirty tigers still inhabit the Tibetan plateau beyond. Like the snow leopard of the Himalayas and the western ranges of China,

---

* The record is said to be 6ft 3in.

these creatures are threatened by human encroachment, whether poachers, prospectors or – as seems inevitable – package tourists.

For years the mountains were mined for jade, reputed the best in China. Now the quest is for gold. In 1988, several hundred poor prospectors headed for the Aqqikkol basin, a plateau 14,000 feet up in the Altun Tagh at the point where Xinjiang, Qinghai and Tibet converge. The tableland had been declared a nature reserve by Beijing, but that deterred nobody. Two years later, there were 30,000 people panning the streams, and the terrain was firmly in the hands of 'gold bosses' who, according to a Chinese report, 'have divided the area among themselves and rule like kings'. Their rule was strict. When a gold boss named Mo from Qinghai heard that a prospector from Gansu province had been panning on the wrong side of the line, he sent a posse of his men to punish the unwitting offender by hacking a chunk of flesh from his calf. The men of Gansu retaliated and dozens were wounded in the ensuing battle. When it was over 'the two sides shook hands and made up, as if nothing had happened'.[3]

Formerly, the creatures of the plateau were hunted for food; now they are shot also for their skins. Elsewhere in the highland regions of Xinjiang the numbers of Tibetan antelope, wild yak and wild ass have declined rapidly, leaving (says one account) a bone-strewn wasteland. Border troops in areas of disputed control are blamed for the increase in hunting in the Pamir and Karakoram ranges to the west, even though a nature reserve for *argali* sheep, ibex and markhor wild goats, lynx, brown bear and snow leopard has been created around Tashkurgan on the pass to Pakistan. The Tian Shan mountains are home to wolves, elk, bears and lynx, despite the presence of Kazakh herdsmen on their lower slopes. These semi-nomads are less bothered by large predators than by the swarms of locusts which periodically descend on the hills and strip their pastures bare. When a swarm is seen approaching, they call out the emergency services: not crop-dusting aircraft but truckloads of ducks and chickens which are released – a hundred thousand at a time – on to the hillsides and, commanded by blasts of a whistle, attack and devour the locusts.

*

Xinjiang's water supply is stored high up in the rocky fortress which guards it on three sides. The girdle of mountains and glaciers ringing the province includes some of the tallest peaks in the world. Even the outposts are imposing. At the Tian Shan's eastern end, just short of the Mongolian border, Mount Karlik soars to 16,000 feet. Further west, Mount Bogda looms over the city of Urumchi at 18,000 feet. The mountains continue to rise as they circle south and west round the Taklamakan desert. Kongur and Muztaghata stand facing each other across the high plateaux of the Pamirs, at around 25,000 feet each, but the king of them all is the massive Qiaogoli, otherwise known as K2 or Godwin Austen, a few steps short of 28,000 feet and the second highest mountain in the world. Turning eastwards once more to become the Kunlun range, the mountains march off towards Aqqikkol and the Qaidam plateau, still reaching heights of 25,000 feet.

The glaciers, however, are shrinking, and have been on and off since the end of an ice age 70,000 years ago. Climatic change and global warming, coupled with industrial expansion and growing demand in the thirsty oases below, are putting ever greater pressure on the system, with profound consequences for the map of Xinjiang.

Numerous river beds mark the passage of water that flowed in the Tarim basin long ago. But today only twenty-four rivers debouch into the desert, and all but one exhaust themselves in its barren wastes: the survivor is the Irtysh which rises in the Altai mountains, briefly crosses the northern tip of Xinjiang, and joins the River Ob on its way to the Arctic Ocean. Most of the June snowmelt from the high peaks of western Xinjiang is carried away eastwards by the Yarkand river, which becomes the Tarim beyond the oasis town of Aksu. The main artery of Xinjiang, it moves ever more sluggishly – increasingly impeded in modern times by dams – as it progresses towards its own extinction on the far side of the Tarim basin. Of the torrents which descend the Kunlun mountains in the south, only the Khotan, Keriya and Cherchen rivers are of any size, and their flow is seasonal. Largest of them is the Khotan, which is navigable by four-wheel-drive vehicles. A mile wide in places and crossing the whole desert from south to north on its way to join the Tarim, for most of the year it is dry but for a few isolated pools. A low fringe of half-dead trees and tangled undergrowth marks its hazy shores, from which the occasional antelope emerges in search of water, while the sun beats down on the cracked grey plates of mud which comprise its bed. Running parallel to it 80 miles to the east is the Keriya, a narrower stream but a more generous one. Its banks are occupied by small settlements of goatherds who live in huts of poplar and reed. After struggling northwards for 120 miles the Keriya disappears into the sands. Smaller neighbours still further east survive no more than 60 miles before they, too, give up the fight. Wet or dry, these river beds nonetheless provide the only punctuation in the desert: corridors of life in a lifeless waste.

In the days before geography became a science the Chinese believed the Tarim and the Yellow River to be one and the same. The mighty Yellow River rises in the Tibetan mountains and loops crazily across the Middle Kingdom, dragging half the Gobi desert with it before emptying into the Yellow Sea south of Tianjin. According to legend the Tarim, after crossing the Taklamakan from west to east and flowing into Lop Nor (*nor* is Mongolian for lake), ran on under the mountains to emerge in China proper. A hundred and fifty years ago, a Kyrgyz storyteller told his visitors about a youth from Lop, the no man's land between the Taklamakan and Gobi deserts, who decided to explore beyond the lake:

> After going down the stream for seven days he saw a mountain ahead, and on going closer he found the river entered a frightful black and deep chasm in the rocks. He tried to stop his boat, but the swiftness of the current carried it into the chasm. At its further end he saw a small black hole inside the mountain and had only time to lie down in the bottom of the boat, when it was drawn into the dark passage. The top of the boat scraped the roof of the channel and bits of stone continually fell upon him. After a long time he emerged from the darkness into the light, and found the bottom of his boat strewn with nuggets of gold. He went down the river for some days, and eventually found himself in Peking [Beijing].[4]

The Yellow River, as erratic as any, did at one time meet the sea near Beijing. But it was never part of the Tarim. The Tarim's real terminus was a riddle which provoked one of the great geographical controversies of the nineteenth century. And when at last the riddle was solved by the Swedish explorer Sven Hedin, it brought him great acclaim.

The story of the wandering lake, as Hedin called it, is really the story of a wandering river. For the Tarim has changed course twice in the last two millennia. Until about AD 330, it ran more or less due east into a salt lake which was all that remained of the great prehistoric sea that had filled the Tarim basin. Then, owing either to the continual movement of the earth's tectonic plates or to the accumulation of its own sediment, the river started to move southwards, shifting the lake by about sixty miles or nearly a whole degree of latitude. In 1921, however, the Tarim swung back on to a more northerly course – though not quite the same one as before – taking the lake with it. Hedin compared it to the action of a pendulum with a brass weight at the end. The remarkable thing about this exploit was that Hedin predicted the second change in the lake's position more than twenty years before it happened, and he was able to go and see the proof for himself in late middle age. By 1972, twenty years after Hedin's death, the lake had dried up altogether owing to colonization of the Tarim further upstream and the need for irrigation canals, sluices and reservoirs. All that remains of the wandering lake today is its ghost, a vast and glimmering saltpan in the desert of Lop.

Grey, bleak and empty, the area round Lop Nor has been compared to the surface of the moon. The archaeologist Aurel Stein left a vivid description of his trek to the place which he described as 'a desolate wilderness, bearing everywhere the impress of death'. In particular he recalled the struggle of his caravan through the yardangs, rocks eroded by wind-driven sand into strange and artificial shapes. Though yardangs are to be found in deserts from the Middle East to the Americas (where they are called mesas), these structures are a particular feature of western China. They are often described in nautical terms. A yardang looks like nothing so much as the upturned hull of a ship. Its sides are grooved to give the appearance of planking where the flying sand has scoured them. A blunt stern end faces the prevailing wind, and the body tapers away to a prow at the other end. Yardangs can be a few inches high or as tall as a ten-storey building, from a few inches long to a mile or more. Some carry turrets or crests at one end, like the heads of old stone statues or the conning towers of submarines. Groups of yardangs, lying in lines astern like ships frozen at anchor, are known as 'fleets'. Occasionally they take on shapes so distinct and so unnatural that it is hard to believe they are not the crumbling remains of man-made structures. Among a fleet of big yardangs at Miran, for example, south of the Lop desert, are rough-hewn square masses on circular bases which mimic the giant Buddhist stupas that stand nearby. Others look like badly worn versions of the Sphinx at Giza, while the whole agglomeration reminds one of some ruined city.* But these phantoms are simply the result of erosion over aeons. When land is pushed up in desert areas and exposed to an interminable, uni-directional wind, the softer material is etched away, leaving outcrops of harder stuff. This aeolian erosion is what carved out the improbable mass of Ayers Rock, the freak mountain in the central Australian desert. At Miran the confusion between natural and man-made is enhanced because many of the smaller yardangs were burrowed out by the early inhabitants to make pottery kilns. The shards still lie in heaps at their mouths.

The Lop desert provides a kind of geographical hiatus between two very distinct wildernesses: the Gobi and the Taklamakan. Thanks to Marco Polo's book of travels (though whether he himself ever made the journey he describes has become a matter of dispute) the Gobi is a name known to every schoolchild.[5] Its Mongol name is synonymous with the terrain it describes: a pebble desert, interrupted by rock and sand, whose dominant colours are grey, black and dark brown. The terrain is varied and can sustain small shrubs and grasses, wild animals, even nomadic farmers with their herds. Stretching in a great east–west arc for 1,000 miles, its western extremities penetrate Xinjiang to form

---

* One Egyptian geologist has argued that the Sphinx is indeed built from a yardang. Other theories about it are a lot more fantastic.

the Kum Tagh desert in the south and the Dzungarian basin in the north.

Of the unusual creatures which used to inhabit the Chinese Gobi, only one of any consequence remains. The last Xinjiang tiger, a relative of the Siberian, is thought to have survived until the 1950s, about the time when the first Communist Chinese scientists began surveying their 'new frontier'. The wild horse or tarpan, *Equus przewalskii*, named after the same Russian colonel who shot the big *argali* in the Tian Shan, is still alive but no longer truly wild. A stubby creature with markings like a zebra and a mane like a yard brush, it is thought to be the ancestor of all modern horses. For the last thirty years it has been found only in zoos and in a reserve specially created outside Ulan Bator in Mongolia, where attempts have been made to reintroduce it into the wild. The last wild Prejevalsky's horse is supposed to have been shot in 1969. The distinction of bagging it – if distinction you can call it – is claimed by an old Chinese hunter called Zhao Ziyong ('Old Zhao'), who twenty-five years later boasted of his exploit to an English explorer.[6]

Zhao was truly a poacher turned gamekeeper. For in the mid-1990s he joined an expedition to track and save another rare and interesting creature that still survives in the wilds of Xinjiang. This creature, too, was identified by the ubiquitous Prejevalsky.* The wild Bactrian camel, *Camelus bactrianus ferus*, has clung to an independent existence for the 4,000 years that its domestic cousin has been in man's service. Leaner than its relative, it has reddish hair, but less of it, smaller humps and shorter ears and muzzle. Until DNA tests a few years ago, there was no way of proving that the animals seen and hunted in the Gobi and Taklamakan were truly wild and not merely the descendants of domestic camels that had run off into the desert. When Prejevalsky returned to St Petersburg in 1877 with a roll of camel hide in his luggage, claiming it came from a wild camel that he had shot in the Tarim basin,

---

* Prejevalsky was taxonomically prolific: although the camel was not named after him, he has a gazelle, a lizard, a gecko, a poplar tree, a rhododendron and an ephedra to his credit, as well as a horse. He collected 20,000 zoological and 16,000 botanical specimens.

people were disinclined to believe him. But recent laboratory analysis shows that the Russian was right. Indeed, genetic testing suggests that the estimated 800 wild Bactrians that survive in a narrow range of Mongolia and Xinjiang are a separate species which diverged long before camels were domesticated.

Seen through binoculars with inexpert eyes, one Bactrian looks much like another. But the group of seven I saw grazing one autumn under the mountains at the very edge of the Kum Tagh desert were the genuine article, according to a camelophile companion who knew about Bactrians because he looked after them in a California zoo. Two of the creatures were kneeling, but the five that were grazing certainly looked smaller than they should, while the humps of the nearest specimen were odd: the rear hump stood up but the front one flopped over as if punctured. That, explained my friend, was a male living off its fat or suffering a loss of appetite because it was in rut. The very remoteness of the place and the fact that there had been camel footprints in the desert at the previous night's campsite made me only too ready to claim a genuine sighting. Later, by way of reinforcement, it emerged that the animals were in the right place, too – the spot coincided with the southern terminus of the wild camels' migration route plotted by Chinese scientists.

Even in Prejevalsky's day, the wild camel was becoming scarce thanks to the enthusiasm of local hunters. The Russian's guide, a hunter from Charklik, claimed to have killed over a hundred in his time and then was surprised to find that years would pass without sight of one. Prejevalsky himself contrasted the wild variety's 'sagacity and admirably developed senses' of sight, hearing and smell with what he called the 'cowardice, stupidity and apathy' of the domestic animal. But there were more wild camels alive than he realized. When Sven Hedin crossed the Taklamakan from south to north in 1895, he found what he called a 'wild camels' paradise' at the point where the Keriya river disappears into the sand. First he saw a tuft of light reddish-brown hair on a tamarisk bush, then fresh tracks. When the party came up on a small herd, his hunter Kasim let loose with a flintlock rifle and brought down a bull. Later a second hunter called Islam shot a she-camel; she sank to her knees and Hedin rushed up to sketch her. 'She did not look at us,' he wrote afterwards, 'but seemed to be in despair at having to part for ever with her otherwise inviolate desert land. Before she died she opened her mouth and bit into the sand. I now forbade any more shooting.'[7] The sight of the dying female drove the rutting males of Hedin's baggage train into paroxysms. 'They rolled their eyes and bellowed horribly with passion,' he recorded. It was plain to him that no human being had ever come near these creatures before.

The wild camel may have been saved by a combination of natural and unnatural circumstances. One of its talents is its ability to drink the salt water of the Gobi, stuff which no domestic camel, let alone a human, can be persuaded to touch. Then, for a time, it enjoyed extra protection in an already remote area, living as it did in the middle of China's nuclear weapons testing zone. The explosions – at first aerial, later below ground – which prolonged the life of this rare animal were not so kind to humans. Oasis people living downwind of them blame nuclear testing for the high incidence of illness and deformity suffered by their children. China suspended the tests in 1996, and the camels, which endured forty-five blasts, now face the greater threat of poaching and tourism unless the sanctuary promised by the authorities is delivered.

Chinese histories are spiced with anecdotes about this intriguing creature. 'The camel is an unusual domestic animal,' wrote Guo Pu early in the third century AD. 'It carries a saddle of flesh on its back; swiftly it dashes over the shifting sands; it manifests its merit in dangerous places; it has secret understanding of springs and sources; subtle indeed is its knowledge!'[8] Camels were supposed to stop and stamp the ground to show where water lay, and to warn their drivers of impending dust-storms by snarling and burying their muzzles in the sand. Refined Chinese mandarins like Yu Jingzi in the early seventh century AD would employ them to carry tanks full of live fish so that they could dine in proper style on official tours. Still today, as in Hedin's time, the camel is the only vehicle properly adapted to negotiate the sand dunes of the Taklamakan. No jeep or lorry, even when modified to vent its exhaust in the air, gets far in this terrain. And the camel has the right temperament for the work, as its owners' rough treatment of its confirms. Uighur camel drivers do not, for example, train a young or 'green' camel to kneel for loading. Three or four men get together and simply wrestle the creature, frothing and bellowing, to the ground. At the end of one day's march across the dunes of the Taklamakan I saw the big male at the head of the column, as he was being unloaded, give his owner a flying kick with a foreleg which sent the man sprawling in the sand. The furious driver picked up an axe that was lying nearby and leapt at the camel as if to cut off its head but instead turned the blade at the last moment and beat it savagely on the side of the neck.

However rough they may be with their noisy, petulant and sometimes violent charges, the Uighurs know not to overburden or undersupply their animals. For the stamina of the camel is notoriously exaggerated. They are supremely patient workers, but only when properly fed and watered. Bactrians, at least, cannot go for more than three or four days without water. And there is no point testing them to the limit: for once a camel has reached its limit, the end of its tether, it cannot return. Its back is literally broken by the last straw. The British discovered this in the days of Empire when they used camels for military transport and found them agreeably steady under fire. In an animal management handbook of 1908, the War Office's veterinary department set limits to what a camel should be expected to carry, and for what duration:

> It is well to keep this in mind, for the animal's virtues are such that it is easy to unwittingly overtax him. Patient to a degree, enduring hunger, thirst and pain with a stoical courage beyond all others, the first sign a camel may give that he is being asked to do the impossible is to drop down dead, on which account he has been classed as 'delicate'.

Or he will simply break down, like a car with big-end failure, and nothing will persuade him to go on. There where he has stopped he will stay until he dies, with an accusing look in his eye. Etiquette demands a certain procedure, however, when abandoning your beast. Uighur camel-drivers believe it brings bad luck to kill a camel that has been 'thrown on the *gobi*'. For it may be saved by a miracle from heaven, and if you kill it, its ghost will haunt the rest of the caravan. Equally, any show of regret by the driver as he leaves the creature behind is an open invitation to pursuit by evil spirits.[9] Even in death the poor brute has his uses: traditionally the carcass would be set up with the skull and bones pointing the way for future travellers.

If the Gobi is a moonscape, the Taklamakan is a seascape. More inhospitable even than the Gobi, it is by general consent one of the most dangerous and empty places on earth.* For the Taklamakan is a true desert, an ocean of grey-yellow sand sculpted into dunes which billow to the horizon. Self-contained in its geological basin, it has a well-defined shoreline beneath the ramparts of mountains which enclose it on three sides, and an uncomplicated habitat: quite simply, nothing but lowly bacteria can live in it. Normally dour Chinese officials take a rhapsodical pride in the desert's evil reputation, translating 'Taklamakan' to mean 'You go in and you don't come out'. This rendition of the Turkic name, faithfully repeated by Western writers, happens to be wrong. As to the word's true meaning, there is no unanimity, even among Uighurs. A Turki linguist born on the western margins told me that the name means literally 'old home place' or 'end place', while a museum curator from the oasis town of Keriya suggested 'place of the grapes'. A Chinese scientific survey of 1987–91 opted for some derivation from *toghrak*, the Uighur word for the desert poplar. Others prefer 'place of ruins', a mainly Arabic derivation, and say the name belonged originally to Dandan-Oilik, a buried city north-east of Khotan, or to another ancient settlement along the Keriya river. This is the answer preferred by the famous Turki scholar, the late Gunnar Jarring.[10]

By whatever name it is known, the Taklamakan, even in an age of specially adapted vehicles, radio telephones, helicopters and satellite navigation, remains as frightening as the day Sven Hedin made his disastrous first attempt to cross it, losing two of his Uighur guides along the way and very nearly dying of thirst himself. The 30-year-old Swede, full of bounce and optimism, had

---

* Charles Blackmore, who led an expedition across the desert from west to east in 1993, called his subsequent book *The Worst Desert on Earth*.

set off from the village of Merket on the north-western edge of the Taklamakan on 10 April 1895 and reached the open desert thirteen days later:

> There was nothing now but fine yellow sand. As far as the eye could reach only high dunes, quite bare of vegetation, were visible. Strange that I should not be amazed at this sight, and that it did not make me halt . . . I was swept away by the irresistible *desiderium incogniti*, which breaks down all obstacles and refuses to recognise the impossible.[11]

You do not have to be driven by Hedin's passion for the unknown in order to feel the sand sea's enchantment. For the Taklamakan is as beautiful as it is dangerous, enslaving the senses even while preying on the nerves. When describing the experience, nautical metaphors become unavoidable; for the traveller marching over the dunes ahead of a camel-train has much the same perspective as an ocean-going yachtsman. At the start of his voyage, the sea is calm and navigation easy: the caravan is crossing a valley of small dunes. Gradually the storm increases, the sand dunes swelling until they are piling up ahead like tidal waves. Now the camels are forced to make long tacks across the rims of the dunes in order to avoid the worst of the sea. All the while, the big bell on the neck of the leading camel tolls like a warning buoy in a fogbound estuary. When the wind gets up, the desert roars. But in the calm of twilight the mariner hears nothing but the hiss of sand being blown off the ridges. The night sky seems to press down more closely and the stars to shine more fiercely than anywhere else on earth.

Few humans have been there to see the Taklamakan ravaged by storms in spring, baked lifeless by the sun in high summer, or mantled by a freak shower of snow in winter. The desert is an arrested seascape and its motif is death; except at high noon the sand is a cold grey, the putty colour of a corpse, a barren landscape mocking its fertile past. From the smallest ripple at one's feet to the great ridges piled up on the horizon, every shape is a reminder of the life that once flowed here, of sprawling rivers and of the sea that once covered the Tarim. Now and again there are other traces of ancient life. Groves of blackened poplars stand dead of thirst in old river beds, the remnants of forests left high and dry when the water made an arbitrary change of course. Gruesome as skeletons, they raise their twisted and withered branches to the sky as if praying for relief from the eternal heat. In the deep desert can be found odd echoes of other worlds. Sea shells lying incongruously on the sand, more than two thousand miles from the nearest ocean, are left-overs from another geological era. Scraps of twisted metal, the litter of nuclear tests from Lop Nor in the east, are souvenirs of the atomic age. And strange lumps of fused rock, which anywhere else on earth would pass unnoticed, show themselves to be fragments of asteroids flung down from deepest space.

Dead it may appear, but even in the heart of the desert there is water lurking not too far below the surface. Experienced camel-drivers can detect a promising spot by a slight discoloration at the foot of a dune. Such marks indicate the tip of a layer of clay, the remains of an ancient river bed. In depressions between the dunes the water may lie only a dozen feet below the surface. But for a man to dig twice his own height at the end of a long day's march is no joke. The Uighurs use a bracket-shaped spade, the *ketman*, which can shift a big load of sand with each heave. Two men together will carve out a hole the size of a large well and work furiously until the sand darkens and grows damp. By then, they are out of sight. Eventually – if they have struck lucky – a rivulet of liquid, the colour and consistency of mercury, will ooze slowly into the bottom of the pit. The men halt their digging, because there is no point going further. It will take all night for the pit to accumulate enough water to fill half a dozen buckets. At dawn the camels will be led down to the well. Even then, the effort may have been in vain. If the water is too salt, the camels, thirsty as they are, will turn up their noses and refuse to drink.

And the desert sands have a life of their own. Han dynasty explorers called the Taklamakan *liu sha*, 'moving sands'. Its great dunes, driven over most of the area by a prevailing north–north-easterly wind, are marching diagonally towards the southern oases at the rate of a yard a year. They creep like a wall of volcanic lava from some distant eruption, slowly and inexorably devouring the flimsy man-made structures in their path. On the desert's southern shore, their rate of advance is three times faster. Parties of workers are kept employed digging redoubts to stem the encroaching tide, and a system of nets and plantings has been imported from the Alps to protect the most vulnerable oases. In the south-western corner, the movement is contrary, since there the prevailing wind is from the north-west, and in the very centre, at the place where Hedin saw the camels, a confused pattern of dunes has been created by the clash of north and north-westerly winds.

The desert's method of advance is simple. Strong and constant winds, mainly from the north-east, pick up the lighter grains and throw them a few feet into the air. When they fall, the grains disturb others which are picked up and carried by the wind in their turn. By this process, known as saltation, the light grains make their way up the windward face of the dunes. At the crest, they topple down the lee side. The ridge of a crescent dune is firm underfoot, even for a fully laden bull camel, but it takes only one step sideways for the walker to find himself up to his waist in soft sand, like a skier who runs off the piste into powder snow. Indeed, some desert trekkers take ski poles with them. As the sand on the lee side accumulates, the slope gets steeper. When the critical angle of 34 degrees is reached, the sand starts to run down the dune like water, small avalanches occur, or the whole face of the dune may slip downwards in a movement called 'slumping'.* Smaller dunes of course travel more quickly than larger ones, and eventually catch them up and are absorbed by them; but they look and behave much the same. Like fractals in geometry, every ripple of sand on the side of a dune is a miniature replica of the dune chain as a whole – and no doubt, if you could inspect it closely, of the entire desert floor. Although sand moves in a simple way, the resulting dune shapes vary a good deal, stretching the ingenuity of mathematical physicists to explain them.[12]

Of all the phenomena of the desert, perhaps the worst is the storms. They begin with a gentle breeze and a pale veiling of the sky as if the sun has gone behind a cloud. As the breeze strengthens,

---

* Sand avalanches are the paradigm case of the phenomenon called 'self-limiting criticality', a new branch of physics. The behaviour of sand in the lower chamber of an hour-glass is an example.

the whole atmosphere turns to a grey haze, and particles begin to fly. Before long, the wind is roaring and the haze is a bombardment of stinging sand which whips the face and penetrates every stitch of clothing. A storm takes several hours to subside. The biggest occur in springtime and are called *kara-buran*, or 'black storm'. Albert von Le Coq described one he encountered on the desert's edge:

> Quite suddenly the sky grows dark: the sun becomes a dark-red ball of fire seen through the fast-thickening veil of dust, a muffled howl is followed by a piercing whistle and a moment after the storm bursts with appalling violence upon the caravan. Enormous masses of sand, mixed with pebbles, are forcibly lifted up, whirled around, and dashed down on man and beast; the darkness increases and strange clashing noises mingle with the roar and howl of the storm caused by the violent contact of great stones as they are whirled up through the air . . . Any traveller overwhelmed by such a storm must, in spite of the heat, entirely envelop himself in felts to escape injury from the stones dashing around with such mad force. Men and horses must lie down and endure the rage of the hurricane . . .[13]

On the desert margins, the sand is a grey dust which, once stirred up by the *kara-buran*, hangs in the air for days, covering the whole Tarim and its oasis towns, blotting out the sun, swirling up to a height of 13,000 feet and hiding the mountains. Storms are more frequent on the shores of the desert than in its interior: in Khotan, on the south road, dust storms were counted on 202 days of a single year.

Only in the corridors of life provided by river beds, or in the rivers' distant oasis deltas, can people, plants and animals find sustenance. The vegetation of these corridors was described by Hedin as 'jungle', an odd-seeming choice of word. But Hedin's description is accurate: the thickets of poplar and tamarisk, oleaster and camel thorn, ankle-catching caltrops and saltworts, are as tangled and dense as any jungle. One of the strangest plants to be found here is *Cistanche salsa*. Called 'desert ginseng' by the herdsmen who collect it, it is a knobbly root with swollen protuberances that looks like a sweet potato but is mottled like a fungus. It is sold as an organic version of Viagra and commands high prices. Less valuable but certainly more effective – albeit for a different purpose – is a succulent which, when picked by the handful, gives out refreshing amounts of water, enough to wash the dust from face and arms.

In these desert corridors the dust is as fine and clinging as talcum powder. The slightest breeze or disturbance of a vehicle tyre throws up a pall, coating trees and bushes with rime and hanging in the air for long minutes like a fog. And when a desert fox, silver grey in colour, skulks across a clearing with a nervous backward glance, you expect a pack of foxhounds to come crashing after him. At such moments, one might be walking on a cold, damp November day in the muddy shires of England. A few wild boar are said to survive in the more remote of these thickets: the Uighur word *tongguz*, which appears in the name of two remote oasis villages, refers to them. There are also shy Mongolian gazelles which emerge from the scrub to drink at intermittent pools, a local variety of long-eared hedgehog – the only insect-eater – which snuffles along the ground, rats and rabbits, gerbils, jerboas and field mice.[14]

In places so deprived of life it is a wonderful sight to come upon a belt of tall poplars glowing red, orange and gold in their autumn foliage and buried up to their knees in sand. On the desert fringes one may climb a dune expecting to see another just like it and be confronted instead by a blaze of colour from a broad copse of poplars. The well-adapted Euphrates poplar, *Populus diversifolia*, is king of the jungle here and its pedigree reaches back to the riparian forests of the Pliocene age. 'In localities with dense streams in the Taklamakan desert, the Euphrates poplar grows lushly,' enthused the Qing dynasty scholar Xu Song.[15] The desert poplar, quite different from the white poplar of the oasis village, bears two kinds of leaf, and its roots burrow deep to discover underground water channels whose presence is confirmed by the glowing crown above. According to a popular saying, these magnificent trees live a thousand years, stand a thousand years and lie for another thousand sand. As the subterranean water flow becomes more fitful, so the poplars become more sparse. The further they grow from the green corridors, the smaller they become. Where the sand dunes begin to swell, they stand like forgotten sentries. Go further still, and the poplars disappear. Now the only vegetation left is the hardy tamarisk (*Tamarix taklimakensis*). With their feathery branches and slim red flowers, the tamarisks stand like beacons on mounds up to 30 feet high formed from the sand trapped over years among their roots. At last, not even the tamarisk is able to survive. All that remains is the occasional lizard skittering across the sand on its toes like a frantic ballerina – a prudent adaptation in a place where the surface temperature may climb to over 50 degrees centigrade. In the open desert, there is nothing at all – not a bird, not a fly, nothing but the occasional poplar seed floating on the wind.

Yet here, beyond the limits of any creature's endurance, is the strangest phenomenon of all. Sticking out of the sand are the slender trunks of desiccated fruit trees; and beyond, set in rigid rectangles, the corner posts of dwellings. There are lintels and doorways and beams falling across each other, with the mark of the carpenter's adze still clearly on them. A large earthenware pot lies in the sand with its handle broken. Someone once lived here. But who?

2

Kings, Khans and Khojas

S HE IS AS old as Abraham and her skin has blackened with age, but the Beauty of Loulan still commands respect. Unlike some of the corpses around her, she has lost none of her dignity in death. She lies as she has lain for 4,000 years, apparently at peace and with the hint of a smile on her lips. Her closed eyes are deeply set, her nose is sharp and her mouth is tightly shut. She wears a threadbare brown robe of wool and fur with a goose feather sticking jauntily from its hood. On her feet, below skinny shins, is a pair of ragged moccasins.

One of 500 bodies exhumed over the past forty years from the desiccating sands of the Taklamakan desert, the Beauty of Loulan is, for her age, amazingly well preserved. Because of her antiquity – she died around 1,800 BC – she is the undisputed queen of the mummies, and has been raised to the status of racial icon by the Uighur people who call her (with a little justification) 'mother of the nation'. Her state owes nothing to the art of the embalmer. Unlike the mummies of Egypt, the Taklamakan bodies were simply placed in poplarwood boxes, lowered into narrow shaft graves and left to take their chance with nature, tomb-robbers and archaeologists.

Similar finds have been made in Europe, but rarely such magnificent ones. Otzi the Ice Man was exposed in 1991 during an unprecedented thaw on an Alpine pass between Austria and Italy. He was sufficiently well preserved, though somewhat deformed, to be mistaken at first for a climber lost earlier in the century. Otzi proved to be 5,300 years old. Though less antique, at 2,000 years, the bog bodies of Denmark and north Germany are remarkable in their way but have usually been collapsed by the action of peat and water into macabre shapes, mere bags of sinew and skin.[1]

Few can compare, for example, with the imposing figure of

Cherchen Man, found in the southern oasis of that name and now installed alongside the Beauty of Loulan in the Xinjiang Museum, Urumchi. Nearly 6 feet tall, he is dressed in a burgundy robe with handsome white deerskin boots over multi-coloured felt leggings; his knees are slightly raised and his long delicate hands loosely tied with a cord of braided wool. His hair is brown and he has a short beard and moustache. Beside him, lying in the same posture, is the best preserved of the three women who were buried with him 3,000 years ago. She is balding, and her chin strap has failed to prevent her mouth from falling open. Both their faces are decorated with coloured whorls, like tattoos. A baby boy a few months old was found nearby with a bottle and cup, and he has been reunited with his presumed father in the museum. The little body is swaddled and tied with red-and-blue cord, the head is covered with a blue bonnet, stones of the same colour have been placed over his eyes, and tufts of red wool have been put into his nostrils.

More remarkable even than the preservation of the mummies is the character of the faces preserved. For these people look nothing like Chinese. Tall and slender, with aquiline features and high-bridged noses, light brown or red hair and heavy beards, they plainly come from the west. Or, as the inscription beneath one of the glass cases reads, referring to the pathetic figure of a young woman with long reddish-brown hair found in the oasis of Hami, 'The dead is a member of a European race.' Just as suggestive of their western origins are the designs of the mummies' clothes, whether of ragged wool or embroidered silk. The poorer clothes are woven into plaid which looks suspiciously like Scottish tartan, suggesting to some experts a common ancestry for Scottish and 'Chinese' tartans somewhere in southern Russia.[2] Others see the tartans of the Tarim as much closer in style to the Celtic plaids of Hallstatt in Austria.[3]

This meeting – or perhaps collision – of cultures, western and eastern, is delicately recorded in the clothes of two 'kings' of the Tarim excavated within the past decade. One was found at Lop Nor on the eastern edge of the Taklamakan, the other at Niya to the south. Both bodies are relatively recent, dating from the third century AD, and it is obvious from their garments how far technology had advanced since the time of the Beauty of Loulan. The

Lop king wears a white mask under a gold band and his face has never been seen – or so a museum guide told me. He looks taller than the 5ft 11in the label gives him. His red robe is embroidered with yellow flowers, pomegranate trees and some very un-Chinese cherubs, chubby naked figures holding shields over their heads and squaring up to each other with daggers. The Niya king, by contrast, wears a kaftan whose silken edges are intricately woven with figures of dragons, tigers, horsemen and birds – all obviously Chinese motifs, even if you ignore the Chinese characters that surround them.

All history is political, but Chinese history is more political than most. It is an uncomfortable fact for Han Chinese nationalists that the mummies show so little racial affinity with them – that 'Europeans' got to the Tarim basin before they did. In the twentieth century some Chinese scientists tried to re-establish priority by asserting that the Han were the product of white Caucasians descended from the legendary Yellow Emperor, whose pure genes had been polluted by barbarian 'reds'.[4] The discovery of Peking Man in 1933 led others to conclude that migration theories were wrong and that the Chinese were 'the most ancient original inhabitants' of any country on earth.[5]

Like the early civilizations of the Middle East or the Mediterranean, the Han Chinese regarded themselves as occupying the centre of the world. But whereas the ancient Greeks came to tolerate barbarians, the Chinese made no such concession. All around them, in various stages of undress, were the savages, and the further you travelled the more savage they became. Chinese mythology described the people at the extreme periphery as birds and beasts, or half-humans with three heads or three eyes. Closer to lived the 'raw' barbarians, creatures who devoured uncooked flesh and were hairy all over; closer still lived the 'cooked' barbarians who were somewhat less hirsute.[6] The innermost barbarians could still be recognized by their unruly locks and strange habits, such as fastening their clothes on the wrong side.[7] Scholars were still defending the bestial hypothesis in the 1920s: Tibetans were said to be descended ultimately from sheep, and the Chinese word for Muslim, 'Hui', carries in it the sign for 'dog' (the canine radical). Up to the 1930s, government propaganda was describing the Japanese as *wonu* or 'dwarf slaves' covered with hair. For to the smooth-skinned Han, hair was more repulsive than brown or black skin.

Today's occupants of the Forbidden City in Beijing are just as anxious as the emperors of the past to maintain a coherent and flattering record of themselves. In former times, the job was simply done. A new dynasty meant new history books: previous scrolls were destroyed and the past was rewritten to exaggerate the legitimacy of the new god-emperor and his line. These days, 'incorrect' books are impounded and destroyed. The idea that real history is too dangerous for public consumption has itself had a long history, and given the chauvinist cultural tradition of the Chinese, sensitivity about race is easy to understand.* Unfortunately, scholars have had to depend on Han and Tang dynastic records for much of their information about the early history of Xinjiang.

Among scientists at least, this chauvinism is softening. Chinese writing about the mummies today makes no secret of their European – or Aryan – genetic origins, stressing instead the extent of Han influence on ancient artefacts. But dating, of both objects and people, is always according to Chinese dynastic periods, and the presence of Chinese garrisons or administrative posts, however token, is always emphasized. Over the past hundred years archaeological excavations – first by Europeans, later by Americans and Japanese, then increasingly by the Chinese themselves – have helped dispel the fog of myth which surrounded the ancient settlements of Xinjiang.

The answer to the question posed at the end of the first chapter has already been hinted at. The people of the Tarim basin and its abandoned desert settlements were not Chinese at all, but Indo-European. Their ancestors had migrated from the Caucasus and Anatolia to occupy the northern steppes, and from there had descended into the Tarim basin during the Bronze Age (2000–900 BC).

---

* It is not only in the People's Republic of China that human remains make high politics. The oldest known skeleton in the United States, Kennewick Man, was discovered in Washington State in 1996 and identified by scientists as European or 'Caucasoid'. Amid great controversy, it was handed over to American Indian tribes who had claimed it as one of theirs, without further investigation.

They were horsemen and herders who used chariots and may have invented the stirrup.[8] Their descendants in the Tarim spoke an Indo-European language which modern scholars call Tocharian. Found only in fragments, Tocharian had different variants used at Turfan and Kucha, but proved to be closer to the languages of western Europe than to the eastern branch of the family. The people who spoke it also came to be known as Tocharian.

These Indo-Europeans were joined in about 1200 BC by a wave of immigrants from what is now Iran who took up residence mainly on the southern and western sides of the desert. The Aryan features they bequeathed to their descendants made a deep impression on early modern visitors. A British traveller in the late nineteenth century described the people living in the hills above Yarkand as tall and fair-faced, with light eyes and sandy whiskers and hair. They were, he exclaimed, a 'purely Aryan group, who only require to be put into coat and trowsers to pass, so far as outward appearance goes, for the fairest Englishman'.[9]

Only later did Sino-Mongolians arrive from the east. A recent investigation of skeleton remains by a Chinese scientist confirmed the early appearance of 'western racial elements' followed by eastern Mediterranean types. He suggested that 'until several centuries BC the eastward movement of the Western race to Xinjiang was more rapid than the western movement of Mongoloid people.'[10] Genetic research by the Chinese has concluded that today's Uighurs are more than half Caucasian: 'The blood of the Xinjiang mummies runs through the veins of the current population.'*

The Tocharians have been equated with the people whom the Chinese called Yuezhi and who were their nearest neighbours in the west. Both suffered the depredations of the most powerful of the nomad tribes, the Xiongnu, who constantly battered at China's northern borders in the first two centuries BC. There seems to be no proof but these Xiongnu are said to be the ancestors of the fearsome Huns who in the fourth and fifth centuries AD swept from central Asia across the Russian steppe as far as modern France,

---

* The Kazakhs were about a third Caucasian, and the Hui (Chinese Muslims) of modern Ningxia province less than one-sixth.[11]

destabilizing the Roman empire.[12] According to the Chinese annals, in about 170 BC the Xiongnu drove the Yuezhi out of their homeland, forcing them to make a great circle northwards and westwards until they ended up beyond the Tian Shan and Pamir mountains. Eventually the Yuezhi settled in the Graeco-Indian kingdom of Bactria (today northern Afghanistan). By this circumambulation, they were once more able to wield influence over their old homeland, but from the opposite point of the compass.

The Xiongnu were the cause of endless trouble, as the story of the Lady Wenji illustrates. In about AD 200 she was abducted by the Xiongnu from her father's house in Henan province, carried off and forcibly married to one of the tribal chiefs. The plaintive beauty of her lamentations for a lost homeland and her pride in her superior background (as put into her mouth by later poets) have made her popular down the centuries. Her story is told in 'Eighteen Songs of a Nomad Flute', a marvellous series of paintings and poems on a fourteenth-century scroll now in the Metropolitan Museum of Art in New York; it is a copy of an even earlier scroll commissioned by the Southern Song Emperor Gaozong in AD 1130.

'Alas, how a pretty face has made me suffer,' sighs Lady Wenji after being carried off, riding side-saddle on a dappled grey. The artist has made sure that under her bee-keeper's veil and clerical hat Wenji looks thoroughly depressed. The nomad chief, who sports a little black moustache and goatee beard, gazes back at her with narrowed eyes.

His abducted bride finds the smell of the barbarians particularly loathsome:

I was taken on horseback to the ends of the earth;
Tiring of life, I sought death, but death would not come.
The barbarians stink so. How can they be considered human?
Their pleasures and angers are like the jackal's and the
    wolf's – how unbearable!
We travel to the end of Tian-shan, enduring all the frost and
    sleet . . .

Her captor is no savage, however. His nomad's yurt is luxurious, and there are servants on every hand. But nothing can comfort

Wenji. In the fourth painting of the scroll she is seen standing lonely, stiff and vulnerable in a hilly grassland at night with a maid-servant behind her holding her Chinese lute in its case. She gazes at the moon, pleading: 'In the vast barbarian sky my cries are not answered. Yet the bright moon is my Han moon, which should recognize me.'

In the fifth picture the party is camping by a stream:

I sleep by water and sit on grass;
The wind that blows from China tears my clothing to pieces.
I clean my hair with mutton fat, but it is seldom combed.
The collar of my lambskin robe is buttoned on the left;
The fox lapels and badger sleeves are rank-smelling.
By day I wear these clothes, by night I sleep in them . . .[13]

There is more in the same vein, but by episode ten Wenji is coming round. She confesses that when she found herself pregnant with her first barbarian child, she wanted to kill herself. But now her hatred for her odd-looking husband has turned to love. So when a ransom mission arrives in episode twelve she faces a horrible dilemma. Twelve years have gone by since she left 'through the pass'. Should she stay with her husband and two little sons or go back to China? Picture thirteen shows her parting. The nomad prince is crying, the little boys are crying and tugging at Wenji's robes. But by choosing country before family, Wenji became for evermore a symbol of Confucian loyalty to ancestors and state.

The Xiongnu were the reason for China's first official foray into the remote and inhospitable west, reached through the Gansu corridor, a long valley shaped like the neck of a bottle which runs between the northern edge of the Tibetan plateau and the Gobi desert, so giving the Chinese their only manageable approach to the barbarian lands.

In 138 BC the Emperor Wudi sent his ambassador Zhang Qian to persuade the Yuezhi, now in Bactria, to join forces in a pincer movement against the Xiongnu. The long-suffering Zhang was captured by the Xiongnu both on the way out and again on the way back, spending years under house arrest each time. His mission to the Yuezhi was a failure, but on his return twelve years later he enthralled the Chinese court with descriptions of the wonders of central Asia, especially the 'heavenly horses' that he had seen in the Ferghana basin (now in modern Uzbekistan) which he said were so mettlesome that they sweated blood. One thing China lacked was horses, for the soil of inner China does not contain the minerals that are essential for breeding them success-fully. Yet if the Chinese were to get on equal terms with the nomad cavalry, they too needed to be mounted. It can have been no surprise to the people of Ferghana, therefore, when a few years later the Chinese reappeared on a buying mission, or turned up twice more to take horses by force. In later centuries state stud farms were to be set up in Gansu and other western provinces, but these were difficult to defend against raiders. As a result the import of horseflesh – usually paid for in silk – became a vital element of China's trade and tribute system, not to say a heavy drain on the imperial exchequer.

Like many who followed him, the Emperor Wudi enjoyed early military success in central Asia but soon overreached himself. Garrisons were reasonably cheap, but maintaining large armies in the far west was ruinous – and occasionally disastrous.[14] According to Han chronicles, an expedition of 104 BC sent from Dunhuang to take control of the northern oases as far as Ferghana comprised 60,000 men, transported with their supplies by tens of thousands of horses, camels, mules and donkeys and no fewer than 100,000 oxen. Only 10,000 men of this army came back.[15] Garrisons were nonetheless set up at Turfan, Karashahr (near modern Korla), Loulan and Yarkand, only to be lost again during the interregnum of the usurper Wang Mang (AD 9–23).

So enormous were the distances and so difficult the terrain, it is no wonder that few Chinese generals succeeded in winning the west. Those who did so became – and remain – national heroes. The Han dynasty general Ban Chao was the first of only three men to achieve that feat during the following two thousand years.

Ban Chao had first to beat the Xiongnu in Mongolia before he could turn his attention to the Tarim. It took him thirty years to subdue the oases, and he finally captured Kashgar in AD 94. Like Alexander the Great in western Asia, Ban Chao employed only a small core of Chinese soldiers and used local mercenaries as cannon fodder. Like Alexander, too, he left local rulers on their thrones provided they acknowledged his suzerainty. And he ended his career almost as gloriously as the young Macedonian – not quite as King of Asia, but certainly as Viceroy of Central Asia.

Ban Chao is reputedly the author of a famous Chinese maxim: 'Use barbarians to fight barbarians' – a prescription which Beijing still finds useful in foreign affairs. He was also, as was Mao Zedong in the last century, a disciple of Sun Zi whose *Art of War* states that a general who has to fight a battle in order to defeat his enemy is an unsuccessful general. Ban Chao deserves to occupy a footnote in world history: his western campaign gave China temporary control over the Silk Road and paved the way for the phenomenon which today we call 'globalization'.

The Silk Road, first so called by Ferdinand von Richthofen in 1877, is a collective name for the trade routes which linked the capital of China with the west. They carried traffic between Loyang and Chang'an (modern-day Xian) at one end and Antioch and Constantinople at the other. Three routes crossed what is now Xinjiang. The lower road, which was the most difficult but also the most protected, ran from Dunhuang along the southern shore of the Taklamakan desert, with a branch at Yarkand that led over the high Karakoram pass to Leh and northern India. Another branch continued to Kashgar, and thence over the Pamirs to Bactria and Transoxiana (modern Uzbekistan). An alternative route from Dunhuang took the traveller north and west, skirting the Taklamakan south of the Tian Shan mountains to join the lower road at Kashgar. The quickest but most hazardous road led through the mountains near modern Urumchi before turning west along the steppe. These routes carried not only silk but also luxury goods of all kinds – precious stones, spices, fur, amber and beeswax. And other things travelled these routes too – fashions, crafts, technologies and religious beliefs.

The Silk Road extended back into the mists of time, and lasted until the fifteenth century when new sea routes opened by the Europeans made it uncompetitive. Few people travelled the length of it. Goods were normally carried over short stages; and because of the confusion of currencies and languages *en route* specialists were required to do the trading. At the time of the first Chinese incursions during the second century BC, the Parthians in what is now Turkmenistan were exploiting their strategic position between two empires to make money from the passing caravans. Later, most of the business was arranged by Sogdian merchants from Transoxiana who became expert linguists and translators of new ideas.

At the far end of the Silk Road, beyond even Constantinople, was the place the Chinese called Da Qin: Rome. How much they really knew about this great empire in the west is hard to say. The imperial court in Chang'an and the senate in Rome were certainly aware of each other, if only because of the trade in silk which bound them together. The luxury-loving Romans were at this time running a large trade deficit with Asia and were sensitive to any political upheavals at the far end of the line.

After capturing Kashgar in AD 94, General Ban Chao's soldiers crossed the Pamirs and marched on westwards to the Caspian Sea – nearly 4,000 miles from the Pacific and the furthest point ever reached by a Chinese army. Now the general seems to have conceived an ambition to push on to Rome. He instructed an ambassador to map a route for him. According to the annals, the ambassador reached the Gulf and was about to charter a boat when the Parthians, anxious to protect their monopoly as Silk Road middlemen, persuaded him that the journey was much too dangerous.[16]

If he had but known it, General Ban could have talked to some Romans face to face. For, according to Homer Dubs, a distinguished Oxford University professor, there was a colony of them living inside China itself, and not far from the general's starting point.[17]

In the Gansu corridor, near the modern city of Yongchang, there was a town called Lijian, an ancient Chinese name for Rome and the Roman empire. How could a Chinese town more than

4,000 miles from the Mediterranean have acquired such a name? Lijian was first recorded in the Han register of AD 5. Then, during the Wang Mang interregnum of AD 9–23, when place names were altered to suit their own history, the town was rechristened Jie Lu, meaning 'captives [taken in] storming [a city]', or 'captives raised up'. Who were these captives?

Dubs has suggested that they were Roman legionaries, survivors of the stunning defeat inflicted on Marcus Licinius Crassus by the Parthians fifty years before. The battle took place in 53 BC at Carrhae on what is now the Turkish-Syrian border. As usual, the Parthians refused to engage; their mounted archers galloped towards the enemy ranks and let fly as they wheeled their horses away – the famous Parthian (or 'parting') shot. The disciplined Romans would usually put up with this tactic, waiting for the enemy to run out of arrows. At Carrhae, however, the Parthians were particularly well supplied: the rain of arrows continued all day. Although the Romans adopted their testudo, or tortoise, formation to protect their bodies they had not yet learned how to guard their heads and feet on uneven ground and suffered terrible casualties. By the time night fell, Crassus had lost not only his own head but also 20,000 men killed and 10,000 taken prisoner.

Eighteen years later, the Chinese were besieging a fortified town on the Talas river (north of the Tian Shan in modern Kazakhstan). Among the defenders were seen about a hundred men drawn up on either side of the city gate in a 'fish-scale pattern' and practising complicated manoeuvres. Dubs argues that the fish-scale pattern was undoubtedly the effect produced by soldiers interlocking their shields in the testudo formation. And there was only one army in the ancient world whose troops used the testudo – the Roman army. The Chinese attackers also came across a double palisade, a typically Roman fortification. In taking the town, they killed 1,518 people and took 145 captive, among them perhaps the men first seen outside the gates: 'They had probably remained in formation, a formidable body of men ready to defend themselves, as only professional soldiers would do.'[18]

How did these Roman legionaries – if that is what they were – get to the Talas river? According to Pliny, the prisoners taken at Carrhae were sent to serve on Parthia's eastern frontier, 1,500 miles to the east where, says the Roman poet Horace, they probably married barbarian women. Once there, they were not far from the Talas river. Perhaps they escaped from the Parthians and, with no possibility of getting back to Italy, went to serve as mercenaries. After their capture they would readily have accepted an offer from the Chinese to relocate them in a town of their own under the Emperor's favour. Lijian, the Roman colony in China, appeared in the records for another 400 years and may have lasted until the year 746, when the Tibetans overran the area and destroyed it.

China's control of the Silk Road was good for her trade with Rome and the west but it made surprisingly little impact on the culture of the oasis people through whom the trade passed. The strongest influence on the Tarim – one which would spread across Tibet, China and south-east Asia – came up the road from the other direction.

Buddhism began arriving over the Karakoram mountains during the first century AD, carried first by Indian traders, later by monkish missionaries. A democratic breakaway from Hinduism, it promised an escape from the endless cycle of death and rebirth through 'enlightenment'. The new creed had struck a particular chord with the people of Bactria and of Gandhara, in the valleys of what is now northern Pakistan. They were the first to fix the image of the Buddha and spread the texts which were carried into the Tarim basin, where monasteries and cave shrines proliferated.

Buddhism had been adopted by King Ashoka as the official religion of India in 220 BC but it had never really taken root in its country of origin. North of the Himalayas, however, it was well received. The nomadic people (whose shamans, or witchdoctors, are not yet extinct) found it sympathetic to their animist beliefs, while the Chinese seemed to think Buddhism was their idea in the first place, a version of the teachings of their sage Laozi that had spread abroad and come back to them in garbled form.[19] Naturally, Buddhism's arrival in China was marked by legend: it was said that the second Han emperor, Mingdi, had a vision of a resplendent figure entering his palace. When told that it was the Buddha, he sent delegations to India to bring back the sacred books. Buddhism prospered in China until the ninth century, when it was seen as a threat to the state. Then the monasteries were dissolved, their property seized, and thousands of monks and nuns were sent back to civilian life.

When Aurel Stein began to excavate the buried cities of the southern Taklamakan in 1901, he knew of course that Bactria was the probable source of the Buddhist civilization he hoped to uncover. He also knew that Bactria had formerly been under the rule of Macedonian Greeks and had a thriving Greek culture.* But even he was startled by what he found. Digging in a rubbish tip at Niya, Stein turned up large numbers of wooden tablets sealed with clay stamps: 'It was a delightful surprise when, on cleaning the first intact seal impression that turned up, I recognised in it the figure of Pallas Athene, with aegis and thunder bolt, treated in an archaic fashion.'[20] The next showed a 'well-modelled naked figure of pure classical outline' which looked like Eros. Another portrayed Hercules with club and lionskin, just as he appears on Macedonian coins. It was impossible to say which of the seals had been made locally and which imported, or what kind of official used them. But there was no doubting that the 'stationery' was local. Stein had not expected to find the Hellenistic style so far east – 'half-way between western Europe and Peking', as he put it.

Alexander the Great had conquered Bactria in 329 BC, and the province was ruled by Greek satraps for nearly 200 years. Although his soldiers reached the Indus and modern Tashkent, they did not get as far as Xinjiang. (Macedonian traders may have done so in about AD 100.) Alexander's influence, however, was pervasive. There are people today in the Chinese Pamirs who claim descent from him or his soldiers, and many Uighur parents name their boys Iskander after him.

Just as the mummified features of the Tocharians revealed a western genetic origin, so the Buddhist statues and frescoes uncovered by Hedin, Stein and their successors betrayed their

---

* Homer and the Greek tragedies were required reading for Bactrian children, and even Parthians liked to stage Greek plays. Plutarch describes how, after killing Crassus at Carrhae, they took his head and used it as a prop for a performance of Euripides' *Bacchae*. It was kicked about the stage in the final act when the mother of Pentheus, gripped by a Bacchic frenzy, tears off her own son's head.

Indian and Greek background. These traces can be seen in the cave shrines at Kizil, near Kucha; or at Bezeklik, north of Turfan; less so at the Mogao caves near Dunhuang, known as the 'Sistine Chapel of Chinese Buddhism'. Not only the iconography but even the architecture of the buried cities has classical motifs, like the poplar-wood architraves carved into Corinthian columns and volutes.

Albert von Le Coq, who excavated some of the most important sites on the north side of the desert and in the Turfan depression, declared that it was 'impossible to find anywhere the slightest suggestion of Chinese influence in either the architecture, painting, or sculpture of these . . . peoples. All their forms are Indian or Iranian on a late classical basis.' And this was in spite of the military power which China exerted at times of dynastic strength.

It was tempting of course for classically educated Westerners to place so much emphasis on the Greek and other western influences they found in China, though nobody could deny that the further east these styles travelled, the more Chinese they became. But what archaeology had shown, once again, was that Xinjiang – at least up to this point in its history – owed much more to the west than it did to the east.

Great though they were, Ban Chao's military triumphs did not secure Chinese rule in the far west. By the year AD 200, the Han dynasty was nearing its end, its decline accompanied by the customary infighting of mandarins and eunuchs inside the court and peasant revolts without. Even the Xiongnu rallied, invading China itself in AD 304. The people of the western deserts were once more left to their own devices.

But now their lives were to be disrupted from an unexpected quarter. At about the beginning of the fourth century, their water supply began to give out. The glaciers were shrinking and the annual flood from their snowmelt was growing weaker. Not only the Tarim basin but all of China succumbed to a drought so severe that the Yellow River and the Yangtze could in some places be forded on foot. Some of the Tarim basin rivers changed their course, leaving delta settlements high and dry; in other places deforestation coupled with the demands of a growing population were to blame. Everywhere, it seems, there was a shortage of people to maintain the irrigation channels, perhaps due to the upheavals that followed the end of the Han dynasty.[21]

Whatever the causes, the garden cities of the Taklamakan began to dwindle and die. Aurel Stein discounted later stories of the Sodom and Gomorrah sort, in which great sandstorms were said to have overwhelmed the people at night to punish them for their impiety. Karadong, excavated by Stein in 1901, was abandoned in the fourth century. The town seems once to have been a staging-post for travel between the north and south sides of the desert. What is today an arid bowl surrounded by dunes was then an attractive riverside town. And the Keriya river, which today disappears into the sands many miles short of Karadong, once flowed on to the then important religious centre of Kucha. (Another, smaller, settlement was recently discovered some miles further north of Karadong.) Other cities, like Dandan-Oilik which Stein found between the Keriya and Khotan rivers, survived until the eighth century. In all, according to some estimates, up to 300 towns were lost to the sands. The desiccation was to resume in the modern age, first in the seventeenth century and again, but at an accelerating rate, in the twentieth. Today there is only one desert delta where a settlement of any size can be found.

After the collapse of the Han dynasty, China broke up into separate kingdoms under rulers of different races. Control over the western regions passed to Turkic tribes and other nomad groups such as the Hepthalites, or White Huns, who conquered the Tarim oases towards the end of the fifth century. Not until AD 618 and the advent of the Tang dynasty was China reunited; and the new emperor, Li Shimin, set about reconquering the lost domains. Forty years later, the Tang armies had reached as far as Samarkand and Bokhara. But now they too faced 'barbarian' enemies on both sides: Tibetans in the south, and Turks in the north.

The Tibetans had united in about AD 600 and were spilling out of their mountain fortress in all directions. In 662 they inflicted a serious defeat on the Chinese at Koko Nor on the Qaidam plateau. It is hard today to imagine the Tibetans as a warrior nation. But for nearly two hundred years they fought the Chinese armies tooth and nail, descending from their icy plateau to seize control of the desert to the north. At Miran they built an imposing fort which still stands among the houses and stupas of the Buddhist city. Stein gathered a great haul of records from rubbish pits beneath the north wall. Although they were a thousand years old they still stank when they were disturbed. In 790 the Tibetans marched up the Khotan river to seize a Tang fort perched on the red rock of Mazartagh, now marooned and guarding nothing but a dry river bed in the middle of the Taklamakan. A year later they beat the Chinese and their Turkic allies again at Beshbalik, near Urumchi. The Tibetans held the region until the middle of the ninth century, and they still commemorate the era when they were a force to be reckoned with. Among the adornments for her wedding, today's Tibetan bride carries down her back a symbolic arrow twisted round with ribbons of many colours. This, according to a Tibetan writer, recalls the marriage of King Songtsen Gampo to a Chinese princess in the seventh century; she had brought with her just such an arrow.[22]

Meanwhile, out on the steppe, the normal hum of nomad traffic had been rising to a roar. Since the fifth century everyone – Huns and Turks from the north, Avars from central Asia – had been on the move, all heading westwards and pushing each other out of the way. A tidal wave of migrants displaced tribes like the Goths who were forced away from the Black Sea and down into the Balkans and Italy, and the Vandals, who were squeezed out of Gaul into Spain and North Africa, and who came back to attack Rome by sea.

To our sedentary societies these great movements of the past seem almost incomprehensible. True nomads are virtually extinct in Eurasia today, even though seasonal transfer – transhumance – is still practised by Kazakhs in the Tian Shan mountains and by Kyrgyz in the Pamirs. Yet one has only to glance at the physical map of Eurasia to see that above the 46th or 48th parallel, north of a belt of deserts, mountains and seas, the steppe road is wide open all the way from Mongolia to northern France. Armed riders and traders could range freely back and forth across vast distances, and for a horseman averaging a modest 40 miles a day it would take a mere three months to ride from, say, Ulan Bator to Berlin. Not until faced with rifles, artillery and bombs – first from the Russians, later the Chinese – did the nomads lose the tactical supremacy they had acquired over centuries.

Around the year AD 540 came the first sighting on the Chinese horizon of a world-shaking new entity that had not been identified before.[23] The Turks, in their various guises, were to become for most of the next thousand years the dominant race not only of central Asia – including of course east and west 'Turkestan' – but also of the Caucasus and Anatolia, capturing Istanbul and extending their rule as far as the Balkans in eastern Europe.

The Turks (often written as Türk to avoid confusion with the people of modern Turkey) were hunters and fishermen as well as pastoral nomads. As far as is known they originated in Siberia and Mongolia, and were racial cousins of the Mongols, whose glory days were yet to come.* Their name meant 'helmet', metallurgy being their speciality, and their own runic script can be seen in the records they kept of their doings engraved on stone stelae beside the Orkhon river, which rises due west of Ulan Bator in modern Mongolia and flows north to Lake Baikal.

Turkic Muslim historians like to trace their descent from Noah's son Japhet who, after the Ark came to rest on Mount Ararat (now on the Turkish-Armenian border), was sent east by his father with a jade stone. One of Japhet's sons was Türk. Some generations later, according to legend, the land allotted to Türk was divided between two sons, Tartar and Mughol (Mongol).

Like the Jews, the Turks saw themselves as God's chosen people. According to Mahmut Kashgari, an eleventh-century Uighur poet and composer of the first Turkic dictionary, God himself gave the Turks their name, regarded them as his private army, and put them in charge of 'troublemakers in the east' – the Chinese, presumably – thus demonstrating that they were 'superior to all other beings'. He gave them the loftiest place in the world to live in, and the purest air to breathe. 'Moreover, one can observe among them

---

* Their origin is ill-determined: for example, Turkic speakers were identified north of the Black Sea in the fifth century before they were heard of in Mongolia.

such praiseworthy qualities as beauty, friendliness, good taste, good manners, filial piety, loyalty, simplicity, modesty, dignity, bravery.'[24] Mahmut Kashgari is buried on the edge of Opal, a pretty oasis south-west of Kashgar, with a long view of the Pamir mountains; his people gave him a fine tomb.

Coming closer to verifiable history, the first Turk empire was founded by two brothers, an event commemorated by an unknown author on the stone stelae by the Orkhon river: 'When high above the blue sky and down below the brown earth had been created, betwixt the two were created the sons of men. And above the sons of men stood my ancestors, the Kaghans [kings] Bumin and Ishtemi.'[25] They set out to conquer everyone within reach, and between the years 552 and 744 they built an empire that stretched in a long, narrow swathe of territory from Mongolia to the 'western sea' (the Caspian) and from the borders of China to the edge of the Byzantine empire.

However, in 581, several decades before the Tang dynasty reunited China, a family feud resulted in a rift between the eastern and the western Turks. A chronicler of the short-lived Sui dynasty which preceded the Tang noted with satisfaction: 'The Turks prefer to destroy each other rather than to live side by side. They have a thousand, nay ten thousand, clans who are hostile to and kill one another. They mourn their dead with much grief and swear vengeance.'[26] The author of the Orkhon stelae, deciphered by the Dane Vilhelm Thomsen in the late nineteenth century, admitted that it was the Turks' own fault. There had been a period of disorder, of unwise rulers and incompetent officials, he explained, aided and abetted by 'the cunning and deceitfulness of the Chinese' who seduced the leaders with empty titles. Noblemen's sons became slaves and 'their ladylike daughters became servants'.[27]

Relations with the Chinese oscillated. Raids and retaliation were followed by truces sealed with royal marriages and tribute – usually of horses in exchange for silk. When the Turks had their final falling out, the Chinese decided their best policy was to befriend the more distant branch, the Western Turks, who controlled the Tarim basin, the better to control the Eastern Turks who were closer. It was a repeat of the Han dynasty tactic of courting the distant Yuezhi in order to control the nearer Xiongnu. But as their new dynasty grew stronger, the Chinese were able to defeat the Eastern Turks in 630, and thirty years later they wrested the Tarim from the Western Turks. Xinjiang was divided into four or five administrative regions, a governor was posted to Kucha to oversee the local rulers, and garrisons were built at strategic sites. The Chinese called the territory Anxi, the 'pacified West', but as usual, the west did not remain pacified for long.

By AD 680, the Turks were on the march again, their moral fibre apparently renewed by a leader called Elterish. On his staff he had a famous vizier, Tonyukuk, a pragmatic nationalist who declared that Buddhism and Daoism were for milksops, not warriors, and that the Turks could only survive by remaining nomads – by 'following the water and the grass', as he put it. Bilga, a son of Elterish, described his father's campaigns on a stele:

> My father the kaghan set out with 17 men, and as the word spread that he had set out and was advancing, those who were in the plains went up into the mountains and those who were in the mountains came down; they gathered, and there were 77 men. Because Heaven gave them strength, the arm of my father was like wolves and their enemies were like sheep. Leading campaigns to the east [Manchuria] and to the west [Transoxiana and Tocharistan], my father gathered the people and made them rise. And all together they numbered 700 men . . . He led 47 campaigns and fought in 20 battles.[28]

Brave as they may have been, the Turks were no match for the Tang armies. But now another piece was added to the chessboard of the central Asian power struggle: the Arabs. Their presence was the catalyst for a chain reaction that changed the course of history for China in the west.

With their Prophet and the Quran to guide them, the Arabs were the emerging power beyond the Pamir mountains. Muhammad had died only a hundred years before, in 632, and the Arabs under their general Qutayba bin Muslim had already invaded western Turkestan, taking Bokhara in 712 and Ferghana in 713.* In 750 a

---

* Claims that Qutayba reached Kashgar seem to be exaggerated. He was eventually recalled to Merv and was killed in a plot in 716.

Chinese governor in Xinjiang, Gao Xianzhi, was rash enough to provoke them by intervening in a dispute between the rulers of Ferghana and Tashkent. Governor Gao marched across the mountains, sacked the city of Tashkent and had its ruler executed. The ruler's son fled to Samarkand for help, and Gao found himself facing an Arab army. With Turkic troops in support, he confronted the Arabs on the River Talas, north of Tashkent in modern Kazakhstan, where the 'Roman legionaries' had been captured 800 years before. But the Turkic troops changed sides at the last moment and the Chinese were defeated.

The Battle of the Talas was not a big battle but it had far-reaching consequences. It scotched China's ambitions for a western empire, putting eastern Turkestan beyond her grasp for the next thousand years. Some historians argue that Gao's meddling with the remnants of the western Turk khanate removed the only serious opposition to Islam and the Arabs.[29] If that is right, then it was a Chinese official who inadvertently helped create the 'Muslim problem' which haunts Beijing today. There was positive gain for civilization, however. Among the Chinese taken prisoner after the battle were paper-makers, and through them the craft reached the Islamic world and Europe.

In the event the victory of the Arabs proved more cultural than military. They were pushed back by a Turkic dynasty, the Karakhanids, whose reach extended into Kashgar and the rest of the Altishahr (the six cities of the Tarim), where their descendants still carry their names – names such as Bughra, 'the camel', and Arslan, 'the lion'.

Westerners tend to equate the word Turk with 'barbarian'. But in Asia it stood for unity and a common language. The civilization of the Turks was exceptionally complex, and their role in the history of central Asia was pivotal. One could add that there are many rulers in Asia and the Middle East who to this day – with however little justification – fear some sort of pan-Turkic revival. The government of China is one of them.

Out of the welter of Turkic tribes, one name stands out which is important to our story – the Uighurs. In AD 744, the Uighur tribe, comprising ten clans, took over the leadership of the Eastern Turks, itself a confederacy of nine tribes. They built themselves a new capital at Karabalghasun on the upper reaches of the Orkhon river, and settled down to a more sedentary – and civilized – life. The Uighurs were in those days a specific group whose name meant 'joiner', 'follower' or 'supporter'.* In its modern sense, however, the designation Uighur is generic, comprising all those present and recent inhabitants of the Tarim who are not Mongol, Kazakh, Kyrgyz, Tajik or (of course) Han Chinese.

The new leaders were well disposed towards the Chinese, and seven of their thirteen khans took Han princesses as wives. Uighur khans, like Chinese emperors, believed in their divine right and styled themselves Tangri Khan, 'King of Heaven'; and they insisted on courtiers and visitors performing their own version of the Chinese kowtow. Although they affected to despise the Son of Heaven in the Chinese capital they recognized his prestige. He, in turn, liked to pretend that he was responsible for appointing the Uighur khans. In fact, the relationship was one of equals, whatever the official histories might say. The picture of the Chinese Emperor sitting magnificently on his throne while terrified ambassadors laden with gifts from barbarian lands grovel at his feet is a misleading one. Like China's earlier neighbours, the Uighurs were people who had to be humoured because they could not be conquered.† But in order not to lose face, the Han talked of exacting 'tribute' from their neighbours when in fact they depended on them for trade – and sometimes for protection, too.

The line between trade and diplomacy in the exchange of gifts (and indeed of princesses) was hard to draw. 'Probably no other country in the world has ever made such an effort to supply its neighbours with presents, thus elevating the gift into a political tool', an historian has written.[30] By lavishing gifts on the barbarians the Chinese hoped to corrupt them with luxury, and so break up

---

* Sometimes spelt Uygur, or Ouighour. The latter is clumsy but gives the best sense of the pronunciation.

† For long periods of their history the Han Chinese were not their own masters but were ruled by a succession of foreign dynasties such as the Wei, the Jin, the Liao, the Yuan (Mongol) and the Qing (Manchu). At times they were forced to pay tribute – real tribute – to others.

the tribal confederations. Far from being dragged as vassals before the Emperor, the nomads were only too keen to send envoys – so much so, that at times the Chinese suffered serious balance of payments problems, could no longer stand the expense of hosting the embassies and were forced to turn new applicants away.

The Uighurs were especially persistent.[31] Trading horses for silk, grain, cloth, weapons and tea, they 'raised extortion of the Tang state, what the Chinese historians justified as "tribute", to a fine art'.[32] As for political marriages, which were common practice right down to the time of the Manchus, everyone knows the (probably apocryphal) story of the Chinese princess who gave away one of the greatest industrial secrets of all time by smuggling silkworms and mulberry leaves in her headdress when she was sent off to the far west as a bride for the King of Khotan.

Not only were the Uighurs as culturally sophisticated as the Tang, there were occasions when the Chinese had to turn to them for assistance. Twice they helped the Emperor recapture his capital from the Tibetans. And in 762, Uighur soldiers were billeted in the Chinese capital to help put down a serious internal rebellion. They made themselves unpopular by staying on for the whole winter, looting the shops and beating up the locals.

It was on a visit to the capital that the Uighur khan first came into contact with Manichaean missionaries from the west and was converted. With a change of religion came a change of attitude and remarkable enthusiasm for the new, more compassionate ethic.[33] The khan's conversion was noted in the annals: 'Let the people accept the Religion of Light . . . Let the state where men kill be transformed into a kingdom where good works are done.'[34] Now everyone, or at least those living in the Uighur capital, was expected to follow the khan's example. In their enthusiasm to be seen as sophisticated westerners, the nobles did so, to the extent of renouncing their manly diet of meat and turning vegetarian. The army officers were reluctant, however, preferring to continue consulting magicians, oracles and magic pebbles.

Manichaeism had arrived with refugees from Sogdiana (modern Uzbekistan), who now enjoyed influence at the Uighur court. The religion was founded by a Mesopotamian prophet and painter, Mani, who was born in AD 216 and was much influenced by Buddhism. His doctrine of good and evil as equal and opposite forces, the good being equated with spirit and light, evil with matter and darkness, was immediately popular. It was regarded as heretical in the west (where it surfaced among the Cathars, or 'pure ones', of Albi in southern France and the Bogomils of the Balkans) but was more easily acceptable in the east because of its Buddhist echoes.[35]

When the Tang emperor Taizong died in 779, the Sogdians persuaded the khan to seize the opportunity to invade China. The khan's cousin, Tun Bagha, prevented him by the simple expedient of killing him and taking the throne himself. But now the Uighurs began to lose their battles. After Tun's death a regent was humiliated trying to recapture the important outpost of Beshbalik (a city near modern Urumchi where the Chinese had a governor) from the Tibetans, and by the end of the century the khanate was in decline. A severe winter in 839 which killed large numbers of the Uighurs' livestock was seen as an omen; for the following year a rebel chief betrayed his khan and invited the neighbouring Kyrgyz to take over.

The Kyrgyz, traders in mammoth furs and walrus tusks, lived in their original homeland in the Altai mountains, far from the Pamirs where they are to be found today. They killed the khan, seized his capital and scattered his subjects, putting an end to the Uighur empire in the north.[36] Perhaps it is going too far to blame vegetarianism for the collapse; but the pacifist doctrines of Manichaeism must have played a part. There were other causes: the difficulty of adapting to a new culture, a rift between town and country, luxury at court, and enemies like the Tibetans who were still on the rampage without.[37]

The Uighurs did not simply disappear. Indeed, they were to have an even more important influence on Xinjiang. Driven out of Mongolia, they moved south to Gansu and Turfan, which had been under their control since 760. They set up a new capital at Kocho in the Turfan depression, absorbing the local Indo-European culture and Buddhism. Although their leaders had converted to Manichaeism, as we have seen, a number of their subjects, just to confuse things, had chosen to become Nestorian Christians. This schismatic version of Christianity followed the teaching of a fifth-century Syrian bishop, who became patriarch of Constantinople, that Christ had two natures, one human, one divine. The heretics broke away to form their own church with its seat at Ctesiphon (near modern Baghdad) and from there Christianity was introduced into China by Iranians and the same Sogdian merchants who had brought Manichaeism along the Silk Road. With its community of many faiths, not to mention a Buddhist past, Kocho was a powerhouse of religious painting and writing. Albert von Le Coq, who excavated Kocho in 1904–5, found what he described as a 'marvellous body of Christian manuscripts', including fragments of the Nicene Creed and St Matthew's Gospel. This and other discoveries prompted him to exclaim that the inhabitants of Turfan 'must, like their ancestors, be looked upon as a nation of entirely western civilisation'.[38] The only Chinese influences he could detect lay in the use of brushes to write and chopsticks to eat.

A charming account of the Uighur kingdom of Kocho as it appeared at the end of the tenth century was left by Wang Di, a Chinese ambassador from the Song emperor. Commenting – as many have since – on the extreme heat in summer, and the people's habit of taking refuge underground, Wang Di said that the Uighurs still behaved in many ways like the nomads they once were:

> The nobility eat horseflesh, while the rest of the population eat mutton, ducks and geese. In music, they play a sort of mandolin and a five-chord guitar. The men enjoy horseback riding and archery . . . Those who like to take long walks never forget to bring along a musical instrument . . . There are no destitute people in the kingdom; those who cannot provide for themselves are cared for by public welfare. Many people reach advanced age.[39]

Wang Di added that there were about fifty Buddhist monasteries and a Manichaean temple served by Persian priests called the Temple of the Pearl.

Gradually the native Tocharian language died out and Turkic took its place, but the Uighurs gave up their runic script in favour of a modified Sogdian one. Little of Kocho remains today but an expanse of grey mud walls. For centuries the grape farmers of the local village, Astana, used it as a source of loam for their fields; the practice was stopped by an enlightened village headman only a few years ago. The kingdom was remarkable for its stability and longevity – it was still functioning, more or less, in the 1930s – and the love of music persists.

Islam, the new religion sweeping all before it on the western side of the Pamirs, had made scarcely any impression on eastern Turkestan. But Muslim historians are as revisionist as any, and as eager as Chinese annalists to assert priority. They ascribed the conversion of the kingdom of Kashgaria, covering the western Tarim, to one man, and to a single, early date.

The man was Satuk Bughra Khan, and the date 957. Satuk was 12 years old according to the Muslim chronicler, waiting to succeed his late father to the throne of Kashgar, and plainly destined for great things. Not only was he precociously wise, but on the day of his birth there had been a great earthquake: flowers blossomed, even though it was winter, and springs gushed forth.

On the same day, on the other side of the Pamirs, a merchant called Abu Nasr Samani had a vision of the Prophet who told him to perform religious exercises for twelve years and then cross the mountains on a special mission. As the day approached for Abu Nasr's journey, Satuk was out hunting near Kashgar. 'A hare started from under a thorny bush, and Satuk, bow in hand, giving chase got separated from the others. The hare now suddenly stopped, and assumed the form of a man, and thus addressed the youth.' This sage, or angel, warned the boy that if he failed to acknowledge Allah and His Prophet, he would suffer hellfire, scorpions and other tortures. But if he did, he would qualify for paradise, replete with beautiful girls and boys and fine wine. A few days later, Satuk met Abu Nasr and after only a short discussion, the boy was converted.

Meanwhile Satuk's uncle Harun, who was acting as regent, had a dream about a tiger cub which he identified as his apostate nephew. He ordered the boy's execution. Satuk's distraught mother begged him first to prove the boy's conversion by waiting to see whether Satuk would carry out a planned engagement to lay the corner stone of a Buddhist temple. Naturally, as a good Muslim Satuk no longer wanted to take part in the ceremony. But Abu Nasr advised him to go ahead: so long as he pretended he was in a mosque while he recited the prayers, said his mentor, Allah would forgive him.

Seeing Satuk's compliance, Harun spared the boy's life, but he soon realized his mistake. The battle that followed lasted seven days and seven nights, with terrible losses on both sides, and Satuk proved invincible. His sword stretched 40 yards when drawn against infidels, and long flames belched from his mouth when he charged at them. Coming upon his uncle while he was asleep, the young victor woke him up, gave him a chance to convert and, when he refused, chopped off his head and threw it out of the window on to a dung-heap. Emerging from the palace, he proclaimed himself king, and Islam the official religion of Kashgaria.

After a career of conquest in which he carried Islam as far as Turfan, Satuk fell ill. Before dying he took a rose from a tray and sniffed it, an apple and ate it, and a goblet of sherbert and drank it. He then stood up and recited the Muslim creed, turned round three times and sang a Persian song: 'A drop taken from the ocean makes it none the less, and a soul quitting its body rends but its covering veil.' He died in the Muslim year 430, or AD 1037.[40]

The progress of Islam was nowhere near so rapid or so widespread as Satuk's story implies. For many years there were Buddhist Turks (the Uighurs) in the eastern part of Xinjiang, and Muslim Turks (Karakhanids) in the western part. The Karakhitai and Mongol invasions of China interrupted the advance of Islam, as did the oasis people's attachment to their old religion. Their resistance can be read into the Turki legends about Khotan: how a flying imam came from Mecca to convert the city; how four imams arrived from Kashgar but were foiled by the local sorcerer who made the city invisible; how the villagers of Ujat disguised themselves as dogs and ate the harnesses of a mounted Muslim army which had come to convert them.

No new religion succeeds without absorbing the symbols and rituals of the old. Just as Christian churches were built on pagan sites in England, so Buddhist stupas were reallocated to Muslim saints in eastern Turkestan. Even the legends themselves had to be taken over. The story of the flying imam is suspiciously like the story of the giant image which flew from India to announce the death of the Buddha more than a thousand years before. And the story of the villagers of Ujat who ate the harnesses is like the story of the golden rats as big as hedgehogs who saved the kingdom of Khotan from the invading Xiongnu. Led by a rat-king, they 'destroyed overnight all the leather of the harness and armour of the invading host, which then fell easy prey to the defenders'.[41]

The Tang emperors had failed to hold their western empire, and the dynasty came to an end in AD 907. There followed a period of confusion in Xinjiang, of alliances, betrayals, battles and massacres which it would be tedious to relate. For the next 300 years the region was variously under the control of the Karakhitai, or Black Khitans, whose leader Gorkhan founded the Western Liao dynasty; the Western Xia dynasty based on the Yellow River, in what is today Ningxia province; and the Nayman Mongols, Nestorian Christians led by their chief Kuchluk. The latter enjoyed persecuting the newly converted Muslims, forcing imams to recant by hanging them upside down from trees outside their mosques.* Kuchluk's reign came to an end when the son of one of his victims turned to a superior power for help. 'Superior' is an understatement: it was the most ambitious, aggressive and terrifying power the world had yet seen.

The twelfth century was coming to an end, and far out in the grasslands the Mongols were mobilizing. They had come to dominate the steppes under their 13-year-old leader Temujin, and in 1206 the tribes held a great rally on the upper Onon river, north-east of modern Ulan Bator, to declare him chief of chiefs under the new name of Genghis Khan.

Within five years Genghis had descended on the Chinese

---

* Another Nayman chief, who married a Uighur princess, became a legend in Europe, where he was seen as a possible ally against the Muslims whom the Crusaders were trying to drive from the holy places in Palestine. They called him King John, or Prester John. But envoys who went looking for him came back empty-handed. Prester John was later supposed to be in Africa.

empire, taking control of Manchuria and Beijing in 1215. He
pursued and defeated Kuchluk at Kashgar, chased him to Khotan
and decapitated him. The Mongols' terror tactics are well known:
a witness from this period is said to have marched for three days
along a hill 'white as snow with the bleached bones of the slain'.
The ground was 'black and grimed with their gore, the stink of
which killed some and poisoned most of their party. At the city
itself, under one of its towers, he saw a pile of bones, said to be
those of twenty thousand virgins who had been cast from it to
escape by such death the fury of the Mughol soldiers.'[42]

There is no need to follow the progress of the Mongol hordes
nor dwell on the methods they used to get as far as Hungary and
Austria. It is interesting to note, however, that not all their casualties were the result of massacre: for they have been held responsible
for bringing the Black Death to Europe. Bubonic plague was
borne by the fleas carried in the fur of the steppe marmot, and was
endemic among the nomads. According to modern historians, the
Mongols, laying siege to the city of Caffa in the Crimea, which
was then a Genoese colony, threw some of their plague-ridden
dead over the city walls. Many of the besieged then fled by ship to
Italy, taking the disease with them. From there the plague spread
and wiped out a third of Europe's population.

Eastern Turkestan was conquered in 1218 but was spared the
worst of the Mongol terror. The Uighur khans submitted quickly,
and many of their soldiers joined the nomad army. But the
Uighurs' contribution to a brutally achieved Pax Mongolica went
further than mere submission. The Mongols were illiterate, and
when Genghis came to write down his people's customs and law,
the *yasa-yusun*, it was the Uighurs who supplied him with their
Sogdian script. They took on much of the new rulers' administrative and clerical work, just as in modern times the Palestinians ran
the affairs of the uneducated bedouin sheikhs of the Gulf. When
not at war, the Mongols were tolerant and adaptable people: they
made no fuss about religion, often adopting the beliefs of their
subjects. In this way, Buddhists and Christians in western China
were able to resist Islam well into the fourteenth century.

Inner China was still not fully conquered, the new capital of
Beijing was not completed and Genghis himself was long dead

when the Mongols set up their Yuan dynasty in 1271. Before his death in 1227, Genghis had divided his empire between his four sons. Eastern Turkestan was included in the middle part of the realm allotted to Chagatai, described by the nineteenth-century Hungarian traveller and scholar Arminius Vambéry as a bigoted Buddhist and confirmed drunkard.[43] His reign was peaceful. From his capital at Almalik in the Ili valley near modern Gulja, he controlled not only the Tarim and Dzungarian basins, renamed Mugholistan, but also Transoxiana and former Bactria.

After Chagatai's death anarchy ruled. The emperors of the native Ming dynasty which replaced the Mongol Yuan dynasty in 1368 had limited ambitions outside the Middle Kingdom and were in any case powerless to intervene. For a short time the region was controlled by Timur the Lame, or Tamerlane from Samarkand, who set up camp in the Ili valley and captured Chagatai's capital.

Not much is recorded about the eastern side of the Tarim basin after the end of the Yuan dynasty. But Turkic histories of western Kashgaria tell us that for most of the next 400 years the oasis farmers were again subjected to a succession of cruel and quarrel-some – if colourful – Muslim princes. Heirs fought each other for the succession, wives and daughters were given as presents, alliances and betrayals ended in decapitation and war, battles were settled by single combat in front of armies. The first rulers were descendants of Mongol khans who had converted to Islam; later they were Turki religious nobles ('khojas') from western Turkestan who claimed a bloodline back to the Prophet Muhammad himself.

One of them was Muhammad Khan (1408–16) who was so jealous of the turban of Islam that he refused to let the peasants wear it: if they did so, he had their fur caps pegged to their heads with a horseshoe. Then there was Pir Muhammad, nicknamed 'Bangi' for his constant intoxication from marijuana. Cruellest of them all, however, was Abubakr, who took Kashgar in 1460 but had his capital at Yarkand. Although affecting great piety, Abubakr would have entire families mutilated for the offence of one member, cutting off the feet of thousands of his subjects. His cruelty was witnessed by Mirza Hydar, one of his generals, whose own family were taken prisoner. One brother was put under the guard of eunuchs until he was 15 years old when, says Hydar, the khan 'staked him to a wall of his chamber by an iron rod through the belly and thus left him to die and rot'.[44] Greedy as well as cruel, Abubakr used chain gangs of male and female convicts to dig through the ruins of desert cities in search of buried treasure. He ended his days wandering the Tibetan plateau, where he was ambushed and killed.

Not all rulers were vicious. Khan Mansur (d. 1542) was a rare case of a Muslim leader who was devout and went to bed early to pray. Mansur employed a chanter of the Quran, a sort of private chaplain, who, although he had perfect intonation, a clear voice and an unfailing memory, was 'slovenly in dress, filthy in habits and beastly in practices'. The courtiers wanted him dismissed, alleging that he had been 'taken in an unnatural crime with a cow'. But the khan retorted that he kept the man to teach him how to read the Quran, not how to rape cattle.[45]

From the year 1560 Kashgaria was at peace. Travellers were able to journey without escort all the way from Hami in the east to Andijan in the Ferghana basin, 'finding hotels at every stage of the road'. But as the Mongol line of Genghis's son Chagatai ran out, the succession became more and more troublesome. From the late seventeenth century it was fought over by two factions of khojas: the Karataghlik ('black mountain') khojas and the Aktaghlik ('white mountain') khojas. The problem was that both factions traced their descent from the Prophet, and indeed from the same man, but they were the product of different mothers.* Nearly a hundred years of turmoil ensued. The resolution when it came was bloody, and it put the people of Kashgaria under a foreign yoke which, but for brief periods, they were never again able to throw off. For it brought back the Chinese, whose presence had hardly been seen or felt since the middle of the Tang dynasty nearly a thousand years before. The Chinese returned to the far

---

* Or possibly of different sons. The common ancestor was Makhtum Azam, a Naqshbandi sufi and theologian from Bokhara who went to Kashgar in the fifteen century, where he became the protégé of the then ruler, a descendant of Genghis Khan.

west, and there – in spite of repeated uprisings against them – they remain to this day.

The new imperialists were not themselves Han Chinese. They were Manchus, steppe nomads from the north who called themselves after the Chinese province of Manchuria which they had first conquered. Once in control of the whole north-east, the Manchus had descended on Beijing in 1644 and proclaimed a new dynasty, the Qing. In contrast to the rulers of the later Ming period, the Manchus and their famous regiments of bannermen were vigorous, outward-looking and expansionist, and just as capable of savagery as their allies the Mongols who had conquered China 400 years before them.

The building of a great Qing empire in the north and west was begun by the Emperor Kangxi largely in response to a challenge from Mongol tribes. Among these were the Dzungars, Buddhists living in the Dzungarian basin, who joined forces in 1676 under a leader called Galdan. Since Galdan's ambition was to conquer not only the Tarim basin and Mongolia but also China itself, a collision was inevitable.

As Galdan's armies fought their way east, allies of the new Manchu dynasty appealed for help. The Emperor Kangxi sent his soldiers north almost to the shores of Lake Baikal; there they confronted Galdan's army and, with the help of cannon designed for them by Jesuits, defeated it in 1690. A protracted campaign against Galdan's confederacy was mounted by General Yue Zhongqi, military governor of Shaanxi and Sichuan, who was a favourite of the succeeding Manchurian emperor, Yongzheng. Although General Yue persuaded the Uighur khan of Turfan to submit, his campaign suffered many setbacks, and the cost of the war fell as a great burden on the people of the western provinces of China.* Heavily taxed, with their women forced into prostitution, and facing starvation, they took to the hills as brigands. Among them were

---

* This khan's fidelity to China is recorded in a modern dedication put up by the Communist authorities at the Emin minaret in Turfan.

women of legendary strength and ferocity with names like Jade Woman and Purple Cloud; known as the 'rouged bandits', they were said to be able to leap huge distances in spite of their bound feet, and to ride beneath galloping horses.[46]

When, after Galdan's death, his nephew tried to capture the oasis of Hami on China's border in 1715, the Manchus went on the offensive. An army was sent into the Dzungarian basin, beating the Mongols near modern-day Urumchi. A treaty was signed in 1724. But the peace was disrupted by the inevitable contest for the succession. One of the contenders was a chief called Amursana, who promised the Chinese that Dzungaria would submit to them if they would help him on to Galdan's throne. The Emperor Qianlong sent his bannermen all the way to Gulja in the Ili valley to enforce Amursana's claims. As soon as he was installed, however, the devious Amursana seems to have changed his mind about vassalage. At any rate, he was taken under guard to Beijing but escaped and made his way back to Dzungaria to start an uprising in 1757.

The Manchus' revenge was terrible. In the mopping-up operations that followed, the Dzungars were virtually exterminated. Historians estimate that a million people were slaughtered, and the land so devastated that it took generations for it to recover. Crossing the Tian Shan, the Manchu army moved through the Tarim, where the 'white mountain' and 'black mountain' khojas were busy fighting one another, and took control of it in 1759.

Thus the Chinese secured their conquest. Their success alarmed Muslim rulers all over central Asia who were disturbed to find the Chinese right on their doorstep. Even the warlike Kyrgyz in the mountains above Kashgar were terrified into submission. Just over a thousand years had elapsed since the Chinese were sent packing by the Arabs and Turks at the Battle of the Talas.

By acquiring an empire, China under the Emperor Qianlong was developing at least the outlines of a superpower, even if that status would take another 200 years to achieve. Her territory was now larger than it had ever been – or would ever be again.[47] It is perhaps idle to wonder whether, if Galdan had been less greedy or the Muslim rulers of Kashgar less quarrelsome, the people of the far west would have secured their independence and still be enjoying it today. In the event the region formerly known to the Chinese as Huijiang ('Muslim-land') now acquired a name to reflect its change of status: Xinjiang, meaning 'new frontier' or 'new territory'.

3

The Fragrant Concubine

Among the emperor Qianlong's trophies from his conquest of Xinjiang was a girl called Iparhan. She was a beautiful Kashgari whose body was said to give off an intoxicating scent without any help from ointments or powders; and when Qianlong heard about this beauty he ordered his general to seize her for the royal harem. She was stolen from her husband (or perhaps her father), one of the Muslim leaders of Kashgar who had resisted Qianlong's army, wrapped up like a piece of precious porcelain and placed in a litter for the long journey to Beijing. Along the road her fragrant body was washed every day in camel's milk and polished smooth with butter. When she arrived in the capital, the Emperor was besotted, Iparhan was renamed Xiang Fei, and the legend of 'The Fragrant Concubine' was born.

The story of Iparhan is one of the most popular in China. Restaurants are named after her; operas, films and books have been written about her. She has been called, next to Wuer Kaixi, the leader of the 1989 Tiananmen student rebellion, the best-known Uighur outside central Asia.[1] She is said to be the young woman in Manchu armour and crested helmet painted in Beijing by the Jesuit missionary Giuseppe Castiglione in the eighteenth century. Modern copies of this famous portrait by a local Uighur artist are on sale at the Kashgar mausoleum of the Khoja Apakh, who may (or may not) have been her great-uncle. The tomb became a place of pilgrimage after claims were made that the miraculous body of Iparhan was buried there – a claim now recognized as false.

The Fragrant Concubine has become a symbol as well as a heroine. But to the Han Chinese she symbolizes one thing, to the Uighurs quite another. And the contradictory accounts of what transpired between Iparhan and Qianlong, between mistress and master, are eloquent: they tell us much about the relationship between Xinjiang and China.

In a version recounted to the British missionary Mildred Cable in the 1930s, the Emperor gives Iparhan a gilded room in the imperial palace and a magnificent garden to walk in. But she is too homesick to enjoy her luxurious new quarters and spends her days crying and complaining. The Emperor builds her a miniature oasis to remind her of her village. Still she weeps. He builds her a mosque whose minaret is visible from her windows, and a Muslim bazaar outside the walls so that she can hear and smell the sounds and scents of home. Still she is not pacified. He erects a pavilion in the garden from whose roof she can gaze towards the west. All to no avail. 'What's the matter now?' demands the Emperor. 'I long for the fragrance of that tree whose leaves are silver and whose fruit is gold,' the girl replies. So messengers are sent to Kashgar to find the plant, a silver-leaved sand jujube, or oleaster, with golden fruit. At last the Emperor's concubine is reconciled to her lot.[2]

Victorian England heard the story from George Carter Stent whose poem, 'The Captive Maiden', begins:

> 'Tis very like my home. From yonder tower,
> Breaking the stillness of the twilight hour,
> In the soft accents of my native tongue,
> I hear the ballads of my country sung.
> But that is all, there the resemblance ends
> That only makes me grieve and crave for more;
> I long for other voices, those of friends;
> 'Twould then be like the home I had before.[*]

The American journalist Harrison Salisbury located the Fragrant Concubine's retreat in the Tower of Yearning, situated near the south-west corner of the Forbidden City. Only the gate of

---

[*] Posted to China at the end of the nineteenth century, Stent made a name as an expert on imperial eunuchs. There were still 2,000 of them at court during his time, and his monograph 'The Need for Eunuchs, How They Were Castrated, and Their Lifestyle' included clinical details which Chinese histories had been too shy to print.

the tower, renamed the Gate of New China under the Republic, still stands. In 1972 Salisbury noticed two soldiers outside it and learned that the gate led to Mao's private apartments in the Zhongnanhai compound, the enclave of houses, lakes and pavilions next door to the Forbidden City where China's leaders still live. It was through the same gate that the student demonstrators tried to reach them in 1989.

Uighurs prefer another version of the story. They remember Iparhan as forever pacing her apartment in the Forbidden City, with little daggers hidden up her sleeves to prevent the Emperor from molesting her. One day, at the time of the winter solstice when Qianlong was away performing rites at the Temple of Heaven, his mother the Dowager Empress warned the truculent concubine that if she did not yield she would be 'granted the favour of death' – that is, forced to commit suicide. Iparhan chose death rather than dishonour. In an alternative ending the Emperor rushes back to the palace to find the door locked while the love of his life is strangled by a pair of eunuchs.[3]

The legend of Iparhan is complicated by the fact that there was indeed an imperial concubine from the west, a favourite of Qianlong. Chosen for the harem in 1760, she was 35 years old when she reached the highest rank with the title of Rong Fei. She, or someone like her, was indeed painted by the Jesuit father Castiglione: the portrait was exhibited in the Yu De Tang bathhouse of the imperial palace in 1914 where it created a sensation and did much to spread the legend of the Fragrant Concubine. According to the Chinese authorities in Kashgar, this Rong Fei died of illness in 1788 aged 55 and was buried in a royal tomb south of Beijing.

The abduction of Iparhan became for the Chinese a symbol of the annexation of the western lands which they had twice before conquered – under the Han and Tang dynasties – but never really controlled. The Fragrant Concubine represented the barbarian but exotic west – the 'mysterious occident' – and a backward people finally reconciled to a superior civilization. The story began to capture the public imagination only at the beginning of the twentieth century, at the end of the Qing dynasty, when she was used as a literary device for familiarizing China with its western empire.

When the dynasty fell, Iparhan or Xiang Fei came to be seen as a resistance heroine, exploited by the corrupt feudal order; and in her new guise, of course, she appealed to Communist propagandists after 1949.[4]

Today her story continues to carry very different meanings. But however she is portrayed, to us Iparhan gracefully illustrates a dangerous ambiguity in the relationship between Beijing and Xinjiang – the province which is part of China but is not Chinese, the 'autonomous region' which has no autonomy, the homeland of a people who are called Chinese but who call themselves Muslim, Turki or Uighur.

By 1759 the great Qianlong was master not only of Dzungaria and the Tarim basin, but also Tibet, modern-day Mongolia and Taiwan. Building on the expansionist policy of his predecessor Kangxi, he had pushed China's borders out into the steppe, in the north-west up to the shore of Lake Balkhash, in the centre almost to Lake Baikal, in the north-east well beyond the Amur river. Burma was subjugated in 1769 and Nepal was occupied in 1790 in retaliation for its attacks on Tibet, thus bringing China face to face with the British in India.

The logic of the Qing conquests seems to have been mainly strategic. In order to protect his Manchurian homeland, Qianlong had to suppress the Mongols; and to keep the eastern Mongols quiet, the western Mongols had to be beaten, which meant taking Dzungaria and the Tarim. To protect *them*, Tibet had to be subdued. There was no material incentive behind the campaign. The mineral wealth of Xinjiang was hardly recognized in those days, and there was little trade with China proper, most of it being conducted with Andijan in the Ferghana basin and Russia. The main advantage of holding Xinjiang was that an aggressor would have to traverse great areas of unproductive territory, across which reinforcement was difficult, before he could actually reach China.[5] In other words, Xinjiang was once again cast in the role of buffer state, but this time a buffer state with a Chinese tenant. Historically speaking, 'China' is an ill-defined name: it was the Manchu conquest of the western and other borderlands that marked the beginning of a transition from Qing empire to Chinese nation-state.[6]

The region comprising Dzungaria and the Tarim was now annexed, divided into northern and southern territories, the *beilu* and *nanlu* ('north road' and 'south road'), and given its new name. For almost another century, however, Xinjiang continued to be referred to in government documents as Huijiang or 'Muslim-land', perhaps in order not to offend the Turkic people, who hated to be reminded of their defeat and colonization. The old name was only dropped after the region's incorporation as a province in 1884.

Administration was put into the hands of the army, but in accordance with Manchu policy the region was not absorbed into China, nor were the Han permitted to settle there. Like other Manchu conquests, the 'new frontier' enjoyed considerable auton-omy. A viceroy was installed at Gulja, near the former regional seat of the Mongols, with deputies at Urumchi and Yarkand. Law and order were the responsibility of a small – and increasingly slovenly – garrison of reluctant soldiers, while most local government was delegated to native *begs* (beys) who used their office to get rich at their compatriots' expense. This duplication of labour reflected the Manchus' picture of themselves as a master race. All over China they had installed their own people to supervise the work of better-educated Han officials, just as later the Communist Party was to install politically correct but technically unqualified com-missars in every factory, military unit and municipal office.

A fort was built in the Ili valley, and the 7,000 remaining Muslim families were reduced virtually to serfdom. The devastated area of Dzungaria was repopulated with settlers and exiles from Gansu province. Mongols who had formerly lived in the area but had emigrated to the Volga region were invited back; many were killed by the Russians and Kazakhs as they tried to return, but nearly 70,000 reached Ili.

Although a master race in their own eyes, the Manchus were all too conscious of being barbarians in the eyes of the Han, and they felt intellectually inferior to the mandarins they employed. But their treatment of the 'barbarian' Muslims was generally benign. The Manchus considered the Muslims aliens who could not be assimilated, and made no effort to impose Chinese civilization on them. A passage from the 1772 *Huijiang zhi* (*History of Xinjiang*) gives an idea of how they were regarded:

> The Muslims' natural character is suspicious and unsettled, crafty and false. Hard-drinking and addicted to sex, they never know when they have had enough. They understand neither repentance nor restraint, and wild talk takes the place of shame. They are greedy and parsimonious. If husbands, wives, fathers or sons have money, they each hide it away for themselves. If even one cash falls into a drainage ditch, they have to drain, sift and dredge until the coin is retrieved. They enjoy being proud and boastful, exaggerating their reputation. They prefer ease to industry, considering an opportunity for inactivity and sleep a great boon, and a drunken binge from dusk to dawn a great joy. Their character is lethargic, and they lack foresight. They do not know what it is to learn skills or to store grain, thus they must have someone to rely on in order to survive. Still, they have their good side: they can endure hunger and cold, will take any insult, and can be happily frugal.

For the Manchus the label 'barbarian' was not a fixed one, and promotion from the category of subhuman could be quite sudden. On 26 February 1760, an edict went out banning the use of the 'dog' radical in the word Hui in official documents. From now on, the Turkis were not to be called barbarian (*yi*); for the Emperor Qianlong did not regard the Jiayuguan Gate at the end of the Great Wall as marking the limits of civilization, merely as a boundary between different groups of his subjects. The Turkis now joined the Han, Manchus, Mongols and Tibetans as one of the 'five people under Heaven'.[7]

As occupiers, the Manchus tried at first to be discreet. They did not force the Turkis to shave their foreheads and wear the pigtail, or 'queue'. They did not want them provoked, so they said, by crimes of 'hair, sex and money'. Moneylending created racial friction, and soldiers fraternizing with local girls in the remote villages or resorting to Turki prostitutes enraged the Muslims. So the Manchus built their garrisons away from the old cities, calling them 'Manchu-town' (*mancheng*) or 'newtown' (*xincheng*). (Modern Chinese historians have revised the former to *hancheng*.) Although they allowed the Han Chinese to trade, they did not appoint them as officials nor let them settle for fear of antagonizing the natives. Segregation was imposed after a revolt in 1765, and Chinese traders were supposed to live close to the army posts where they could be supervised. (Two years earlier, and for similar reasons, the British Crown had drawn the Proclamation Line in America, forbidding English settlement west of the Appalachian mountains.)

Not even the great Qianlong could make his conquests secure, however. Just as the 'topping out' of a luxurious new corporate headquarters is said to mark the peak of a company's fortunes, so Qianlong's triumphs heralded a long slide in the dynasty's share price. An ominous warning was the revolt which broke out unexpectedly in the oasis of Ush Turfan, near Aksu, in 1765. The people of the town had become resentful of their exploitation by Chinese-appointed Muslim overseers and were infuriated by the Chinese governor's abuse of local women, whom, they said, he had allowed his servants to gang-rape. When a detail of 'volunteers' working outside the town was conscripted to transport oleaster saplings – which the Emperor had ordered, it was said, for the Fragrant Concubine in Beijing – the men refused and mutinied. The first weapons to come to hand were the oleasters, which botanists call *Elaeagnus angustifolia*. Having beaten off their military escort, the workers went back to their oasis where the villagers joined them in killing their oppressors. Manchu soldiers then laid siege to the town and, when finally it surrendered, banished the women, children and old men over the mountains to the Ili valley. The revolt had taken six months to suppress and had shaken the confidence of the new conquerors. From now on, the Manchus tried to keep the Chinese and Turkis apart as much as possible.

As the imperial dragon grew weaker, the fire from its jaws could no longer sweep the perimeter of its huge domain. Some historians date the start of the rot to as early as 1774 when there was an uprising in Shandong province, followed by another in Henan. Rebellions became more numerous, and secret societies were revived. Luxurious living spread among the upper class, and because the pay of public servants was cut, corruption began to infect the court, encouraged by the ageing Emperor's favourite, a young and incompetent general called Heshen. No doubt many provincial officials were honest men, but a highly centralized bureaucracy prevented them from responding to local grievances. Instead they were tied down by 'a tyrannous mass of legislation'.[8]

It was not just the cost of conquest and the need to hold new territory which sapped the empire's strength, nor even the luxurious living and frenzy of palace building. Both were affordable. What could not be controlled was the rapid increase in China's population, which grew from about 60 million in 1578 to over 400 million in 1850. Each family needed 70 *mu* (10 acres) of land to live on, but unoccupied land was increasingly difficult to find and there were no technical advances to boost farmers' productivity. In previous eras the Han had gone south to find land; but now the south was full up. The pent-up pressure was graphically illustrated at the end of the nineteenth century when Manchuria, hitherto the preserve of the 'master race', was opened to Chinese immigrants. Some 25 million people moved in over the course of a few decades in what has been described as the greatest mass migration in human history.[9]

The weakness of the empire was savagely demonstrated by the Taiping Rebellion of 1850–64. Organized by a village schoolmaster who decided that he was the younger brother of Jesus Christ sent to rid China of the Manchu 'demons', it lasted fourteen years and cost 20 million lives. Trouble within the empire was compounded by trouble from without. Pirates had always been a scourge in the South China Sea, but now it was the Western powers who wanted to dominate the China market. In the forefront of them was Britain.

The English East India Company had been running large tracts of India since the seventeenth century and trading its opium for China's tea and silk. In 1793 the British government sent a diplomatic mission to China under Lord Macartney armed with samples of manufactures, in the hope that the Emperor could be persuaded to formalize trading arrangements. The Son of Heaven was unmoved. Matters came to a head half a century later when the Chinese tried to stop the opium imports and Britain declared war. After bombarding and capturing a number of ports, the British forced the Chinese to open coastal cities to foreign trade, to give up the island of Hong Kong, to cede jurisdiction over foreign merchants, and to pay a large indemnity.*

Other Western powers soon followed suit. In a series of what the Chinese still call 'the unequal treaties', trade and territorial concessions were to be exacted from China well into the twentieth century. They were humiliations which the Chinese people have never been allowed to forget and which influence Beijing's foreign policy to this day.

Meanwhile, on China's western borders, the Russians were building their own Asian empire. Russian entrepreneurs licensed by the tsars had already opened up Siberia, reaching the lands of the Yakuts in the far east in the 1630s. The settlement of northern Kazakhstan was begun a century later, Tartars being employed as merchants and mediators to pave the way for colonies of Russian farmers. It was another hundred years before the Caucasus was finally occupied, and the Russians began moving on western Turkestan in the 1850s. Fort Vernoe north of Lake Issyk-kul, precursor to today's Almaty, was established in 1853. Tashkent fell to the Russians in 1865 when General Chernaev watched a Muslim army of 20,000 men turn tail on seeing their emir hit by a musket ball. The state of Kokand in the Ferghana basin fell the next year and Samarkand in 1868. Completed in 1881 with the defeat at Geok-Tepe of the Turkmen – one of the few peoples to put up a real fight – the Russian conquest of central Asia resembled not so much the winning of the American West as the European scramble for Africa.

With the Manchu dynasty under increasing pressure on all sides, it was not surprising that others should have seen an opportunity to extend their power.

On the western side of the Tian Shan mountains the khojas

---

* They also had to exempt the British from the kowtow, the obeisance which required a visitor to kneel three times and prostrate himself nine times as he approached the Emperor.

driven out of Kashgar by the Manchus were plotting from a temporary power base in Kokand. (At this point the Russians had not yet appeared on their horizon.) The khojas deeply resented losing their leadership of the western Tarim, and they were further enraged by reports that their kinsmen's wives and daughters were being violated by the conquering Chinese. The people of the western desert looked to the khojas, not to Beijing, for economic support and religious guidance. At the same time it became obvious that the western garrisons established during Qianlong's long reign had been enervated by the climate, softened by lack of training and distracted by the need to meet the farm quotas set them by the state.[10]

The state of Kokand in Ferghana, host to the refugee khojas, enjoyed special trading privileges in the Tarim oases, sending tribute to the Qing emperor in return. Now, Kokand felt entitled to better terms. And when its demands were rejected, the ruler unleashed the khojas to preach holy war against the *kaffir*, the infidel Chinese.

In 1825, the spark of their rhetoric burst into flame. A 'white mountain' khoja called Jahangir, who had been organizing guerrilla raids from a mountain village, succeeded in ambushing a small Chinese expeditionary force and killing almost every man in it. The local tribespeople, Uzbeks, Kazakhs and Kyrgyz among them, rallied to Jahangir's banner and marched on Kashgar. In their fort 7 miles from the city, the Chinese were too weak to respond. Jahangir executed the Governor of Kashgar – a Turki appointed by the Chinese – called himself 'sultan', and decreed that turbans be worn in place of the official Chinese headgear.[11] This was the signal for revolt all along the south road, in Yangi Hissar, Yarkand and Khotan, and for a massacre of Chinese civilians caught anywhere outside the walls. In 1826, after a seventeen-day siege, Jahangir took the Kashgar fort. The Chinese governor and his officers committed suicide, and 8,000 soldiers were reportedly massacred, though 400 saved their skins by converting to Islam on the spot.

A huge force of 80,000 Dongans (Muslims of Han descent) and steppe nomads from the north and east was amassed the following year by the Chinese viceroy at Ili. Jahangir went out to meet it near present-day Maralbashi, north-east of Kashgar, with 50,000 men. But now, instead of throwing their armies at each other, the two generals decided – or so local lore has it – to settle the issue by single combat of champions. This was an ancient custom, of course, popular in Persia from where the story of Sohrab and Rustum, father and son duellists, was taken by Matthew Arnold for an epic poem. The description of the two champions left us by H.W. Bellew, who researched the history of the Tarim in the 1870s, is hardly less dramatic:

> That of the Chinese was a giant Calmac archer fantastically dressed like a devil dragon; whilst the champion on the side of Jahangir was a noted Khokandi warrior equally versed in sword and rifle practice and clad in gaudy silks and chain armour. The two advanced to the contest on the open plain backed by their respective supporters. But whilst the Khokandi was adjusting his rifle, the Calmac shot an arrow through his chest and out between the shoulders, and his adversary fell dead on the spot. A skirmish followed between the supporting parties, but the Kashgar army, disheartened by the untoward commencement of the contest, soon broke and fled in disorder. They were pursued with great slaughter and loss in captives . . .[12]

Jahangir, who had ruled for nine months as Sultan of Kashgar, fled into the Pamir mountains where he was betrayed by his former allies the Kyrgyz, captured and sent to Beijing for execution 'with torture'. After taking the usual reprisals, the Chinese removed 12,000 Turki families to help repopulate Dzungaria (where, as we saw in the previous chapter, a million people had been slaughtered during the Manchu conquest of the 1750s). These new immigrants were called Taranchis, or labourers.

A few years later, in 1830, Jahangir was followed by his elder brother Yusuf from Bokhara. Yusuf's excuse for invading the Tarim was that he wanted the Qing to lift a trade embargo. This invasion was memorable chiefly for the rare investigation by the Emperor's officials into the reprisals against Muslims which followed it.

During Yusuf's attack on the fortress at Kashgar a number of

Chinese merchants began killing Muslims who had taken refuge with them, thinking them to be in league with the forces outside. During the night, however, a mob of Chinese went out to pull more Muslims from haystacks and ice cellars, killing over 200 and setting fire to buildings. After the invading Kokandis withdrew, a crowd of Turkis who had not taken any part in the attack appeared outside the fort with presents for the Chinese. They were hoisted into the fort individually and killed on the ramparts. Seventy or eighty men died in this way before the Manchu governor stopped the slaughter. The investigators were told that this savagery against loyal subjects was in revenge for the deaths of Han and Dongans killed at Kashgar during the previous invasion by Jahangir. But the Han merchants were later absolved, because they had fought against the invaders.[13]

Yusuf's occupation of the Muslim city lasted a mere three months, but it again exposed the weakness of Manchu authority in the region. The Emperor agreed to let Kokand appoint an inspector at Kashgar and *aksakals* (literally 'white beards') as consuls to collect religious subscriptions and represent the Andijani traders in principal towns. In return Kokand promised to restrain the khojas.

Two more uprisings of note occurred before the Chinese lost control completely. The first, in 1846, was known as the Revolt of the Seven Khojas and lasted seventy-five days. Its main feature appears to have been the seizure of the wives and daughters of fellow Muslims who had been serving as officials under the Chinese; so that when the Chinese put the rebellion down – with the help of 3,000 criminals marked with a scar on the left cheek – the khojas were denied refuge by their co-religionists and were obliged to flee over the mountains to Kokand.

The second revolt, in 1857, was led by the cruel hashish-smoking Wali Khan who seemed determined to set new records for cruelty. Bellew describes him as 'the most licentious tyrant and bloodthirsty maniac of that ambitious and selfish fraternity' whose barbarities shocked even those who had been accustomed for centuries to 'deaths and tortures in their worst forms'. Wali Khan's adventure began early one morning when he set fire to the Sand Gate, or south gate of old Kashgar. The city yielded without a struggle and once again the citizens took the opportunity to hunt down and murder Chinese. The Turki governor took refuge in the Manchu fort while the rest of his officials were executed and their wives and daughters handed out to the rebels like so many tombola prizes.

Wali Khan achieved a certain notoriety abroad, for among his victims was an early European explorer, the German Adolphe Schlagintweit, one of three scientist brothers who were (probably) the first modern Europeans to reach eastern Turkestan. Robert Shaw, a British adventurer and later commissioner in Ladakh, who arrived in Yarkand in 1868, told how an official apologized to him, saying he felt ashamed of the murder of the 'Englishman'. Schlagintweit was seen going towards the gate of Yarkand with his servants and baggage and was stopped by the local ruler's men who led him 'with honour' to Kashgar. But the dope-crazed Wali Khan, instead of honouring the stranger, fell into a fury and ordered his execution. The wretched explorer's head was raised on a pole on the riverbank above the Kizil bridge, where it remained for many weeks. Shaw says Wali Khan was regarded as a djinn or demon who would execute his courtiers if they merely raised their eyes in his presence. He once had a muezzin killed for raising his voice in the call to prayer.[14]

Wali Khan was no more successful than the rest of the khojas. After seventy-seven days he and his army of 20,000 were routed by a Chinese force of 12,000. One defeat was enough for his allies who were so disgusted by his behaviour and terrified of his bully-ing that they deserted him. Violence breeds violence, and the revenge taken by the Chinese was no more judicial than that visited upon them. Wali Khan's father-in-law, keeper of the shrine of the Muslim saint Satuk, was crimped like a mackerel before being disembowelled and his still beating heart thrown to the dogs. Then his head was cut off and put in a cage on the main road into the city along with those of his allies. His eldest son suffered a similar fate, but three other sons (who staged their own uprising in 1862) lived to tell the story to the Englishman Bellew.

Bellew's attempt to explain to his superiors the reasons for the turbulence in the region contained some prescient judgements. The khoja clans, he said, were already divided among themselves; and their rivalry was intensified by their subordination to a greater power – first to the nomad khans of Dzungaria, later to the

Emperor in Beijing. Meanwhile, local government was inherently unstable because different groups of citizens fell under different systems of law, all of them more or less corrupt: the Muslims under shariah, the Chinese settlers and traders under Chinese law, and the Andijani merchants under Kokand rule. Equally disruptive was the Chinese style of occupation – a network of military garrisons whose troops were charged with keeping order, ensuring taxes were collected and protecting trade but who were kept away from the people they were policing. The soldiers lived in forts some distance from the oasis cities, while the civilian Chinese lived and worked mainly between the forts and the cities, and so failed to mingle with either traders or peasants. This separation of communities, of occupier and occupied, was not always rigidly enforced. But the principle was never abandoned, with consequences we shall see later.

As for Wali Khan, he went over the pass to Kokand where he was brought to trial by the relatives of those he had murdered. He was acquitted on the grounds that he was a *sayid*, that is, a descendant of the Prophet, and his accusers were fined instead. However, the cruel khoja came to the sticky end he deserved. He was assassinated some years later in Kashgar by the most successful Muslim challenger yet to the empire of the Manchus and the only man, before or since, who succeeded in creating and maintaining an independent unitary state in eastern Turkestan: Yakub Beg.

Events conspired to make Yakub Beg important. The British had been thoroughly alarmed by the rapid advance of the Russians through central Asia, fearing that the Tsar – or at least some of his generals – entertained an old ambition to drive them out of India. As the British were themselves pushing up into the Punjab, the forward positions of the two empires were coming ever closer, and Yakub Beg's kingdom of Kashgar occupied a gap between them. The 'Great Game' was under way. And that explains why in 1873 a British envoy, Sir Douglas Forsyth, having crossed the Karakoram mountains, found himself in Yangishahr, the new town 5 miles outside Kashgar, waiting for an audience with Yakub Beg, the self-styled King of Kashgaria.

Forsyth and his small party were conducted by a chamberlain through a number of outer courtyards populated with 'gaily-dressed soldiers'.

We passed into the penetralia, a small court, in which not a soul was visible and everywhere a deathlike stillness prevailed. At the further end of this court was a long hall with several window doors. Ihrar Khan [the chamberlain] then led us in single file, with measured tread, to some steps at the side of the hall, and, entering almost on tiptoe, looked in and returning beckoned with his hand to me to advance alone. As I approached the door he made a sign for me to enter, and immediately withdrew.

I found myself standing at the threshold of a very common looking room, perfectly bare of all ornament and with a not very good carpet on the floor: looking about, I saw enter at a doorway on the opposite side, a tall stout man, plainly dressed. He beckoned with his hand and I advanced thinking that it must be a chamberlain who was to conduct me to 'the presence'. Instinctively, however, I made a bow as I advanced and soon found myself taken by both hands and saluted with the usual form of politeness, and I knew that I was standing before the far-famed ruler of Eastern Turkestan.

After a few words of welcome the Atalik [Yakub Beg] led me across the room and seated me near him by the side of a window. At this moment a salute of 15 guns was fired. His Highness asked in an eager tone after the health of Her Majesty [Queen Victoria] and of the Viceroy, and soon after called in a low voice to Ihrar Khan to bring in the other officers. They came in one by one, and each was shaken by the hand and made to sit down by my side. Then there was a long and somewhat trying pause, during which the Atalik eyed each one of us with intent scrutiny; I had been told that etiquette forbade the guest to speak much at the first interview, and that it was a point of good manners to sit perfectly still, with downcast eyes.

When it is remembered that the oriental posture requires the visitor to sit upon his heels, with feet well flattened under him, the excrutiating [sic] agony of having to keep perfectly unmoved in this position for perhaps half an hour will be appreciated.[15]

Another Englishman had preceded Forsyth. Robert Shaw, then a young tea-planter, paid Yakub Beg an unofficial visit in 1868. He too was taken through the courtyards, where he was particularly impressed by the sight of the Mongol archers among an 'assemblage of thousands'. Despite the Englishman's lack of credentials, Yakub Beg was friendly, crooking his two forefingers together to show how close the two men already were. He talked about the weather, and he appeared put out to learn that the Viceroy of India reported to a female superior in England.

Shaw had a second interview which took place at night in a pavilion lit by Chinese lanterns. Yakub had recovered his diplomatic aplomb. This time he grasped the top of one finger to show how small he felt himself by comparison with the Malikah Padishah, Queen Victoria. 'The Queen of England is like the sun', he said, 'which warms everything it shines upon. I am in the cold, and desire that some of its rays should fall upon me.' Behind the flowery language, which must have thrilled the young adventure-seeker, there was a careful calculation. Yakub Beg was afraid, not of the Chinese but of the encroaching Russians, and he wanted English protection. Even more to the point – as he would subsequently make clear – he wanted guns.

The ruler of eastern Turkestan now apologized for the murder of the 'Englishman' Schlagintweit, as the official at Yarkand had done. Shaw replied that he was not to blame because he had not been in power at the time, and he pointed out that in any case the murdered man, though a guest of the British in India, was a German. Yakub Beg concurred, holding up six fingers to show how recently he had come to the throne, and Shaw riposted with a rhetorical tribute: 'Those kings who succeed to thrones by right of birth obtain their power by no merit of their own. But those who, like Timoor and Sikander [Tamerlane and Alexander], obtain great kingdoms by their own deeds are looked upon with admiration.'[16]

Shaw must have known that Yakub Beg fancied himself descended from Tamerlane and he cannot have been surprised to find himself rewarded with silk robes and bags of gold and silver which he later estimated to be worth £690 – or about £32,000 in today's money.

Yakub Beg was already styled Atalik Ghazi ('Guardian Warrior') and Badaulet ('Blessed One'), and he was shortly to be upgraded by the Sultan of Constantinople with the title Emir Mohamad Yakub Khan of Kashgar. Laden with these honorifics he clearly enjoyed the dutiful abasement of Queen Victoria's subjects, whether official or unofficial. Little did he guess that the British, who had come so deferentially to woo him into a trade treaty with gifts that included working models of a sewing-machine and a steamboat, would in the end be the agents of his downfall.

The self-styled king was not a native of Kashgar, nor even a rebel against Chinese rule. He was a soldier and courtier of the Emir of Kokand and – unlike the Kokandis of previous years – he turned up in Kashgar in 1864 not in a personal bid for power but because he had been sent by the Emir as an aide. Though the tool of other men's ambitions, Yakub Beg showed the wit, strength and ambition to grab any opportunity presented to him. The opportunity in his case had been a massive uprising within the Chinese empire two years previously.

The rebels were Muslims: not the Turki Muslim farmers of the Tarim oases, but the Muslims of Chinese descent called Dongans who lived mainly in the provinces of Gansu and Shaanxi. Although they shared a religion, the Turkis and the Dongans were quite different in character. Early European visitors to Chinese Turkestan observed that the Turkic Muslims (today's Uighurs) were a generally peaceable, even passive people compared with, say, the mountain Kyrgyz or the Kazakhs of the steppe. Clarmont Skrine, British consul at Kashgar in the 1920s, described what he called the lethargy of the Turkis. 'Although Muhammadans they had none of the fanaticism of other groups of their co-religionists, and apart from sporadic rebellions, which were usually led by outsiders, they were content to be governed by the Chinese.'[17] He recalled how his appearance at an organized dog-fight on the south desert road was enough to send the Uighur participants scattering, even though what they were doing was perfectly legal. 'No wonder', he added, 'that a handful of Chinese with a paper army keeps perfect order throughout Kashgaria.'[18]

The Dongans (now known as Hui) were another matter. They

were a puzzling, paradoxical people. Distrusted, even today, by the Turkis who regard them as unclean Muslims and enforcers of Han rule, they were treated patronizingly by their fellow Chinese, who saw them as misfits. Dongans often served the Emperor as soldiers, but they were sensitive to any slight against their religion, and far readier to respond with violence.

Contemporaries saw the Dongan rebellion as an Islamic revival motivated by fanatical opposition to modernization of any kind. Certainly, fatwas authorizing holy war were issued in some cities, and Qing sources claim that in Urumchi the revolt had been planned for over a year and weapons stockpiled in the mosque.[19] But the Muslims – whether Dongan or Turki – had no lack of material grievances. For over a century the Dongans had borne the brunt, financially and militarily, of the emperors' attempts to pacify Dzungaria. Their discontent proved infectious. As for the Turkis, they had become tired of paying for the Chinese garrisons that controlled them. There were sales taxes, poll taxes and forced labour in mines and canals – the feudal system of *corvée* which, it will be recalled, sparked the oleaster incident at Ush Turfan in 1765, the first uprising after the Manchu conquest. (The system goes on to this day: large bands of Uighur 'volunteers' can be seen digging ditches and repairing dykes on their day off.) The people felt exploited by the Chinese merchants – it was said that several debtors were thrown into the Khotan river each day because they could not pay – and they were fed up with the machinations of the Kokandi consuls and agents whom the Chinese had allowed to operate among them.

So when in 1862 the Dongans of Gansu took up arms, the people of eastern Turkestan were in a mood to support them. The trigger seems to have been a rumour which began circulating in Kucha soon afterwards that the Chinese governor-general at Ili, or even the court at Beijing, had ordered the extermination of the Muslims. Whether such a genocidal order was ever considered, let alone issued, or whether it was invented by the Gansu rebels in order to whip up support in Xinjiang, is not known. But its effect was devastating.[20]

The strength of the natives' anger was matched only by the weakness of the Manchu garrisons. A quaint description left by an exiled Manchu eyewitness at the military headquarters in the Ili valley explains exactly why the empire was in no state to deal with what was about to befall it:

The Manchus, having lived quietly in cities for a hundred years, lost all their martial spirit and were physically weakened so much that they could not even pull the bows; the arrows shot by them did not go far and did not penetrate the thickly quilted clothes of the Taranchis [local Muslims]. The effeminate Manchu officials neglected teaching soldiers how to use the bow. They dressed fashionably and led a debauched life. In the battle with the Taranchis and the Tungans [Dongans] their bulky clothes hampered their movement. On top of this, the soldiers were starving since there was no food . . . The horses of the Manchus were also emaciated from hunger because they could not get fodder. They could not gallop in deep snow. The Taranchis and the Tungans caught the Manchus stuck in snow and killed them.

The [Manchu] officials did not care for the soldiers and the soldiers also held them in contempt. When the rebellion broke out, they did not attempt to lead the army and suppress the rebels bravely. Instead, at the sight of the rebels they ran away. They worried about preserving their own lives and they did not realise that all in all they would be annihilated and their wives and daughters would fall into the hands of the rebels. How pitiful all these are![21]

Even if they had been fit there was little the garrisons could do. They could not easily be reinforced, since the rebellion had blocked the Gansu corridor, cutting their lifeline to Beijing. They were in the same predicament as the soldiers of the Tang emperor more than a thousand years before who, finding themselves over-whelmed by the Tibetan invasion, could only lock the gates and pray. The explorer Aurel Stein found texts and graffiti at Endere on the southern desert road, where the Chinese garrison had been cut off in AD 781. He wrote: 'They managed to transmit pathetic appeals for help to the Imperial court, from which, however, there came no succour, only grants of laudatory titles and liberal acknowledgements of official merits.'[22] In 1862, the chances of help from Beijing looked even more remote because mainland China was still convulsed by the Taiping Rebellion, which had another two years to run.

From Gansu the Dongan revolt spread to Kucha, which erupted on 4 June 1864, followed by Urumchi, Yarkand, Khotan, Aksu and Kashgar. Khotan rose in response, it is said, to the execution of some drunken Muslims who had boasted to the driver of a Chinese official that a revolt was being planned. The impotence of the occupation forces was bloodily demonstrated at Yarkand. Following an argument between Han and Dongan soldiers in the garrison, the Chinese magistrate decided to disarm the Dongans. When the plan leaked out, the Dongans outside probably suspected that this was the prelude to the rumoured extermination. They turned on their Han colleagues, killing 2,000 of them. Then they marched into the city, calling for a massacre of the Chinese. It was 10 August, one of the hottest days of the year. 'A mob of ruffians, gamblers and drunkards, and others who were more or less in debt to the Chinese traders, rushed all over the city and with their knives killed every [Chinese] man, woman and child they could lay hands on, and plundered their houses,' wrote Bellew. 'So rapid was the work of their destruction that by noon not a [Chinese] was left alive in the city except for a few who had found concealment in the house of Musalman friends.'[23] In the streets 7,000 lay dead.

News of the massacre spread like wildfire across the Tarim, and the bloodshed was repeated in any town where Chinese lived. The inner citadel of the Yarkand fort continued to hold out for several months. When it fell, the magistrate, his family and his chief officers thought it wiser to decide their own fate. They assembled in his reception room. The magistrate took out his pipe and emptied it on to a trail of gunpowder which started at his feet and ran out to the magazines on each side of the citadel square. The remaining Chinese soldiers hurried to place themselves close to the explosion. According to locals, for three days human limbs and heads were seen flying as the hidden mines went up.

At Kashgar the flag of independence was raised in late 1864 by a Kyrgyz leader, Siddiq Beg, who had been sent by the district governor to restore order but who joined in the plunder himself. (The Kyrgyz had a reputation as brigands who would serve the master who rewarded them most.) Hoping to legitimize his coup, Siddiq asked the Emir of Kokand to send a khoja over the mountains to be Kashgar's king. With the Russians now breathing down his neck, the Emir chose Buzurg Khan, last surviving son of the 'white mountain' khoja Jahangir who had led the unsuccessful revolt of 1825. In November 1864, Buzurg left Tashkent, and in his train, serving as liaison officer and army commander, was Yakub Beg.

'Among the officers of Buzurg's army was a clever and audacious youth who had begun life as a dancing boy,' reported the British missionaries Mildred Cable and Francesca French.[24] In fact, Yakub Beg was already nearly fifty when he crossed the Tian Shan, and a rich courtier. He was a soldier, too – but not a very successful one. As for his vocation as a dancer, that seems, sadly, to have been an invention.

Yakub was born some time between 1810 and 1815 in Kapa, near the city of Andijan in Kokand. As a youth, he was called *bacha*, which does indeed mean 'dancing boy'; but so, too, was his eldest brother. It is most unlikely that the son of a magistrate would have been allowed to earn money as a professional dancer, and pictures of dancing boys of the region make the story more improbable still. A photograph taken in Bokhara by L.S. Barshevsky around 1890 shows an androgynous youth in bare feet and a striped woman's dress, poised daintily on a kilim beneath poplar trees. His head is shaved in front, and an Alice band holds back long, flowing tresses. Behind him stands a small crowd of turbaned, bearded and very male onlookers. It is more likely, then, that *bacha* was used in Yakub's case as a term of endearment for a good-looking youth with a fine singing voice who might have frequented the teahouses in his home town.[25]

Destined to become a weaver, Yakub escaped instead to his father's home town of Pishkent and became a civil servant. Promotion followed his sister's advantageous marriage to the governor of nearby Tashkent, and by the age of 35 Yakub was in command of the White Mosque fort on the Jaxartes river, and in a position to supplement his salary with the tolls levied on passing caravans.

At about this time Yakub began to show his opportunistic flair. He was accused, it seems, of selling fishing rights to the Russians who were busy extending their empire to this part of central Asia; he paid his accusers off with the ill-gotten gains. Later, he was to describe his first military engagement as an heroic defence of the White Mosque fort. Modern research has shown, however, that he was not even present when the Russians attacked the fort: Yakub's part was confined to an earlier skirmish in which his 1,000 men were sent packing by 100 well-armed Russians. For that he was dismissed.

Whatever the truth about his past, his summons from the Emir to go to Kashgar brought Yakub to the brink of a sensational career. This minor khan in a remote central Asian country was to enjoy a walk-on part on the world stage. Endorsed by the Sultan of Constantinople, recognized if not courted in St Petersburg, he dazzled the imagination of European newspaper readers and impressed even members of the British establishment. He is still remembered with pride by Uighur nationalists – and with alarm by Chinese government officials.

Neither the Emir, his employer, nor Buzurg Khan, his new master, seemed to see in Yakub any sort of threat. Arriving in Kashgar at the end of 1864 with Buzurg and his train, Yakub behaved like a model servant. The old city had already been taken by the Kyrgyz bandit Siddiq, but now Yakub set about capturing the neighbouring fort where the Chinese were holding out. When it fell in 1865, he sent the Emir some presents: nine Chinese cannon, nine virgins, nine times nine Mongol horses and the same number of silver coins. But the Emir was not able to enjoy them: he had been killed at Tashkent by a Russian musket ball.

Yakub's greatest challenge came the following year when an army of 26,000 arrived from Kucha to dislodge the Kokandis. Although he had only 2,000 men to pit against it, they were tough mountain fighters interspersed with professional Kazakh soldiers, and he won the battle. As his successes mounted and his popularity rose, more men came over to him. Now Yakub Beg saw his chance. Breaking his oaths of loyalty to the Emir and to Buzurg, he declared himself king in 1866 with the title of 'Blessed'. The guile-less Buzurg was, according to one story, sent on a pilgrimage to

Mecca to get him out of the way. According to another, he was exiled to Tibet.

Marching with his army down the south desert road in 1867, the Blessed One invited the ruler of Khotan to a feast, then imprisoned him. Deceit also helped him to win the strategic town of Kucha in the same year, when the local khojas fell out and their viziers defected to him. Turfan, a bastion of the Dongans, held out for six months and surrendered on 1 November 1870. Aided by Chinese guerrillas, Yakub then marched through the Tian Shan to capture Urumchi which, after changing hands twice, eventually fell to his son Beg Kuli Beg. Now the Andijani adventurer and his Dongan allies held the whole of the Tarim basin, Turfan and the regional capital.

Meanwhile, the fertile Ili valley, which had been laid waste by the rebels and by internecine fighting between Dongans and Taranchis, was snatched by the Russian general Kolpakovsky. He found the canals blocked, the towns ruined and the fortresses gutted. A census taken by the Russians in 1876 counted 132,000 people in the capital Gulja, compared with 350,000 before the revolt. Urumchi, a Manchu and Chinese town of 24,000 households, saw its population reduced by three-quarters. The massacre of the Dzungars a hundred years before had been repeated, though this time it was the Chinese who were the victims.

Yakub Beg's administration was severe to the point of cruelty; but outsiders, especially the British, found plenty to admire. Robert Shaw's impression of eastern Turkestan was that it was much better off than India, 'a kind of Eldorado . . . a modern, thriving state . . . commercially experienced and traditionally outward looking. It felt a bit like Europe.'[26] The London *Times* agreed, declaring after Douglas Forsyth's first, inconclusive mission that 'the people are prosperous and contented with the severe, but in the main wise and just, rule of their new master'.[27] The region was poised to play a major role, it added. The India Office in London was bombarded with demands from chambers of commerce anxious to begin trading. Few British officials in London or Calcutta wanted to become militarily involved north of the Himalayas, and 'masterly inactivity' was the order of the day. But trade with Yakub Beg would both help the Empire and enable the

British to keep a close eye on Russian territorial ambitions. So long as China was weak, Yakub provided a buffer.

Although the Russians received Yakub Beg's ambassador, they were in general less enthusiastic than the British. The explorer Nikolai Prejevalsky, who met Yakub Beg in 1875, described him as 'nothing more than a political imposter' whose subjects could not wait to be governed by Russia. In a letter to his brother he went further: 'Yakub Beg is the same shit as all feckless Asiatics. The Kashgarian Empire isn't worth a kopek.'[28]

Prejevalsky's verdict is characteristically crude and perhaps says more about him than it does about the Turki people, whose language he could not speak. Yet it is true that the normally quiescent oases found plenty to grumble about. The new khan taxed the peasants and merchants more heavily than the Chinese had done, and the people resented the foreign troops imported from over the mountains as much as they did the locally conscripted vagabonds described by a Turki source as a mob of 'villains, unbridled ones, thieves, gamblers, abusers and pigeoners [swindlers]'.[29]

Forsyth and his delegation, however, were mightily impressed by the variegated soldiery on display in the courtyard of Yakub's palace:

here a gigantic Afghan with nut-brown complexion and flowing glossy black beard, there a square-faced, flat-nosed, skew-eyed Kalmak [Mongol] with cheek bones as high as his shoulders; next a fair, full round-faced Andijani with short trimmed beard. Cunning mien and crouching seat of his Kirghiz neighbour, with angular eyes, cheeks and face ending in a short wispy tuft of beard. Our familiar black skinned and oily faced Hindustani Musalman, beard shining as bright as his eyes, and obsequious smile. A muddy-skinned, withered, opium-smoking Khitay [Chinese] whose repulsive physiognomy is the reflexion of his cowed spirit and forced servility. Contrast the bewhiskered and gentle looking Badakhshi, with high full forehead, long arched finely carved nose, and oval face of the true Aryan stamp.[30]

An army of 40,000 was trained by instructors from Turkey and equipped with Lee Enfield rifles from Istanbul and – so the

Russians said – England.* It was financed by taxes more exorbitant even than those imposed by the Chinese, the peasants being forced to sell whatever they had, down to their cooking pots and spoons, to meet the tax assessors' demands. These tax farmers were expected to take tribute to the Blessed One twice a year: the ruler of Khotan, Niyaz Beg, on one occasion sent him seventy camel-loads of gifts and two horse-loads of silver.

Yakub Beg believed in order, and central planning. He set up large state workshops in the towns to make saddlery, weapons and clothes. Milestones and waystations were erected. The government requisitioned a fifth of the gold output of Khotan; and the people there resorted to digging up ancient bricks of tea from the buried desert cities because their supply from China had been cut off. Trade treaties were signed with Russia in 1872 and Britain in 1873.

Security was tightened. Kyrgyz kidnappers found their lucrative business halted and the nomads were prevented from cheating innocent travellers. Forsyth quoted in his report a popular saying of the time: 'If a man drops his whip in the middle of the plain, he will find it there if he looks for it a year afterwards.' Although there is no evidence that Yakub Beg was particularly religious – he had no scruple about dispatching any khojas who got in his way – he lived simply, as Forsyth witnessed, and he rebuilt the shrines of Muslim saints. Shariah law was enforced and squads of religious police went about with whips to punish moral backsliders. The Yarkandis told Forsyth's delegation that life had been more fun under the Chinese and market day 'a much jollier time'. One citizen described a Chinese market day thus:

> There was no Kazi Rais . . . to flog people off to prayers and drive the women out of the streets, and nobody was bastinadoed for drinking spirits and eating forbidden meats. There were musicians and acrobats and fortune-tellers and story-tellers, who moved about amongst the crowds and diverted the people. There were flags and banners and all sorts of pictures floating on

---

* There may not have been an official supply, but it seems the Indian government did on one occasion pay the carriage on 200 cases of guns for a private firm.[31]

the shop fronts, and there was the 'jallab', who painted her face and decked herself in silks and laces to please her customers . . .

Yes, there were many rogues and gamblers, too, and people did get drunk, and have their pockets picked. So they do now, though not so publicly, because we are now under Islam, and the Shariat is strictly enforced.[32]

While Yakub Beg was basking in the admiration of his new foreign friends and showering himself with favours, his nemesis was waiting over the horizon in the person of General Zuo Zongtang.

Yakub, sitting in Kashgar, might have thought his position secure, as many of his advisers considered the Chinese too weak now to unseat him. In fact he was even better off than he realized. A great debate had been in progress at the imperial court since 1865, and it was by no means certain that Beijing was prepared even to try to win its territory back, the question being, in a nut-shell: was Xinjiang worth the trouble? On one side stood the maritime lobby led by Li Hongzhang, who argued that a western campaign would be a waste of money and that the priority was defence of China's coast against Western predators. On the other side the 'steppe lobby' insisted that the protection of the north and west must be put first.

General Zuo, although he had worked on maritime defence and shipyards, was firmly of the steppe persuasion. He was in a line of advisers stretching back to the days of the nomad marauders who saw the far west as a buffer zone protecting Mongolia, which in turn protected the capital. And he had a powerful ally in the person of Prince Yihuan, father of the Emperor Guangxu. His other trump card was his own reputation: he had made his name defeating the Taiping army, and if anyone could mount a successful campaign against the rebels, it was he.

Zuo came from the province of Hunan, and had won the second highest degree in the mandarin examinations. After his success against the Taipings he was made Viceroy of Shaanxi and Gansu provinces in 1865, and there he quelled the Dongan rebellion. Asked by the Emperor what should be done about Xinjiang, Zuo advised that China's coast was not in great danger because

Westerners were only interested in trade, but that it would be folly to retreat from the west and try to hold a line behind the Yumen pass in the Gansu corridor, as Li and his friends were suggesting. He did not win the argument until 1875, but by then most of his preparations had already been made. They had taken him six years, and were surely among the most elaborate ever devised by a military commander.

The first problem had been to supply an army of up to 200,000 men. Even at the best of times Xinjiang and the border regions could not support so many. But now those regions were ravaged. Zuo, however, was not about to make Napoleon's mistake in Russia and run the risk of being defeated by the scorched-earth tactics of an enemy. He began to set up supply lines inside 'mainland' China, a network which eventually covered more than 6,000 miles. Food and weapons were to be brought from five main depots, including Shanghai and Tianjin on the coast, to rear depots in Shaanxi and Gansu, closer to the war zone. From there they would be transferred to wagons or camels and transported across the last 600 miles of desert to the front lines inside Yakub's kingdom. Zuo also borrowed a tactic first used by the Han in their forays into the western wastelands: he instructed his soldiers to plant crops around their garrisons, mend the irrigation channels, build roads and plant trees.[33] More fancifully, it is said that he had trees planted along the route in advance so that his army could find its way home. As a further precaution he planned to use native troops as much as possible, calculating that Han Chinese soldiers would be afraid of the Turkis and the desert, and would refuse to eat the local food. Meanwhile he arranged to buy grain from the Russians, making it plain he had no military designs on the Ili valley which they had grabbed in 1871. The merchant I.O. Kamensky supplied him with 5 million *chin*, or 670,000 pounds, of grain in 1875, and double that quantity the following year. Kamensky did well: flour which cost 10 to 15 kopeks a measure in Gulja could be sold for 8 roubles (about sixty times as much) in Gucheng on the Gansu border.[34]

Zuo's campaign motto was 'move slowly but strike quickly'; in other words, he would make sure he had all the *matériel* he needed before choosing a time and place to attack. Siege warfare was discarded as being too protracted, and therefore expensive. His method of taking a fortress was to run his cannons into position under cover of darkness, open the bombardment before dawn, and throw his infantry in quickly behind it.[35]

The second problem was how to finance the expedition. Provincial subsidies from Beijing on which Zuo relied were £9 million in arrears, and his troops were waiting for their pay. The solution was provided by the very people who had seemed most keen to maintain Yakub Beg on his throne – the British. Not, it must be said, the British government, which maintained a show of neutrality when it came to money, but the servants of the Hongkong and Shanghai Bank.

Imperial etiquette meant that the Emperor could not be seen to be borrowing money, but his servant General Zuo was licensed to do so. Indeed, it seems he was more or less expected to finance his own campaign. After 1868, however, terms had to be approved by the palace. That meant diplomatic involvement, and the appearance of government backing, which embarrassed both the bank and the British Foreign Office. Two loans, in 1867 and 1868, were arranged by Zuo's agent, a merchant banker called Hu Guangyong. But there was 'no indication that the Hongkong Bank participated'. A third was mooted the following year, in which the bank was to take a $1 million share, but it came to nothing. However, the bank's Shanghai office was certainly involved in the so-called 'Kansu [Gansu] loans', the first of which was for 5 million taels (£1.6 million) and was raised in 1877, the year of Zuo's conquest of Xinjiang.[36]

A Foreign Office telegram dated 20 October of that year, when Zuo's army was marching from Kucha to Aksu, confirms the agreement and says it is 'for possible operations in the North-West'. The author, Hugh Fraser, adds: 'There is, I am glad to say, a slight difficulty in the matter at present, for the Imperial decree sanctioning the loan is not drawn up in terms satisfactory to the Bank.'[37] The loan agreement had, in fact, been drawn up in July between Zuo's agent Mr Hu and Mr Cameron of the bank, who had been leaning on the government to use its influence so that the first instalment could be paid quickly. Two further loans were made through the bank: of 1¼ million taels the following year, and of 4 million taels in 1881.

While indirectly involved in the financing of Zuo's campaign, British diplomats were at the same time busy trying to save Yakub Beg's neck. Their fear of Russian intentions towards India compelled them to back both possible outcomes: either an independent Kashgaria which would be a British client state, or a victory by General Zuo which would put the Chinese back in control.

An exchange of government telegrams showed just how intimately the British were involved. Sir Thomas Wade, ambassador to Beijing, was anxious to find a 'modus vivendi', as he put it, which would preserve the dignity of the empire – the Chinese empire, that is. He confided to Douglas Forsyth, now in Delhi, that Li Hongzhang had asked him to write to Yakub Beg telling him to submit. But when Forsyth met Li in Tianjin in July 1876, Li changed his tune. The Emperor, he said, would let Yakub Beg keep Kashgar as a vassal of China if he laid down his arms and sued for peace. Would Yakub have to pay tribute and perform the kowtow? 'Certainly,' said Li. 'Yakub Beg would never do that,' Forsyth replied. 'In that case,' said Li, 'there is no help for it but to defeat him.'[38]

Lord Derby, the Foreign Secretary in London, put forward his own three-point formula: Yakub Beg should be left in control provided he recognized the Emperor of China as his superior; the border between 'Kashgaria' and China should be clearly demarcated; and the two sides should sign an agreement of mutual assistance.

In 1875, while the machinations continued, General Zuo began his westward march with the intention of approaching Urumchi from north of the Tian Shan mountains via Barkul and Gucheng. Hearing that the invasion force was on the move, Yakub Beg left his son Beg Kuli Beg in charge and marched east, with 30,000 to 40,000 soldiers under his command. When Urumchi fell to the Chinese in August 1876, he sent his envoy to London for talks with Guo Songtao, the Chinese ambassador. The message was that he, Yakub Beg, would now accept any position that the Chinese gave him so long as he could keep his kingdom.

Yakub seemed reluctant actually to engage with the approaching army, and the Muslim defenders were quick to make their getaway before their garrisons were attacked. By the winter of 1876, most of the Dzungarian basin had fallen into Chinese hands and Yakub, ensconced at Korla in the north-east corner of the Tarim basin, now gave orders that his troops should not fire on the enemy, not even in self-defence – a curious tactic, which had a devastating effect on morale.[39] His soldiers became even readier to desert. Perhaps Yakub was trying to signal that his offer to parley was genuine. Perhaps he hoped that by giving up territory in the north and east of the province he would be allowed to keep Kashgar and the Tarim for himself. But the further Zuo advanced, the more the attitude of the Chinese hardened. It was too late.

After the fall of Turfan in the middle of May 1877, and as General Zuo was turning south into Kashgaria itself, Yakub Beg suddenly and unexpectedly solved his own dilemma. He died.

The Muslims believed he was poisoned. Some said it was the cold tea brought to cool him off after he had become tired and short of breath from beating a subordinate called Kamal al-Din. He drank the tea, fell to the ground and 'his body became hard, turned blue, and began to crack'.[40] Others said the tea-bearer was in the pay of a rival, Niyaz Beg of Khotan. But Niyaz Beg later wrote to a Chinese general saying that Yakub had killed himself: if he, Niyaz, had been responsible for poisoning the Blessed One, he said, he would have been happy to take the credit for it.

An officer who claimed to have been present said Yakub had flown into a passion after getting a letter from the Chinese which asked why he did not surrender when even his own people had turned against him. He killed the messenger, wounded the man who had read the letter to him, and then took poison. A Turkish officer on Yakub's staff provided a more plausible version. According to him, at about 5 p.m. on 28 May, having beaten Kamal to death, he was about to belabour another colleague when he 'received a blow which deprived him of memory and speech' – in other words, he had a stroke. He lay in that state until he died at 2 o'clock the following morning. The Chinese, naturally, said Yakub Beg had committed suicide because he knew the game was up.

It did not take long for General Zuo to mop up resistance in the rest of Yakub's kingdom. He was helped by a struggle for the succession, which saw the kingdom split into three. Aksu fell in October 1877, Kashgar in December, and Khotan the following January. Victory was announced by the Chinese in the official

Peking Gazette on 26 December 1877: 'Our forces, whose path has lain amid the boundless waste and under the rigours of an icy season, have within the space of a single month accomplished a march of upwards of one thousand miles in length.' The British took surprisingly little notice of the collapse of their client king, but for one languid comment from the Foreign Office. On receiving a translation of the official announcement, Hugh Fraser wrote to the Foreign Secretary to say that if this report was true, the Chinese 'have reason to be proud of the achievement'.[41]

Zuo's achievement was a rare event in China's history, since it was applauded by traditionalists, nationalists and Marxists alike. His recapture of Xinjiang was indeed remarkable, but its glory was dimmed by Yakub Beg's failure to win the support of his own people and to fight for what he had won. It is easy to agree with those who say that if it had not been for Yakub's loss of nerve, and the discontent he created by his exploitative reign, the Chinese expedition might have ended as 'one of the most disastrous military undertakings in modern Chinese history'.[42]

Thanks to China's weakness and his own ruthlessness, Yakub Beg had succeeded where others failed in creating an independent eastern Turkestan. His kingdom lasted a mere thirteen years, but it left a mark on the Chinese psyche which has never been erased. In human terms, the cost was enormous. In little more than a hundred years Xinjiang had changed hands three times, and each change was marked by massacre and devastation. The Emperor Qianlong had annexed the territory, but his successors could not hold it. Now, with the help of British loans and Russian supplies, it had been restored to China.

How nearly it was lost again we shall see, when a routine lunch party turned into a bloodbath.

4

The Baby General

THE DOGS BARKED incessantly the night before Governor Yang was murdered. It was certainly an omen, said one of his ministers afterwards, a warning that the ancient proverb was about to be fulfilled: 'He who slays at a feast shall at a feast be slain.'

Forty years after the death of Yakub Beg, Xinjiang found itself once more under a dictator, but this time one from inside China. The explorer Sven Hedin described Governor Yang Zengxin as the most absolute ruler on earth; and his methods of dealing with difficulties were as cunning as they were ruthless.

An example of Yang's ruthlessness occurred at the beginning of 1916 when he had been in power for five years. A former aide came to Yang with the warning that some of his ministers were not to be trusted. Instead of rewarding the man he denounced him as a slanderer and had him shot in the courtyard of the Governor's mansion. Then he called his ministers together, told them what he had done and declared his absolute faith in them. Mightily relieved, the disloyal officials were thrown off their guard.

They should have known better. When the mid-January festival came round, Yang summoned his ministers to a feast. The guests of honour were to be the Inspector of Education from Beijing and the Minister of Finance of Xinjiang. What happened next is described by Aitchen Wu, an adviser to Yang's successor, who had it from one of those present:

When the cups had been filled a few times the Governor suddenly rose and left the hall. This action aroused no suspicion since it was known that Yang cared little for wine. But in a few minutes he returned, followed by a soldier who held concealed behind his back a long curved sword. The Governor paused behind the seat of Hsia Ting, one of the principal malcontents. Then in a cold, even casual voice speaking typical Yunnanese dialect, he said: 'Behead Hsia Ting!'

The knife flashed, and Hsia Ting fell dead, his blood spouting upon the robes of those who sat at table with him. All cowered in horror, none daring to move; but in calm tones the Governor reassured them. 'This has nothing to do with you. Come, more wine for my guests!'

When the cups were refilled the Governor again left the chamber, but almost immediately he returned, a second soldier at his side. Proceeding around the table they halted at the chair of one Li Yin, and once again the guests heard the dread command. But Li Yin must have feared that his intrigues were known, for he leapt to his feet even as the blade swung upon him and fled from the chamber wounded, his assailant close at his heels. He did not get far. In a few moments screams from the outer hall told the remaining guests what fate had overtaken the second of their number.

The table was in confusion, blood was everywhere. The Inspector from Peking looked on, speechless with horror . . .

Calmly the Governor resumed his seat at the table, called for more wine, and proceeded without the least trace of emotion to give judicial reasons for what he had done. Then, having spoken, he applied himself to the dishes which were set before him, and to the astonishment of the company made a hearty meal, finishing his two bowls of rice as usual.[1]

A Mafia *capo* could not have done better.

Ruthlessness was a legacy Governor Yang had inherited from General Zuo, the hero of the Chinese reconquest. To mark Xinjiang's incorporation as a full province of China in 1884, Zuo, now imperial minister for military affairs, had changed China's policy towards Xinjiang completely.

Autonomy was finished. Now the Turkis were to be assimilated and turned into Confucian Chinese as fast as possible. Remote control was replaced by direct rule, and an aggressive colonization began. Han officials crowded into the Manchu bureaucracy, and Han settlers began to arrive in larger numbers. Many of Zuo's own soldiers had decided to stay behind after their effortless victory; after them came traders from Beijing and Tianjin, bringing simple goods such as towels, linen cloths, brushes and soap. These entrepreneurs risked being robbed and murdered on the way, but the price of their wares rose satisfyingly the further west they travelled. The Tianjin traders prospered most, because they shunned drugs and alcohol. The poor refugees who followed them from overcrowded neighbouring provinces usually succumbed to the ravages of opium.

As the Han became more aware of their manifest destiny to rule the west, so they became more 'orientalist'. The erotic and the exotic were intertwined to mitigate the savagery of the new domain (as has been seen in the story of the Fragrant Concubine). A Turki folksong describing 'big, sweet watermelons' in the same lip-smacking breath as girls with long ponytails and shining eyes, who beckoned Han millionaires to come and marry them, became popular in mainland China.[2]

Just as Thomas Jefferson, a hundred years earlier, had said that Red Indians should change their language in order to become true Americans, so General Zuo decreed that the Turkis must learn Chinese in order to become proper Confucians. He set up charity schools for teaching Chinese language, literature and civilization. Officials tried to whip up support by handing out free pamphlets in Turki, offering grants and exempting from *corvée* and taxes the parents of children who attended such schools. But when the 'turbaned people' were summoned to school, they ran and hid. Teachers had arrived with the army to instruct the locals in the Thousand Characters, the One Hundred Names, and how to compose in eight paragraphs. 'Stunned with amazement, the Muslims just don't know what to say,' one contemporary reported. 'To stop the pupils fleeing, the masters lock them in the classroom and put them in irons.'[3] The children also had to pay homage to the image of Confucius. Not surprisingly, those who turned up were treated as outcasts by their own people. The Uighur nationalist refugee Isa Alptekin recounted how his grandfather sent a local poor boy to the Confucian school in place of his own son, whom he hid in a summer resort. When the ruse was discovered the father was jailed for several months and the boy was sent to school where he was given a Chinese name and made to dress in Chinese clothes and wear a pigtail. The boy's mother could not bear even to touch the pigtail and – so the father said – ceased to love her son.

Adult Turkis were ordered to make Chinese marriages and worship at Chinese temples. They had to show exaggerated respect to Chinese officials by kneeling before them, and if an official was on his way to prayers, they had to kneel at the temple entrance with their hands behind their backs. Officials were given arbitrary powers of arrest, punishment and execution. It is even said that the General Zuo formally asked the Emperor for licence to kill Turkis, armed or not.[4]

A fresh outbreak of Dongan trouble in Gansu in 1885 was put down with a massacre and resulted in a general uprising on the province's eastern border as far as Lop Nor. The Russians threatened to come in and restore order. Then, in 1894, China was attacked by Japan, and was at war for eight months. Four years later, floods and famine in the north-eastern province of Shandong gave rise to the peasant revolt known as the Boxer Rebellion. Within a few years the enfeebled Qing dynasty was finished. The provinces rebelled and declared their independence on 10 October 1911, and the Republic was created at Nanjing the following January, with the revolutionary leader Sun Yatsen as interim President. In March the Emperor abdicated and Yuan Shikai became President. China broke up into a series of fiefdoms. Neither the Republic nor the Guomindang wing of Nationalists who seized power under General Chiang Kai-shek in 1928 could reunite inner China, let alone exert any authority in the far west. Between 1919 and the Communist victory of 1949 China was, in the words of one historian, 'a demoralized country which had lost all hope, a world in which pity and justice no longer had any meaning, where horror had become a daily event'.[5] It was the time of the warlords. Some were brigands on horseback, but many were educated men, military governors who now took the law into their own hands. For the next half century, Xinjiang belonged neither to its people nor to the state. It was on its own – with the Russians breathing down its neck.

To stay in charge during such times took special talents. Yang Zengxin was a meticulous mandarin, born in Yunnan province in 1867. After experience in the western provinces he was appointed *daotai* (circuit commissioner) first to Aksu in 1908, then to Urumchi in 1911, and he seized control of Xinjiang when Yuan Shikai became President of the Republic. Educated in the classical tradition, Yang used to retire in the evenings to read aloud the works of the ancient philosopher Laozi in tones which resounded through the compound. President Yuan said that he possessed 'the greatest mind in China'.

Yang boasted that he was creating 'an earthly paradise in a remote region'. The Governor seemed to radiate a kind of divine majesty. He certainly made an impression on the British missionary Mildred Cable, who – though she naturally tended to see the best in people – was no fool. 'I understood something of the power he wielded,' she wrote after meeting him. She described a scholar and gentleman of the old school, tall and stately in a grey silk gown. 'His strong, intelligent, commanding face revealed one who could grasp a situation quickly and deal with it unhesitatingly.'[6]

As we have seen, this last remark was something of an understatement.

Like all autocrats, Yang was secretive. He was said to keep the key to the telegraph office about his own person. Ever mistrustful, he had surrounded himself with officials from his home province; but by degrees he came to doubt the fidelity of even his closest advisers. Things came to a head when malcontents in Yunnan devised a plot to thwart the ambitions of Yuan Shikai, who seemed set on founding a new dynasty. The plotters canvassed friends in Urumchi for support, and met with some success. Yang would have none of it: hence the festival banquet. After all, he owed his job to Yuan, who had confirmed him in power and who appeared content to let him run Xinjiang as a private kingdom so long as he paid his respects to the capital. The last thing Yang wanted was to see his sponsor pulled down.

He was helped by geography. The great tracts of steppe and desert which separated Urumchi from the rest of China insulated

Xinjiang from the upheavals of the new Republic and allowed Yang to rule as he pleased. His policy for peace was to keep the different races of Xinjiang apart, and his borders tight shut. The only foreign presence he permitted – and then only because he had no choice – was that of Soviet trade agencies in the border areas of the Ili valley and Chuguchak. Although officials and the native *begs* beneath them were allowed to squeeze the populace in the time-honoured fashion, Yang never permitted the exploitation to cut so deep as to cause trouble, and he backed his appeasement of the Muslims with secret executions of officials who went too far.

The chief beneficiary of Yang's 'earthly paradise', however, was Yang himself. Miss Cable and her companions Francesca and Evangeline French caught a glimpse of this side of their hero's character when they bumped into Yang's son on the Soviet border in 1926, smuggling valuables out in a cart and packing them off down the Irtysh river. They learned that Yang had realized his time was up and planned to get his family and riches out via Russia to the British concession in Tianjin. In reality, Yang was bleeding the province to death. He printed his own, worthless, money which he forced traders to accept in return for their hard currency receipts from inner China. In just two years, according to Clarmont Skrine, British consul-general in Kashgar, the notes in circulation exceeded the province's annual revenue by six times. Large sums were salted away abroad: Yang was reputed to have a bank account in Manila, safely under US jurisdiction.

Visitors to Xinjiang tended to accept Yang's 'paradise' boast. They saw Yang as a progressive whose regime was firm yet reasonably fair to the natives. Modern scholars are less impressed. They see a reactionary whose regime was merely a seventeen-year prolongation of a corrupt imperial age.[7]

For all his neurotic precautions, Governor Yang found himself saddled with one official he never trusted: an ambitious, Japanese-educated modernist called Fan Yaonan.

When the Guomindang forces took power, entering Beijing in June 1928, they prescribed that 'democratic' advisory councils should be set up in each province. Yang refused to admit his *bête noire* to the Xinjiang council even though Fan was a high-ranking official and an active Nationalist supporter. 'I keep Fan like a chained tiger,' he boasted. According to one of his colleagues, this rebuff was the last straw for Fan. He decided to eliminate the Governor before he was himself eliminated. He was a good pupil and his scheme was crafted, like the plot of grand opera, with tragic symmetry.

The Governor was due to attend a prize-giving day at the Russian Language School in Urumchi on 7 July. Fan arranged with the Dean of the school, a friend of his, to let him plant a dozen or more of his men in the audience disguised as students, with revolvers hidden in their sleeves. Speech Day arrived. The Governor was in a good mood. During his homily, however, an alert member of his staff called Lieutenant Du noticed some strange-looking faces in the audience. The Dean assured him nothing was amiss, and the party adjourned for a banquet. Yang's bodyguards were invited to eat in a separate room and put aside their weapons, which were promptly removed.

Among the guests were the Soviet consul and his wife, and Yan, the Governor's scholarly Minister for Industry, who later described the scene to his friend Aitchen Wu:

> The Governor was anxious to leave as early as possible since he had duties at the Military Academy; he therefore asked that the dishes should be speedily served. In spite of this request there were delays. Yang was, however, in the highest spirits and in a moment of unwonted bending was playing 'finger games' with his neighbours. Suddenly . . . the Dean of the school entered with a new bottle of wine which he set down upon the table with such vigour that all eyes turned towards him, pained by such rough manners in the presence of the Governor.
>
> At that moment Fan asked: 'Are the other wines all ready?' to which the Dean replied: 'All is prepared.' Fan then raised his cup towards the Soviet consul-general to drink his health. As the cups met, shots rang out simultaneously, all aimed at the Governor. Seven bullets in all were fired and all reached their mark. Yang, mortally wounded, but superb in death, glared an angry defiance at his foes. 'Who dares do this?' he questioned in the loud voice which had commanded instant obedience for so many years . . .

When they saw what had happened the high officials stampeded for the door. The Russian Consul and his wife took refuge in the lavatory. Lieutenant Du was shot, and Yan, who was wounded in the shoulder, only escaped by feigning death. As he lay beneath the overturned tables Yan saw Fan standing over the sorely wounded but still breathing Governor, revolver in hand. Two further shots completed the crime.[8]

Yang had enforced the peace for seventeen years. His reign would have been remarkable at any time. It was even more remarkable when the rest of China was in turmoil, Russia was going through its fratricidal Revolution, and the world itself had been at war between 1914 and 1918.

But the death of Yang left Aitchen Wu feeling embarrassed: 'During my travels in Europe I have heard a good deal concerning the barbarism of [Xinjiang],' he wrote. 'The critics of my country were quite right in what they said. Let me admit freely that in the recent history of Urumchi there is much that is terrible. I am myself bitterly ashamed that there should occur on Chinese soil events which approach in horror to the Russian purges, the assassination of Dolfuss, and Hitler's infamous July 30th purge.'[9]

One notable absentee from the death-feast of Yang was Jin Shuren, Minister of the Interior and second-in-command. Jin had excused himself after the Governor's speech, pleading pressure of work. Suspicious minds wondered whether Jin might know something, for it was he, not Fan the chief conspirator, who inherited the feudal mantle. Fan was quickly arrested by the garrison troops who had not been party to the conspiracy, taken as he sat in the Governor's chair. He was led away, and executed by means of the death of a thousand cuts.[10]

Jin now tested Yang's engine of repression to destruction. The new Governor, whose succession was rubber-stamped by an impotent Guomindang regime in Nanjing, was half the man that Yang was but twice as greedy. 'A weak, vacillating opium-smoker' according to Miss Cable, he pandered to the rich and stamped on the poor. 'He was a man beset by fears, alternately too feeble or too harsh,' she wrote, displaying 'that combination of tyranny and vacillation which is the most fatal characteristic that an autocrat can possess.' Even his political adviser Aitchen Wu felt bound to admit Jin's weaknesses, though he ascribed them more to fear than to favouritism.

Yang's Yunnanese courtiers were replaced by men from Gansu, Jin's province. The money-presses clanked ever faster to churn out paper *tael* notes. Internal passports were introduced, censorship and police surveillance were stepped up, and pilgrimages to Mecca (the *hajj*) were forbidden: not that Jin suffered from any religious squeamishness; he probably feared that hard currency would leak abroad. Such restraints as there had been on taxing land were removed. The natural wealth of Xinjiang – gold from Keriya, jade from Khotan, furs and fleeces from the mountains – was scooped up by government monopolies under Jin's control. Jin's profiteering was confirmed by Georg Vasel, a German engineer and Nazi agent. Vasel claimed to have met a German pilot called Rathje in Suzhou who had been employed by Jin to fly a million dollars' worth of his gold bullion from Urumchi to Beijing.*

It was not long before Jin's rule was challenged. The first murmurs of revolt came in 1930 from the sweltering oasis of Turfan, where a local religious leader plotted to set up an independent Muslim state. He sought help from a Muslim Chinese officer stationed with the Guomindang army on the Gansu border. Without his commander's permission this Dongan lieutenant set off with about a hundred men to ride across the desert but, pursued and harried by troops sent to turn him back, he arrived at Turfan with only twenty-seven survivors. The revolt fizzled out. Jin should have heeded the warning, says Aitchen Wu, but instead he did nothing to soothe the restive Muslims: 'Yang had met his end through careless unchaining of an apparently tame tiger; his successor had profited so little from experience that he was boldly tormenting a whole host of obviously wild ones.'[12]

---

*Vasel was building aerodromes in China. Rathje the pilot shared his tent one night and told him the secret of the bullion he was carrying. Next morning the two were trying to get the plane going when Dongan cavalry appeared and demanded to search it. Rathje and the wireless operator tricked them by sitting on the bullion boxes with their own suitcases ready for inspection on their knees.[11]

The tigers broke loose in the large oasis of Hami, close to the Gansu border, a place traditionally reconciled to the Chinese presence. In March 1930, the ruler of the oasis, Maksud Shah, died. Sometimes known as King of the Gobi, Maksud was descended from the Uighur khans who had been lords of Xinjiang a thousand years before. After the reconquest he and a few like him had been allowed to continue with semi-autonomous powers, like the 'native states' in British India.[13] Maksud was thoroughly assimilated, speaking Turki with a Chinese accent and dressing in Chinese robes. The explorer Albert von Le Coq described his palace as decorated with Chinese and Khotanese carpets, embroidery in both the Chinese and the Bokharan style, jade carving from Khotan and Chinese porcelain, a French clock, a Russian paraffin lamp and a cuckoo clock. 'I was astonished', says von Le Coq, 'to find in the house of a Mohammedan prince an enormous quantity of Russian liqueurs and excellent French champagnes. He was continually drinking our health and seemed quite hardened against any of the ill effects of alcohol.' But he did refuse to have his photograph taken.[14] Maksud's grand vizier was Yolbas Khan, known (coincidentally) as the Tiger Prince, who spoke Chinese fluently and was something of a quick-change artist: he was to play an ambivalent role in the coming troubles. Another prominent member of Maksud's retinue was Khoja Niyas, who was to play an even more unpredictable part.

On Maksud's death, Jin was advised by local officials to take Hami in hand, abolish the monarchy, break up the Shah's 6,000-acre estate and introduce land reform. Yolbas and Maksud's young heir were summoned to Urumchi to swear their fealty, probably under duress. Although oppressive to his subjects, Maksud's rule had been far from intolerable. But Jin's men in Hami showed themselves especially generous with the Turkis' property. 'Reform' turned out to mean giving Turki lands to about a hundred Han refugees from Gansu, and compensating their owners with tracts of poor soil on the desert's edge. Wu called it 'sheer robbery only thinly disguised as law'. The Muslims were incensed and telegraphed a petition to Urumchi, which either never arrived or was ignored.

It was the folly of one of Jin's tax collectors in early 1931, however, which really unleashed the tigers. A young man called Zhang Mu was stationed in a small village north of Hami. There he seduced a Muslim girl. Following the inevitable outcry he offered to marry her. One version of the story has it that he was invited to discuss terms over dinner at the house of the girl's father. When he arrived he and his thirty-two bodyguards were set upon by Turkis and killed. Another version is that a marriage was agreed, and the youth and his bride were killed on their wedding night. Whatever the truth, the murder was the signal – planned or not – for a general riot. With a few captured rifles, the Turkis now descended on the old city of Hami and began slaughtering the Chinese. Among the first victims were the families of Gansu immigrants who had been settled on Turki land. Their heads were cut off and buried in their ill-gotten fields.

Jin decided to take the severest reprisals, although he must have been aware of the Turkis' material grievances even if he did not understand the insult caused by his abolition of the Hami monarchy. He refused the Muslim leaders' surrender, forcing them to look about for support. This they now did. And among the supporters they found was someone who, though still a youth, had already shown himself a daring, savage, charismatic and dangerous adversary.

Ma Zhongying was a Dongan warlord from Gansu, born in about 1910 into a clan of warlords whose chiefs were known as the Five Ma. Though only 21 at the time of the Hami revolt, he was already a veteran, having joined the army at the age of 14 and become a commander a year later. He had marauded through north-west Gansu, terrifying the towns with his butchery and the country with his pillaging, and had spent a short time at the military academy in Nanjing where he was said to have impressed Chiang Kai-shek. Now he was in control of north-west Gansu, and his reputation was enormous. Ma is short for Muhammad, the name of the Prophet, and therefore a very common surname among Chinese Muslims. In Chinese it sounds like the word for 'horse', hence Ma's nickname of Big Horse used by Sven Hedin and others. But to the men of his army who worshipped him and thought him invincible Ma was always the Little General or the Baby General.

Like Yakub Beg before him, Ma came to Xinjiang from outside to assume the leadership of a revolt that had already begun. The approach in his case was made by the Tiger Prince of Hami,

Yolbas, whose aim seems to have been a limited one: to get a more sympathetic governor in Urumchi and restoration of the Hami royal family. In his memoirs, Yolbas claimed that he had not set out to involve Ma; he had been on his way to Nanjing to ask the Nationalist government to do something and had dropped in on Ma at Suzhou 'by chance' where he gave away the secret of his mission. Ma promised to help 'in the name of Muslim brother-hood'. But he had much bigger ideas.

It was not a simple situation. The Turkis were in revolt against a provincial governor whose allegiance to the Nationalists was only nominal. But they were about to be aided by a Muslim Chinese warlord who knew and admired Chiang Kai-shek and saw himself as the true representative of the Nationalist regime in Nanjing (which later recognized him as such). At the same time, the Turkis and Dongans, despite their shared Islamic faith, were far from natural allies.

True to his word, the Baby General dashed across the Gobi at the head of 500 cavalry in June 1931, arriving in Hami just as a convoy of European motor-lorries pulled up. This was the French Haardt-Citroën Expedition which had struggled over the Karakorams and was on its way to Beijing. It quickly left again. According to one of the expedition's engineers who stayed behind, Ma first sent two messengers to the Chinese garrison commander demanding surrender. Only one returned, carrying the head of the other. On 3 July, Ma's army attacked the fortress of the old city with gunfire, yells, drums and trumpets, followed by a rush of men to the glacis. Chinese peasants were driven forward with scaling ladders by Dongan soldiers carrying huge curved swords. Up went the Dongans, to be greeted with pikes and axes, rocks and hand grenades, followed by an enfilade of machine-gun fire.[15]

The siege of Hami went on until November, by which time the garrison, having eaten the last of the camels, horses and mules, was reduced to flour and opium. For weapons they had only swords and fire arrows found in a secret arsenal left by General Zuo sixty years before. A relief force arrived, headed by 250 White Russians whom Governor Jin had recruited from the Ili valley where they had settled after the Bolshevik victory in the Russian civil war. The White Russians had plenty of military experience and when

Ma went out to meet them he was seriously wounded, being shot in both legs. Hami was reprieved, but the Chinese reprisals were so savage – devastation in the Turki villages and mass executions in the town – that fuel was only added to the flames of rebellion.

The Baby General retired to nurse his wounds at Anxi, in Gansu. There he summoned the three English missionaries to visit him.

Mildred Cable, Francesca French and her sister Evangeline were at Dunhuang, south-west of Anxi, where they had been held under virtual arrest by Ma's soldiers. They knew all about the Baby General and his methods. These intrepid women had crossed the area controlled by his Dongan troops and had witnessed the terror they inspired in the people. Village women would sit all day long on the *kang* (the raised bed of wood or clay with a fire underneath, still seen in rural north China), dressed in their best clothes and clutching their possessions, ready to flee at the sound of the village gong. The missionaries themselves got used to decamping in the middle of the night when the alarm was raised by a horseman galloping through the village.

On one occasion, having left an inn shortly before the other guests, the ladies were stopped on the road by a raiding party and were saved only by the appearance of an officer who knew them. The bandits moved on, shooting travellers as they went. On another occasion the women were sitting round a brazier eating fried dough-cakes with a farmer and his family when they heard the rap of a riding whip on the door. In strode a Dongan officer. He demanded five bushels of wheat. When the farmer protested that everything had been taken in previous raids, he received a lashing with the whip. The old man went to the corn bin and swept out what was left in the bottom. The officer departed. 'Our host, without a word of anger or of complaint, took off his cotton coat and with his hand felt the weals on his neck and shoulders, then he came and joined our circle round the brazier again. Such', reflected Miss Cable, 'is the patient endurance of men who have never seen human rights maintained.'[16]

The Dongans' expropriations were so severe that the people of Dunhuang were reduced to beggary; typhus raged in the streets and its victims lay in their delirium croaking for water, while dogs and wolves mangled the corpses of the poor in their shallow graves. The women saw a press gang in action: local youths, snatched from their homes, were marched into town, their hands tied behind their backs with nooses running round their necks. The many opium addicts among them had to face cold turkey. Three times a day they were taken to the drill yard, and when they were fit, they would be sent up to Anxi for a passing-out parade in front of the Baby General himself.

Receiving the summons to Anxi, a hard march across the desert, the women set off on a cold November morning in 1932. They arrived four days later, were quizzed by a cheeky boy sentry on the city gate and shown to their lodgings. Next day they were admitted to the presence.

The 'slim, delicate-featured youth' they encountered, far from frightening the women, seems to have elicited a kind of matronly disapproval tinged with affection. Miss Cable thought there was good in the young man. But if for a moment she imagined Ma was interested in hearing the words of Jesus, she was quickly disabused. Ma was anxious to resume his campaign and needed the missionaries' miraculous Western medicine.

Ma's behaviour towards the supplicants who streamed into his audience chamber was very different. Miss Cable observed, as she prepared dressings at a side table, the 'callous, flippant youth' dispensing justice according to his mood. One old man came begging for his son's life. Ma never deigned to look at the poor wretch crouching before him, but toyed instead with a hunting knife as the petitioner pleaded:

> 'Spare my son's life, Your Excellency.'
> 'Why should I spare his life?'
> 'He is my only son, Excellency.'
> 'The boy is disobedient, and my orders are to punish disobedience with shooting.'
> 'I promise he will never do it again, Excellency.'
> 'He has done it once, and that is enough. I do not change my mind. You may go.'
> The simple fellow bent forward until his forehead touched the raised dais on which the General sat, and the body-guard hustled him away.[17]

Miss Cable does not say what she prescribed; but, whatever it was, the warlord was soon able to ride again. 'He always treated us with civility,' she wrote, 'probably owing to the fact that we were the only people who never flattered him and were obviously not afraid of him.'[18]

In private Ma was much less decisive. Surrounded by sycophants and advisers, he was pulled this way and that. Aitchen Wu met a pair of them called Yin and Yang, who behaved rather like Rosencrantz and Guildenstern, the clownish courtiers in *Hamlet*. There were also two Japanese on Ma's staff, whose duties were obscure. They were the object of the greatest suspicion, however, since the authorities in Urumchi feared that Japan, which the year before had occupied Manchuria, had designs on the whole of northern China. Ma also had two Turkish military advisers from Istanbul, one of whom claimed to have fought in the First World War, the other to have graduated in political science in Paris.

These latter two had befriended the missionary ladies earlier in their travels and now proved useful, persuading Ma to let his prisoners return to Dunhuang on condition they promised to stay there. Mildred Cable's account of her final meeting with the Baby General shows her Christian feeling for him. 'My last impression of him remains as that of a slender, elegant man, standing in a room of which the walls were hung with every kind of rifle, and surrounded with a body-guard of turbaned warriors, who watched him narrowly as he took from my hand a copy of the New Testament in Chinese, the book which would speak to him in his own tongue, rebuke him and, if he would but repent, convert and remake him. He saluted, I withdrew, and we never met again.'[19]

Back in Dunhuang, the dauntless women began secretly to save flour and fodder for their escape. They made their break some months later, while the town was 'taking its early dose of poppy-juice', striking out along a little-known desert track towards the border with Xinjiang, and stopping neither by night nor by day. Three days later, they were overtaken by Ma's soldiers who had followed the tracks of their cart; but they bluffed their way out, producing flamboyantly stamped Chinese passports which the soldiers took to be from Ma's hand. When they saw the documents the guards stood to attention, saluted, and promised safe conduct. By the time the mistake was discovered, the women were safely inside Chinese lines.

Meanwhile, Jin Shuren, the governor in Urumchi whose mismanagement had given the Baby General the *casus belli* he was looking for, had been trying to strengthen his position. He turned to the Soviet Union – not to distant Nanjing – for tanks and aeroplanes and other military supplies, signing an illegal treaty in October 1931 which gave the Russians a virtual monopoly of trade in return. He also, even more fatefully, appointed as commander-in-chief of the provincial army Sheng Shicai, a highly trained Manchurian soldier and senior army officer in his mid-thirties who had been posted to Xinjiang by the Nationalist regime.

In the meantime, convalescing at Anxi, the Baby General appointed his adjutant Ma Shiming to take over operations in Xinjiang. In the following year there were skirmishes at Turfan, which the new Chinese commander Sheng managed to recapture. But in the winter of 1932, the position of the Chinese in Urumchi began to look desperate. Ma Shiming started to march on the provincial capital. At the same time Aitchen Wu, the eloquent chronicler of this chaotic time, was making a long journey from the coast of China towards the threatened city.

Wu set off without an inkling of the trouble awaiting him. The new adviser's real name was Wu Aizhen, and he was a scholar from a family of literati in Fuzhou, opposite the island of Taiwan, who for five successive generations had graduated as *juren*, the highest provincial degree awarded under the old mandarin system. After university in Beijing and several years in the United States – where he acquired his Westernized name and dress – Wu had joined the civil service and been appointed by the new Guomindang government to advise Jin Shuren.

Rather than head west across China and face the perils of the Gobi desert, Wu and two companions decided to take the quickest and easiest route, involving a 7,000-mile detour. Embarking at the port of Tianjin, they took a ship round Korea to Kobe in Japan, and

another ship back across the sea to Vladivostok. There they caught
a train along the Trans-Siberian railway, changing at Novosibirsk
and heading south through Semipalatinsk on the recently completed 'Turk-Sib' line. Finally, they took a lorry down to the
Xinjiang border at Chuguchak, and so on to Urumchi which they
reached after only thirty-six days, on Christmas Day 1932.

Wu's duties were vague, and in his memoirs he describes himself
as a guest. Most likely he had been sent to persuade Governor Jin
to pay attention to his new political bosses in distant Nanjing. If so,
he failed.

Wu liked to be thought of as a mild person (the 'Ai' in his name
means 'gentle') and certainly he was no warrior. He preferred to
keep his head down while the action was afoot, and re-emerge
when it was time to clean up. But the conventional picture of the
Chinese mandarin as soft and other-worldly is not altogether
accurate. These gentlemen had to be tough to undertake the jour-
neys they made. William Drew, an English missionary who first
met Wu in Urumchi, said that he saw him in a flaming row with a
junior: 'His eyes, always bright and eager, were ablaze, his visage
contorted with rage, and his speech like bursts of gun-fire.'[20] The
Confucian diplomat was nevertheless a humanitarian, free of racial
and religious prejudice, respectful of Christianity and with keen
organizational instincts. His powers of analysis, says Drew, were
not, however, as great as he imagined.

Wu was to be found in characteristic mode when the Dongans
descended on Urumchi on 21 February 1933, taking the Great
West Bridge and putting the town under siege. We see him sitting
in his room, dressed, as usual, in a Western suit and patiently
copying out extracts from the *Illustrated Encyclopaedia of Xinjiang*
in an attempt to calm his nerves. Artillery fire rattles the
windows. The Muslims are at the gates and the only hope of survival lies with a tough, vodka-swilling cohort of 300 White
Russians under their commander Colonel Pappengut, a former
Tsarist staff officer.

Outside the locked gates of the city, the Russians fought with
'disciplined fury', Wu recorded. But thousands of refugees from
outlying areas had been caught in the battle. They had sought
shelter in what the Chinese called the Street of the Small

Religion (Islam), which the rebels now occupied. To dislodge them, the Chinese commander ordered that it be set alight. The scene that followed was too frightful to describe, said Wu. 'As the flames swept down the long lane of wooden structures they became an inferno of horror, for the roar of the conflagration was added to the rattle of gun-fire, and the hideous shrieks of those who were trapped. The rebels sought safety in flight, and as they crossed the open were machine-gunned . . . but the fugitives had nowhere to fly to and perished to the last man, woman, and child.'[21]

At least 2,000 Dongans and Chinese were killed – or, as Wu put it, one for every five words he had copied from the *Encyclopaedia*. The city was saved, however, by the arrival of Sheng Shicai and his troops. The rebels pulled back, still keeping control of the surrounding country, the city gates were opened on 3 March, and Wu set about organizing the burial of the dead.

A month later, on a sunny afternoon in April 1933, the Governor's adviser was once more sitting indoors, reading an English translation of the Quran. It had been given him by his friend George Hunter, a Scottish missionary well known in Urumchi. Suddenly, the silence was shattered by a burst of rifle-fire. The shots seemed to come from the direction of the Governor's mansion, and were followed by the sound of galloping hooves. A servant went up on to the roof to investigate, and reported seeing a figure clambering over the wall of the Governor's compound.

Wu began to ask himself what he should do if his master were to be murdered. He was right to be worried: what he had heard was the White Russians repaying Jin for his incompetence and ingratitude. Though they had defended the city and were the only fighters of any experience in it, Jin had refused to give them the best horses – or indeed any horses at all. Now they were taking the law into their own hands. About two hundred of them had stormed the mansion, and the figure Wu's servant had seen climbing over the wall was none other than Jin himself, stripped of his uniform and making a run for it.

Although he was the official Guomindang representative, Wu was in no hurry to get involved, least of all to aid the fugitive Governor. He told his panicky Chinese colleagues that he had no standing in the matter and that they should work something out with the White Russians. 'I told them to pull themselves together and act along the lines I had suggested. Then I went home and continued to read the [Quran],' he recalled.[22] But he did consent to join a committee formed to appoint a provisional successor as governor, an ineffectual minister called Liu Wenlong. (Jin, after lurking in the region for a while, escaped to Chuguchak on the Soviet border and made his way back to Tianjin via the Trans-Siberian railway. There he was arrested and imprisoned for his illegal dealings with the Soviet Union.)

The committee's first choice for defence minister was the commander of 2,000 soldiers from Manchuria who had arrived in Urumchi at the end of March, bolstering the city's defences.* But he refused, saying he and his men were only visitors. So the job was offered to Sheng Shicai, who also went through the motions of refusing. He was only a common soldier, he said, and had no political ambitions. Sheng, who was suspected of having lobbied for the post through his pretty and ambitious wife, was on his way to becoming the real ruler of Xinjiang.

Still in neighbouring Gansu, the Baby General decided it was time to resume operations in Xinjiang himself. His press-gangs had replenished his private army and his confidence had been boosted when Nanjing gave it official status in 1932. It was designated the 36th Division of the National Army of China, and he, its 22-year-old warlord chief, commanding officer. In May 1933, he sent his younger brother to mop up in Hami, following himself by lorry and moving towards the capital along the northern side of the Tian Shan mountains. The nervous occupants of Urumchi radioed to Nanjing for help, but communications were not good. The Marconi long-wave radio stations at Kashgar and Urumchi had been damaged by rebels, and the thousands of miles of telegraph line were vulnerable to tribesmen who stole the wire for their own uses.† Wu realized that there was no hope of his superiors sending

---

* They had been fighting the Japanese who had invaded Manchuria in 1931, and they had escaped via Siberia.

† Attempts to link China and Russia across the Tian Shan were frustrated by bears. They knocked down the telegraph poles, mistaking the humming of the wires for bees.

reinforcements, but – true civil servant that he was – he wanted to do the correct thing. 'If I were to be slain,' he wrote afterwards, 'I wished it all to be done in orderly fashion.'[23]

However, after suffering a military rebuff outside the capital, the Baby General decided not to make a fight of it and put out peace feelers instead. The new governor was anxious to listen, and General Sheng summoned Aitchen Wu and asked him to join a delegation to Gucheng, above the mountains to the east, where the Baby General was camped. Wu demurred, pleading that he did not understand local politics sufficiently to be of any use as a negotiator. A few days later, however, while he was sitting in his courtyard reading the maxims of Confucius, he was approached by a group of Dongans, Uighurs and Manchus who begged him to reconsider. 'It is your duty to go,' said one of them, a rich merchant. Wu objected that he had no official status. 'My friend,' said the merchant, 'our highest duties are appointed by God.' Wu gave in. Confirming his assent to the Governor, he pondered on what he had let himself in for: 'My next hour was a bad one. I knew this was no ordinary diplomacy on which I was engaged. In his sudden rages [the Baby General] was scarcely human: torture, murder, and massacre were the commonplaces of his existence.'[24] Wu had every reason to be nervous. The German engineer Georg Vasel claimed to have seen Ma throwing hand grenades about as a joke to frighten his men, and personally decapitating five soldiers accused of desertion.

The Governor's idea was to persuade Ma to withdraw from the north of Xinjiang and turn his attention to the south, where (the delegation was to imply) he would be licensed, as official commander of Guomindang forces, to begin carving out the empire he dreamed of. Of course there was a danger that Ma would use the south as a base for attacking the north again. But for the Governor and his general at that moment, a war deferred was as good as no war at all. They advised Wu to appeal to Ma's weaknesses, his ignorance and his vanity, to flatter him by treating him as a scholar and a statesman as well as a warrior.

Arriving at Gucheng, the members of the delegation were summoned to the presence even before they had had time to wash. Wu recounts how the party was driven to a typical Muslim dwelling.

They sent in their visiting cards and were told they would be seen immediately. As they crossed the courtyard they were halted by guards, told to put their hands up, and searched thoroughly:

> Word then came that we were to enter. Dusk was upon the plains, and one by one the flickering oil-lamps were being lighted in the houses. I led the way. A door swung open. Rising from a couch in the middle of the room, 'Big Horse' came to meet us.
>
> My first impression was that of a rather slight but very wiry figure, boyish in walk, but with the assurance and determination of a man. He did not indulge in any ceremony.
>
> '*La – ye – wei – sze – Wu-Hsien-sen*?' he asked. ['Which of you is Mr Wu?']²⁵

While Ma was reading the letters the delegation had brought, Wu studied him. He saw a young man with a thin face and bright eyes, and a perfect physique which he compared to the look of a trained racehorse. In negotiation, however, Ma rambled, pretending a vast knowledge which was based on a few scraps of information. Wu thought his self-confidence bordered on insanity. He had 'the dreams of a schoolboy of genius who had made a large part of China his playground and now coveted the rest of the world'.²⁶ But even in his most extreme flights of fancy there was, according to Wu, a leavening of common sense.

Others have confirmed this assessment. Georg Vasel describes Ma as extremely handsome by Asiatic standards, with dark expressive eyes; sinister, but with a charming and generous side to his nature. His pride was extreme, and childish. When Vasel produced his wind-up gramophone and played German military marches for him, the Baby General watched closely, then insisted on changing the records himself. He put in a new needle, but the wrong way up:

> The blunt end of the needle produced nothing but a hideous scratching noise from the record. Ma looked at me with mouth agape in a puzzled fashion. I quietly pointed out to him that he had inserted the needle upside down, whereupon he put on the

brake, and readjusted the needle. He took care to assure me that his mistake had been due to inadvertence – not through ignorance of the method of manipulating a gramophone.[27]

Ma's love of music was genuine. He took an old, asthmatic harmonium with him everywhere, and would spend hours playing Muslim hymns on it. Another of his amusements was to gallop through the streets, standing like a circus rider on the saddles of two of his magnificent horses, and with his Mauser pistols pick off targets set up for him along the road.

Vanity, cruelty, naïvety and indecision were the main traits of Ma's character. He quoted as his models Genghis Khan, Napoleon, Bismarck, Hindenburg and Zuo Zongtang. But for precociousness and ambition – if not for tactical genius and drinking capacity – he more nearly matched the great hero of central Asia, Alexander of Macedon.

Like Alexander, he was obsessively fit and physically brave: and it was these disciplines, coupled with the savagery of his methods, which made his army so feared. For the narcissist Ma, physical training was like a religion, something to be pushed to the limit. Almost the first thing he did after receiving the delegation from Urumchi was to have them escorted down to the parade-ground. There they saw about a hundred boys dressed in vests and shorts, and drawn up in ranks before a set of parallel bars about six feet from the ground. On the bars could be seen a slender figure going through a difficult exercise routine. It was Ma himself, proving that he was the best athlete in his army. There followed sword drill, the youths shadow-fencing in pairs with great speed and accuracy. When they had finished Ma came up to the party, his face shining with enthusiasm: 'Do you like it?' he asked. Wu replied that it was a pity these young men were soon to die. 'That is the fortune of war,' replied Ma. 'War is always misfortune,' retaliated the diplomat. However, to show their gratitude for the spectacle, the delegation presented the troops with forty sheep, four hogsheads of sugar and two cases of tea.

'I have never seen troops in China train so hard,' commented Peter Fleming, who passed through Dongan-held territory in the southern Tarim in 1935. Fleming watched the soldiers practising siege work on a high wall of planks, and the cavalrymen carrying out the manoeuvre of wrestling their mounts to the ground and taking cover behind them, all in unison.[28]

The cavalry was Ma's pride and joy. On the move, the Dongan army was led by his personal regiment. 'The broad iron swords of the dragoons clanked as they rode along on their magnificent white horses,' wrote Georg Vasel, who only weeks before had watched the army setting off for Xinjiang, 'while on their shoulders they carried carbines of the most varied and antiquated patterns.' A 'white' regiment was followed by a brown, and then a black, each composed of 2,000 horsemen. Behind the cavalry came the infantry in column 'keeping perfect time with their shrill, high-pitched, mournful Asiatic marching songs'. The raw recruits were sandwiched between the columns to stop them running away. The baggage was carried by high-wheeled ox carts and hundreds of camels, the bells around their necks clanging. Nearly 2,500 of these soldiers were to die crossing the Gobi desert.[29]

The delegation appeared to have won its case. Ma agreed to a ceasefire, and to take himself off to the south of the province. But once they had gone, he changed his mind and continued to press forward. In June 1933 he met Sheng's troops at the town of Zilichuan, north of Mount Bogda. The armies were evenly matched, and Ma seemed on the point of victory when a freezing hailstorm broke overhead, lashing the lightly clad Muslims and turning the tables against them. Ma withdrew in good order along the road he had come, and made his way south and west, halting at Turfan. Here again he seemed ready to talk, offering to withdraw to Hami if the government would pay his troops. Sheng, in an effort to buy him off, made him 'garrison commander of the East' – and, in theory, under his command.

In December, however, Sheng's new subordinate suddenly appeared on the western side of the capital to launch a surprise attack. The Chinese commander took up position on an eminence called One-Shell Victory Hill, so called because sixty years before when the city was occupied by Yakub Beg's soldiers, one shell was allegedly all it took to force a surrender. This time, too, the Muslim enemy withdrew, with hardly a shot fired.

Sheng Shicai had meanwhile shown his true colours. Soon after his June victory, he came back to Urumchi and called an extraordinary meeting of the provincial council, or cabinet, in the garden of his mansion. Wu, although suffering from dysentery, made a special effort to attend and so witnessed the whole affair. He had been worried by the atmosphere of political intrigue in Urumchi, yet had no idea what was in store. The peonies and azaleas were at their best on that sunny morning. 'Peacocks spread their finery amid the blaze of flowers; parrots screeched in the branches. I shall never forget those thin cries in the hot air.'

Turning up early for the 10 o'clock meeting in a garden pavilion, he noticed guards on the inner gate of the compound. Sheng was sitting alone and very still outside the pavilion, fan in hand. Inside, there was a strange silence of presentiment. Suddenly, there came the sound of heavy boots outside. A messenger arrived for Sheng, who sent him off again. A few moments later there was the sound of seven shots. 'Sheng came slowly in from the terrace, his figure black against the sunlight as he paused a moment at the door. Then he came and sat next to Liu [the Governor], looking straight before him, ignoring questioning glances, waiting till the whispers at the far end of the table had died away.' He rose to his feet and announced that he had ordered the execution of three ministers, the Chief Secretary, the chief of staff and the aviation minister for their part in a conspiracy. Sheng then declared he could no longer be controlled by a committee, and would resign.[30]

His intention was, of course, the exact opposite. He had simply eliminated those who would resist a complete takeover. It happened that a special commissioner from Nanjing was in town, and two of the murdered men were friends of his. This man, to save his own skin, had little choice but to recommend that Sheng be confirmed in his position. Liu was confirmed also but resigned, as was intended, a month later.

Sheng Shicai had tightened his grip, but the rule of his even more ruthless adversary, the Baby General Ma Zhongying, was about to be severely curtailed. In late 1933, Sheng did what his predecessor Jin had done, and approached the Russians. A delegation was sent to Moscow, where Stalin proved keen to oblige.

Stalin may have heard rumours that the Dongan fighters were a front for the Japanese – perhaps because Ma had two Japanese on his staff, one of whom was captured during the hailstorm battle – and been persuaded that it was only a matter of time before they came marching out of Manchukuo, their new colony in Manchuria, to threaten Xinjiang. He may also have feared that Dongan successes would stir up his own central Asian subjects.

At all events, Ma's troops suddenly found themselves, in January 1934, facing Soviet bombers, tanks and heavy artillery. It was later claimed that some of the bombs contained poison gas. Two brigades of Red Army troops disguised as Chinese regulars, a total of 7,000 men, advanced to the Tutung river, west of Urumchi. The Dongans fought with their customary bravery, crawling through the snow camouflaged in sheepskins and storming the Red Army machine-gun posts with their curved swords waving above their heads. But they were no match for the Russians. Retreating they encountered a column of the Red Army. They engaged it hand-to-hand, and managed to roll some of the armoured cars off the mountainside. Ma was forced back to Korla, where he seized lorries belonging to the explorer Sven Hedin, who was on his last expedition to China, and made off along the north desert road to Kucha and Aksu. As the convoy of lorries bumped along Ma was cracking jokes and singing songs, more like a schoolboy at the start of the holidays than 'a great general facing ruin'.[31]

Meanwhile, in the south of Xinjiang, things had developed rather differently. In 1915, Governor Yang had appointed as his henchman in Kashgar the loathsome Ma Fuxing, a Dongan usually known by his title, Ma Daotai. Clarmont Skrine, the British consul-general, described him as 'a short, grizzled, monkey-like man with a long wispy moustache and fierce eyes' whose known cruelty made his *opera buffa* appearance more sinister than amusing.[32] Ma was illiterate and a drunkard, and insisted on being called *padishah*, or 'king'. He kept a harem of Turki beauties, was an expert extortionist, and annexed the mineral wealth of the Tarim basin – oil, coal, copper and jade – for himself, but was careful to send tribute of gold, diamonds and cash to his master in Urumchi.

Ma Daotai's real specialities, however, were mutilation and crucifixion. He kept a hay-chopping machine with which he amputated his enemies limb by limb. According to a Russian visitor, Paul Nazaroff, he would nail the amputated arms or feet to the city gates with notices stating whose they were and why they had been removed. Sometimes the owner was chained up beside them. Eventually, Yang decided that Ma Daotai had gone too far and in 1924 he sent another Dongan, Ma Shaowu, to remove him. The *padishah* was given a taste of his own medicine: he was shot and tied to a wooden cross for two days.[33]

The Tarim remained at peace after Yang's assassination in 1928 and stayed so until 1933. The cruel Ma Daotai's reign had done nothing, however, to help relations between Turkis and Dongans in the south; and this was a decisive factor in the turbulent years that followed. In the north, as we have seen, Dongans and Turkis were allies, at least for most of the time. In the south, they were enemies from the start. Which is not to say the Turkis – or Uighurs as we may call the majority from now on – were united. The old 'black mountain' and 'white mountain' rivalry inherited from the era of the khojas persisted; the former, based at Artosh near Kashgar, were more tolerant of Chinese rule, the latter, at Kucha, were Turki nationalists. Unlike the north, the Tarim remained largely free of Soviet influence; indeed, it was a hotbed of conservative reaction, right-wing nationalists and Islamic traditionalists. Refugees from Stalin's collectivization, like the Kyrgyz who arrived in 1932, were welcomed.

A sense of the Uighurs' feelings about Chinese rule in the south is given in an anonymous petition of 1933 from the Khotan area. Despite its use of words such as 'infidel' and 'martyr' it sounds more like the plea of a desperate man than the fulminations of a religious zealot:

A friend for the sake of friendship will make known a friend's defects and save him from the consequences of his defects. You, who are supposed to rule, cannot even realise this, but try to seek out the supporter of Islam to kill him. Foolish infidels like you are not fit to rule . . . How can an infidel, who cannot distinguish between a friend and a foe, be fit to rule? You infidels think because you have rifles, guns and money, you can depend on them; but we depend upon God in whose hands are our lives. You infidels think that you will take our lives. If you do not send a reply to this notice we are ready. If we die we are martyrs. If we survive we are conquerors. We are living but long for death.[34]

The gold miners of Khotan and neighbouring Keriya were tired of being paid in worthless paper notes, and rose in protest just as the petition had warned. The Baby General's Dongan-Uighur army moving along the north desert road had taken Aksu on 25 February 1933, and three days later the Khotanese killed their Chinese magistrate and some other Han officials. The people of Keriya took over their oasis without bloodshed when resident Chinese agreed to convert to Islam. The city governor of Kashgar found himself being boxed in, and was desperate for help. But Jin Shuren in Urumchi was himself in deep trouble; the best he could do was to ask his lieutenant to send more money to his private bank account in mainland China and to award him a new title: 'Chief Bandit Suppressor in the Rear'. In desperation, the Kashgar governor armed the Kyrgyz bandits from the mountains above, who promptly betrayed him.

There is no room here to follow all the twists and turns of the Tarim revolt, the alliances and the betrayals. Three factions emerged: the marauding Kyrgyz, led by a nomad chief; the Uighurs, led by a wagon driver from Kucha; and the rebel Dongans. Each had their motives. The Dongans wanted to get rid of the provincial governor in Urumchi but were loyal to the Guomindang in Nanjing; the Uighurs wanted to get rid of the Dongans and secede from China; the Kyrgyz wanted to grab as much loot as possible, and go home.

Once this odd alliance had seized control from the Chinese, there was a brief lull in which, according to the British consul, all three leaders 'settled down to the congenial business of accumulating wealth and wives'.[35] The Kyrgyz leader is said to have ended up with a harem of thirty.

As for Uighur independence, that was already on the agenda. Early in the previous year, 1932, a 'committee for national revolution' had been set up by Mehmet Emin Bughra, a scholar in his thirties, and his younger brothers Abdullah and Nur Ahmad. They were joined by a schoolteacher and former magistrate from Gulja, Sabit Damullah, who had travelled abroad – to the Soviet Union, Turkey, Egypt and India. The committee was anti-Communist, anti-Christian, anti-Dongan and anti-Chinese. It grew to 300 members, and boasted 50 antiquated rifles. On 20 February, the committee set up a provisional government with Sabit as prime minister, and Mehmet Emin, the driving force behind the movement, as head of the armed forces.

Another important figure in the movement was Khoja Niyas, an associate of the Tiger Prince, Yolbas, from the court of the late King of the Gobi at Hami. Because of his station, Khoja Niyas was regarded by the Uighur fighters as their spiritual leader. But he could not quite decide whose side he was on. At first, he allied his forces with the Baby General. Then he accepted a post with the provincial government from Sheng. Now he was persuaded to become president of the breakaway Uighur government.

On 16 March 1933, the town of Khotan was taken, shariah law was imposed and the Chinese forced to convert to Islam. A doughty band of Swedish missionaries working in the town was ordered out, and many of the Hindu moneylenders from Kashmir were murdered. Over the next months the Khotan emirs extended their control until they held all the oases of southern Xinjiang, with the exception of the garrison outside Kashgar. Then, on 12 November, they made their move to secede from China. After a debate in which the merchants on the committee expressed their concern at what a Muslim regime would mean for business, the vote was taken and the Turkish-Islamic Republic of Eastern Turkestan was proclaimed. Kashgar was to be its capital, shariah its law. Its flag was to bear a crescent moon and star, and it would have a currency of its own.

In many ways the new republic (TIRET for short) was the spiritual successor of Yakub Beg's emirate.[36] Like Yakub, the emirs turned to Britain for support. The new consul in Kashgar, Colonel J.W. Thomson-Glover, was sympathetic but told them his government recognized only Nanjing. A delegation sent to Delhi was no more successful, and Turkey was wary. The Shah of Afghanistan, Muhammad Zahir, agreed to sell them arms, though few guns actually arrived. It looked very much as if the regime was doomed to fail, since apart from the intolerance of its rule it was hostile to all three major players in Xinjiang: the provincial government, the Dongans and the Soviet Union.

The Muslim revolt was reaching its crisis. Following the battering they had received from Soviet troops and bombers at the Tutung river in January 1934, the Baby General and his army were now hastening westwards along the north desert road in the lorries commandeered from Sven Hedin. However, they would soon collide with the Uighur resistance led by the Khotan emirs. In February Ma's advance guard reached the Kashgar oasis, pushing the TIRET leaders out. Needless to say, Khoja Niyas was the first to change sides. He fled to the Soviet border where he signed a treaty promising to join forces with Sheng, in return for which he was to be made 'Civil Governor for Life'.

Now Ma's Dongans attacked the Old City, killing as many as 2,000 of the Uighurs. While the attack was in progress the British consul's wife, Mrs Thomson-Glover, and a small party went out on to the terrace of the consulate, called Chini Bagh, to watch the Dongans driving out a motley force of Uighurs and Kyrgyz. One of the Dongan soldiers, spying the British spectators from 400 yards away, knelt and took a pot-shot. The bullet hit the consul's wife in the shoulder. In their panic some of the Uighurs climbed into the consulate compound, killing one of the staff and wounding four of the Britons, including the doctor, who later died.

Further south, the TIRET forces were in trouble. Both of the younger emirs were killed in action, and the head of Abdullah was displayed outside the Id Kah mosque in Kashgar. As the Dongans approached Khotan, the revolution's leader Emir Mehmet was forced to flee. First he went with 3,000 supporters to Keriya, then he doubled back, abandoned his escort and with several pony-loads of gold disappeared into the Kunlun mountains and crossed over to India.

Ma himself reached Kashgar in April with 10,000 men. By now he was exhausted, and his state of mind, volatile at best, can only be guessed at. He called on the British consul, looking in vain for support. He called on the Russian consulate where, according to

Wu, he was persuaded that his cause was hopeless and was offered an escape route. By the end of June he had ordered his men to evacuate the city and move on down the south road under the command of his half-brother. But when the day came he himself was not with them. Accompanied by fifty men, including one or two Russians from the consulate, he is supposed to have left Kashgar on 7 July and crossed the border at Irkeshtam into the Soviet Union. Then he disappeared.

He was rumoured to be in Beijing, in India, or back with his clan of warlords in Shaanxi province. A year later Peter Fleming was shown a photograph of him, dressed in the uniform of a Red Army cavalry officer and apparently in good health. He was supposed to have written letters from Moscow over his own seal which were read out to the Dongan troops in Khotan.[37] He was sighted in Moscow in early 1936. But he is thought to have been executed on Stalin's orders two years later.

The Baby General was a mystery to everyone, perhaps even to himself. Variously described as an agent of Japan, of Moscow, of the British in India, his real loyalty was probably to the vision he had of himself as a new Tamerlane. The German engineer Georg Vasel said he was a typical product of inner Asia. 'He was one of those types – half field-marshal and half gangster – who, when successful, are historic heroes, and when unsuccessful end their lives in some dungeon.'[38]

Sheng now had most of the province back in Chinese hands – although it would be more correct to say that he had placed it in Russian hands. As a conciliatory gesture he promoted some of the Uighur leaders to senior posts, and the Chinese stopped calling them 'turban-heads' (*zhantou*) in official communications; instead they were referred to as *weiwuer*, a transliteration of 'Uighur'. The remnants of the Dongan army continued to exploit and bully the Uighur peasants on the south road, making occasional military forays. But in May 1937, Sheng invited in another Soviet invasion force to deal with trouble in Aksu. That was enough for the Dongans in the south, who melted away like the rivers in the desert.

Eric Teichman, a British diplomat who travelled to Kashgar on a trade mission in 1935 and saw things largely through Chinese eyes, wrote of the restoration: 'I fancy that the Turkis welcomed the return of Chinese rule. Chinese methods are not ours, and Chinese rule in [Xinjiang] has been freely criticized by foreign travellers in Turkistan, accustomed to other standards. But, by and large, the Chinese mandarins have a genius of their own for colonial administration; and the Turki peasant probably fares better under a Chinese régime than under native Moslem rule.'[39]

Through Sheng's open back door, the Kremlin now sent a Red Army regiment to Hami, where all the trouble had started in 1931. Its function was to block the way of any Japanese advance and keep Xinjiang detached from its putative landlord, the Chinese government. An assembly plant for Soviet aircraft was built near Urumchi, disguised as a factory for 'agricultural implements'. Soviet goods flooded in at subsidized prices in order to crush competition from British India. Stalin made sure he was paid in full for the help he had given Sheng, with mineral rights, oil and power supplies, and transport.[40] Himself no slouch at asset-stripping, Sheng thought the terms of the various agreements he was made to sign were outrageous. But on a visit to Moscow in 1938 he visited Molotov for cocktails in his dacha, asked for Marxist indoctrination lessons, and enrolled in the Soviet Communist Party. Xinjiang, for so long seen by China as a buffer state against barbarians in the west, was now the USSR's buffer state against the east, and Japan.

Hardly had he found himself back in the driving seat when things began to go wrong for Sheng. In April 1941, Japan and the USSR signed a non-aggression pact, reducing at a stroke Xinjiang's value to the Kremlin. Sheng began to make secret overtures to the Guomindang. Two months later, Hitler invaded Russia from the west, and the speed with which his Panzer divisions advanced made it seem likely that Russia would fall. A deal was done, and in the summer of 1942, Sheng brought his fiefdom back into the Chinese fold. The Russians were told to withdraw all their soldiers and advisers within three months. Sheng conducted a purge of Soviet sympathizers: one of the people he had tortured and executed was Mao Zemin, brother of Mao Zedong, who had been sent to work for him at the height of his pro-Soviet period in 1938.

But Sheng was playing the political stock-market too hard, and misreading the signals. Just as the Guomindang officials began arriving at his mansion, the Russians won their historic victory at

Stalingrad. No longer in need of Xinjiang's oil, they completed the withdrawal demanded of them. Knowing that the incoming Nationalists would not let him stay in power, Sheng took advantage of a big Japanese offensive in China in 1943 to conduct another purge in Urumchi, this time of Nationalists, using the pretext of a Communist plot. Once again, he asked the Red Army to intervene. There was no reply. Or at least, there was a reply, but it came from the wrong direction: a message from the Nationalist government now in Chongqing recalling Sheng to a new post – as minister of forestry and agriculture.

Inside the People's Park in the town of Gulja stands a fine balconied villa of two storeys, decorated in Islamic style with blue tiles round its windows and along its cornices. Behind the house is an overgrown courtyard, and what looks like an outdoor stage. Everything is in a state of disrepair. Inside is a small archaeological museum which few people seem to visit. This building is the former headquarters of the only democratic regime to have appeared in Eastern Turkestan.

A few hundred yards beyond it is a museum whose walls are covered with grainy black-and-white photographs showing a ragged army, groups of men of different races posed like football teams, and studio portraits of officials with their wives. An avenue of trees leads to a broad flight of steps and a stone plinth on which are arrayed nine tombs simply inscribed with the occupants' names and covered with plastic flowers. In front of the tombs stands a pillar with a dedication in both Uighur and Chinese, said to have been composed by Chairman Mao himself. These are the remains of the Eastern Turkestan Republic (ETR), the state created in November 1944 by the last full-scale uprising to take place in Xinjiang.

Although Sheng and his police state had gone, they had left behind a ferment of Muslim discontent. The public's mood was not improved by the behaviour of Sheng's police chief who used a delay in the handover of power to liquidate 400 or more political prisoners. The Uighurs resented the large numbers of troops who were now deployed, and the poor Chinese peasants who were settled on the land. As rulers the Nationalists proved as repressive and exploitative as Sheng and his cronies; inflation took hold and the economy collapsed.

The rebellion seems to have begun with the Kazakh nomads, who for some years had been marauding through the northern steppes. Many of them were refugees from Soviet collectivization: they had preferred to kill their flocks and herds rather than lose them to the state, and they were not now going to let the Guomindang seize them. Under a charismatic leader, Osman Batur, the Kazakh resistance spread down the north-western border of Xinjiang, from the Altai mountains near Mongolia to the Ili valley. Osman was more of a bandit than a freedom-fighter, but he was remarkably successful in skirmishes with conventional troops.

The ground for revolt had been prepared by a 'Xinjiang Turkic People's National Liberation Committee' reportedly set up in Alma Ata in 1943 by Russian-educated Uighurs. When the Kazakh campaign reached the Ili valley the following autumn, local Uighurs also took to the hills. On 7 October, Kazakhs and Uighurs attacked the Guomindang garrison at Nilka, east of Gulja. Then they marched on Gulja itself, where the authorities panicked, arresting and shooting people at random.[41] Here the Nilka brigade agreed to put itself under the leadership of Ahmadjan Kasim, a middle-class, Moscow-educated Uighur schoolteacher who had been jailed by Sheng as a Communist and who was probably the agent of the liberation committee in exile. This Kasim – or Kasimov – sought to make the rising a properly proletarian affair, embracing all nationalities (even the Han), to prevent it becoming a purely Islamic or Turki front.

In Gulja the revolutionaries captured the government and police headquarters, and the power station, and soon a retaliatory massacre of Han Chinese was under way. A British consular official in Urumchi reported that the slaughter of Chinese became less indiscriminate later. Soldiers and civilian officials were nearly all killed, and men from Sheng Shicai's home region of Manchuria were the next most vulnerable: the safest were the descendants of General Zuo's camp followers who were mostly 'sutlers and prostitutes'. Women and children were usually spared.

On 15 November the Eastern Turkestan Republic was proclaimed and its green flag with a white crescent and star was flown from the villa in the park. The ETR was nominally headed by an Uzbek religious leader, Ali Khan Ture, but the real power lay with Kasimov. As well as Kazakhs and Uighurs there were Kyrgyz (who had also suffered from Soviet collectivization), Mongols and minor groups such as the Sibo, remnants of the Manchu garrison brought in during Qianlong's reign 180 years before. There were Russians, too, since apart from its proximity to Soviet Kazakhstan, the Ili valley had been annexed by the Tsar for ten years during Yakub Beg's rule.

The extent of Soviet Communist support for the Ili rebellion has been much discussed by historians. Although denied by the Soviet government virtually until its end, a Uighur broadcast from Radio Tashkent in May 1967 admitted that arms and 'trained commanding cadres' had been provided by the Russians. The rebels wore Russian-style uniforms with the initials VTR, standing for 'Vostochnaya Turkestanskaya Respublika', stamped on them in Cyrillic. Even so, it should be said that the ordinary people, the real resistance, were motivated less by ideology or 'political education' than by resentment, fear and hatred of an occupying force which abused their persons, religion and way of life. In a report which looks prophetic today, the British consul in Urumchi wrote:

> What the Chinese authorities will not accept is the fact that there are ample causes purely internal to [Xinjiang] which do not need supplementary external causes to explain to the fullest degree not merely the present discontents but also a future conflagration of the greatest size.[42]

Massed Guomindang forces were beaten back by the rebels in the winter of 1944–5, causing panic in Urumchi. The British consul phlegmatically observed that unlike their 'incredibly tough opponents' the Kazakhs, Chinese troops were unable to endure the icy winds. Although a Chinese stronghold at Airambek with 8,000 troops continued to hold out, by the end of January 1945 the whole Ili valley was in rebel hands. The fighting was vicious, and atrocities against prisoners were reported by both sides. Osman and his Kazakhs joined in, taking the towns of Chuguchak on the Soviet border and Shara Sume in the far north. A counter-attack at Wusu in September 1945 was surprisingly defeated by the informal rebel army – possibly with the help of a Soviet air attack – and the citizens of Urumchi began to flee to the east while the provincial government prepared to evacuate to Hami.

As the fighting moved into the Tarim, led by the fearsome Kazakhs, Chiang Kai-shek sent an ultimatum to the Kremlin: secure a ceasefire or watch him make an international issue out of this assault on Chinese sovereignty. Surprisingly, Stalin agreed, and in October 1945 the leaders of the mini-republic said they would negotiate: they would give up their ambition to secede if Xinjiang was given self-rule within China. In the south, however, the fighting continued, though whether this was due to a Communist invasion through the passes or was a local affair led by religious nationalists, was not clear.

A treaty signed in the north on 2 January 1946 promised freedom of religion, publication, assembly and speech. District officials were to be elected, not appointed. Uighur and Kazakh would become official languages alongside Mandarin, and non-Hans would use their own language at primary school, with Chinese being compulsory only at middle school. Taxation would be according to 'the real productive power of the people' and 'their ability to pay'. Culture and the arts would be allowed free development. Annexes gave the ETR the right to nominate six of the fifteen locally elected members of the provincial government, with another ten to be appointed by Chongqing. It would be allowed to keep an army of no more than 12,000, with the rest joining the Guomindang national army or a provincial 'peace preservation corps'. The police force would be locally staffed and directed.

The deal suited both major powers. It confirmed the Soviet Union's vicarious hold on the area, and it gave the Nationalists – or so their leaders imagined – leverage against their Chinese Communist enemies who were making ground against them in the civil war which had resumed after the defeat of the Japanese invaders. As for the Communists, they professed the greatest admiration for the ETR as a proto-Communist revolution. In August 1949 Mao Zedong wrote to Kasimov: 'Your struggle over many years is one component of the democratic revolutionary movement of the whole Chinese people.'

The Nationalist general who had liaised with the rebels, Zhang Zhizhong, now became governor, setting right the worst of the injustices and releasing political prisoners. He also made a bonfire in front of his office of 25,000 ounces of opium stored by Sheng Shicai's monopoly trading company. Among his ministers were the former Emir of Khotan, Mehmet Bughra, who after fleeing to India had made his way back to the Nationalist capital; his ally Isa Yusuf Alptekin, a Uighur intellectual who had fled from Sheng; and Burhan Shahidi, a Tartar trader who had served under all three previous regimes and who was to stay in power under the Communists until 1955.[43] In 1947, following Uighur demonstrations, Zhang was replaced by the Uighur Masud Sabri, who had made the same journey into exile and back as the Emir of Khotan and Alptekin but who was regarded by the ordinary people as a collaborator.

Yet the so-called coalition could not be saved, and Xinjiang split once more, with hostile regimes at Gulja and Urumchi; the latter, in an attempt to woo the Uighurs of the south, took the unprecedented step of allowing Mehmet Emin Bughra and Isa Alptekin to publish nationalist journals with titles such as *Flame* and *Freedom*.

At the end of 1947, the Communists in central China were on the offensive, and looked set to win the civil war. By the summer of 1949, the People's Liberation Army had reached the Xinjiang border and on 25 September the Nationalists capitulated without resistance.

But the momentous handover of power was marked by a mysterious event which has still not been properly explained. About a month before the Nationalist troops surrendered, Kasimov and the other leaders of the Gulja regime accepted an invitation to attend the first plenary session of the Chinese People's Political Consultative Conference in the capital. They boarded a plane to Alma Ata in Kazakhstan, from where they would fly on to Beijing. Then they disappeared. Not until December, after the Communist government had been formed, was it announced that the group's onward plane had crashed into a hill in Manchuria on 27 August, killing everyone on board.

In 1979 an anonymous 'former Beijing student' claimed to have heard from the granddaughter of one of the victims that the plane had been sabotaged by the Chinese Communists. According to a press report that year, the Uighur Saifuddin, who had been Minister for Education in the ETR, had 'expressed his doubts about the aircraft reaching its destination and had pleaded illness as an excuse for not joining the ill-fated party'.[44] Kasimov tried to reassure him by saying that a Chinese would be accompanying the party and the Communists would surely not kill one of their own. Saifuddin was not convinced and stayed behind. Whether the crash was an accident or sabotage, it suited the Chinese Communists because it frightened the Gulja revolutionaries and dealt a blow to Soviet ambitions in Xinjiang. The Chinese Communists were later to purge the rest of the Gulja regime, arresting over a thousand people.

Another version of the story has it that the plane did not crash at all and that the ETR leaders were taken off at Tashkent by the KGB and sent instead to Moscow where they were 'liquidated'.[45] A Uighur historian in Ankara believes five men were kidnapped by Stalin and murdered, causing the collapse of the ETR. This revelation, he says, was made in an article published after the collapse of the Soviet Union by one of the KGB officers who had tortured the ETR leaders. Uighur exiles who went to Moscow to check the story talked to a former Kremlin doctor who had also been involved. He told them that the five had been held in the Tsar's stables and killed there.[46]

On hearing of the plane crash an ETR commander in Gulja, Rokhmannov, ordered a revenge massacre of Han Chinese in which more than 7,000 were killed. When the Communists arrived, they took reprisals, killing him and many of his soldiers.

Today, Uighur schoolchildren carrying banners and wearing the red scarves of the Young Pioneers march in crocodile to the tombs of the Ili 'martyrs'. They lay flowers on the graves and have their picture taken. On their way they pass a construction site where a bigger and better martyrs' shrine is being built. The new site is something of a puzzle. Why should the authorities want to spend money honouring Soviet-supported separatists who tried to break with the motherland?

The answer is that the Communist authorities today are ambivalent about the episode. They want to celebrate the leaders of the Ili breakaway republic as proto-revolutionaries, while at the same time condemning them as nationalists, Islamists and Soviet stooges. As usual, history is being made to serve current ends. The new building has probably been designed to offer a reinterpretation of what happened in 1944. Perhaps, after all, the Ili rebels were never anti-Chinese, only enemies of Guomindang 'reaction'. Perhaps they broke free of the motherland the better to embrace it.

Part II
The Barbarian Within

5

Red Dawn

WHEN THE FIRST Corps of the People's Liberation Army marched into Urumchi on 20 October 1949, the natives of Xinjiang had reason to be grateful. The Communists called it the 'Liberation'; and it must indeed have seemed like one after the years of expropriation by warlords and the chaos, punctuated by brutality, of Nationalist rule. Idealists on both sides may have believed that a new day had dawned and that the brotherhood of man would now be the guiding principle of government. At the very least, the Communists' victory in the civil war promised stability. It also meant that after years of submission to local adventurers and dictators, Xinjiang would again be ruled directly from Beijing.

Perhaps nobody foresaw just how tight that control would turn out to be. Anti-Communists – those who had not already fled the advancing troops – might have had their worst fears confirmed, however, by the arrangements that were now made to welcome the victors into Urumchi.

One day early in September, notices suddenly appeared in the city ordering the inhabitants to go out the following morning to the airport, 6 miles away, to greet the advance units. Anyone who stayed behind without a special permit would be shot. Some 130,000 people trudged out in the heat and dust, and waited all day, but no troops appeared. When they got home that evening, further proclamations were issued repeating the order for the following day. Again the masses walked out, and again they were disappointed. Only on the third day did the Communist soldiers appear, four or five thousand of them, ferried in by two hundred Russian aircraft. By this time the people's enthusiasm had grown somewhat stale, but ciné cameras were on hand to stimulate and record the ovation.[1]

To the revolutionaries who inherited it, the western empire won by the Manchu Qing dynasty was something of an embarrass- ment – not because they did not want it, but because they had no ideological excuse for holding it. Sun Yat-sen surmounted the difficulty by saying that within the borders that now made up China there was really only one nationality; the minority races would have to disappear by merging with the Han.*

Chiang Kai-shek took a similar line. He accepted the ancient (and still current) division of the Chinese into five different peoples, all descended from the same ancestors. Their differences were superficial, and due only to religion and geography. Further- more, the great empire was united by a common historical destiny: like Tibet, Mongolia and Manchuria, Xinjiang was Chinese not because of the Qing conquest but by virtue of the gradual assimila- tion of its peoples and territory over 2,000 years.[2]

However uncivilized, Turki and Mongol people were compat- ibly white and could in the long run, therefore, be assimilated. And just as many white Americans considered it natural that red men were doomed to extinction, so Chinese racial theorists of the early twentieth century argued that the red, brown and black races were destined to be eliminated, leaving the final struggle to be decided between the white and the yellow. If they were not careful, the Chinese would be hunted to death as the red barbar- ians in America had been, or enslaved by the whites like the 'lazy, stupid, greedy and sex-mad' blacks and browns.[3]

The warlords who ran Xinjiang made their own policies towards the natives. Governor Yang was strict, secretive but adroit; Jin Shuren was despotic and provocative; Sheng Shicai began by treating them liberally but ended as dictator of a police state. Chiang's policy was dictated mainly by military weakness. In 1942 he made the provocative decision to resettle landless peasants in Xinjiang. Yet colonization did not really take off under the Nationalists, and by the treaty of 1946 which ended the Ili rebel- lion, Chiang was forced to give a measure of freedom to the people of Xinjiang that they would not see again in the twentieth century.

---

* In fact the Han are far from being racially homogeneous, whatever theorists may say.

The Uighurs even witnessed a rare act of repentance by a Han official. General Zhang Zhizhong, the conciliatory governor installed to pacify the province, wondered out loud why Xinjiang was run by the Han, who comprised only 5 per cent of its population. 'Why have we not turned over political power to the Uighurs and other racial groups?' he asked. The behaviour of previous regimes, he added, had been 'entirely wrong', no different from that of imperialist nations towards their colonies.[4] But when leading Uighurs wrote to Chiang Kai-shek suggesting it was time to honour his pledge of eventual self-rule, Chiang was furious.

The Communists seemed to take the opposite view. They charged their predecessors with racism and accused them of drawing up plans for eugenic birth control. Mao declared that dreams of racial supremacy were anti-Marxist, that 'Great Han' chauvinism, as the Party called it, was a counter-revolutionary crime greater than Turki nationalism. He called on his officials to recruit and train up the natives for administration so that the gulf between Turkis and Han might be bridged. Never before in 2,000 years had the Chinese of the mainland made such fraternal gestures towards the barbarians of the west.

However, Mao and his colleagues were less concerned to follow the doctrines of Marxism–Leninism than to consolidate their power, defend the new Republic's borders, exploit the mineral wealth of Xinjiang, and make good use of the wide open spaces now at their disposal. Just as the Bolsheviks had built on an empire won by the tsars, so the Communists would build on the empire won by the Manchus.

There were two obstacles to this programme. One was Turki nationalism, the other Soviet influence. While Chinese Communist power was still weak, it was important not to antagonize the people of the western border or let them fall once again under the sway of the Soviet Union. Uighurs, Kazakhs, Mongols and others were promised not only social emancipation but also political autonomy within one China. Metaphorically speaking, the Great Wall of China was to be demolished; but the Great Wall inside the heads of the Han, constructed over centuries of living in dangerous proximity with the barbarian, could not be torn down so easily.

The following three chapters will examine different aspects of the conflict between the Communists' stated policy towards 'minority nationalities' and their actual treatment of them. This chapter will describe how solidarity between Han and Turki was ruined by racial prejudice and political pragmatism in the rebuilding of Xinjiang up to the time of the Tiananmen massacre and the collapse of the Soviet Union. The next chapter shows how the state's treatment of religion led to a resurgence of protest, and to the reprisals which followed. Chapter 7 charts the physical colonization of the province – principally by means of exile and the gulag. The last three chapters bring us to the present: the plan to overwhelm the Uighurs by means of economic investment; the Uighur diaspora, nationalists and their supposed links with terrorism; and finally the emergence of separate societies in Xinjiang.

Among the first measures ordered by Beijing was a purge of officials to weed out the last of the pro-Soviet Gulja revolutionaries. A programme of mass Han immigration was announced in March 1950, to make good Mao's promise that in building socialism Xinjiang would get all the help it needed from its 'fraternal nationality', the Han. But the first influx was small – no more than 10,000 people – compared with what was to come. These pioneers were technically qualified, keen to teach their skills, and generally welcomed.

In the villages, however, the appearance of Communist apparatchiks was not popular with Turki headmen. The Party set out to destroy their power, alerting the masses to 'feudal reactionary elements' which it said might have to be removed by military force. The Muslim élite – landlords, moneylenders and the clergy, who formed the very structure of Uighur society – were to be reformed. The process was to take ten years, over two stages: first 'democratic reform', then collectivization.

To undermine resistance from the old establishment, its members were divided into sheep and goats. Heading the goats were landowners with political power such as the hereditary Muslim nobles. They were automatically shot. Next in line were landlords and smaller landowners, who were certain to lose their property but who might, if small enough, keep their lives. After them came middle-class enemies who were considered capable of redemption. There were only two categories of sheep: middle-class 'friends' and the unblemished proletariat, or farm labourers.

The system could be bucked by the adroit. One young man, after his father died in 1953, was embarrassed to find himself the sole possessor of a big house with an orchard on the east side of Kashgar, not far from where the Sunday market is held today. He had three brothers who had left home; one was a captain in the Guomindang army who had surrendered and been sent to study law in Xian, and the other two lived in Urumchi. Realizing that he now qualified as a Class Two enemy of the people, and was likely to be shot, the young man set about extricating himself. First he took fruit from the orchard and possessions from his house to the local Uighur magistrate to bribe him into testifying that the house was not his alone, but divided between the four brothers. Then he went to the chairman of the local land reform committee, a Party man, where he was publicly arraigned and told that if he did not tell the truth about his father's legacy he would be shot. When his story was finally accepted, he decided to take no more chances. Abandoning the house, which was made over to a group of poor families, he moved as far away from the city as he could, to the furthest point of Kashgar county, where he was allowed to work as a factory manager.[5]

Those who co-operated or were too influential to execute, such as leaders of the former Eastern Turkestan Republic, were called 'enlightened', and treated more leniently than their equivalents in the rest of China. They were excused the ritual humiliations and persecutions, allowed to make over a proportion of their property and given new jobs. But the recalcitrant or weaker class enemies were targeted as 'counter-revolutionaries'. The influence of the clergy was tackled by the creation of a Party agency to supervise it: the China Islamic Association. Some of the mosque lands and assets were confiscated, and the religious courts were merged with the secular People's Courts. Imams were appointed and paid by the state, not elected by parishioners. Redesignated 'patriotic religious activists', they were sent on ideology courses and ordered to hang pictures of Chairman Mao in their mosques and to give sermons on such topics as 'the international solidarity of the working class'.

A campaign against rents and 'serfdom' was launched in 1950. Cadres were sent out to educate the peasants in class struggle with their landlords. 'Excess' rents had to be repaid in kind, and over-priced loans were forfeited. It was claimed that in the next two years about a sixth of the province's landlords were taken to court. But even in these heady early years Party bosses had doubts as to how quickly the ethnic minorities could be assimilated. A correspondent on the *Xinjiang Daily* complained of the conservatism of the countryside which he said harked back to the days of the Manchu empire. He quoted a 'proverb of Uighur landlords' to illustrate it: 'The water in the river flows on but the stone beneath remains still.'[6]

The rent campaign ended in May 1952 and was hailed by the official media as 'a great victory'. It was followed immediately by land reform. Over 7 million acres of land were distributed to 2 million peasants, and landlords were dragged into 'grievance' sessions, where their tenants were instructed to bring accusations against them. The nomads were told to give up their feudal habits, but at this stage the authorities did not try to change their way of life for fear – a prescient fear – that mass slaughter of livestock would follow. For the oasis farmers, however, small co-operatives of twenty to forty families were set up. In 1955 Mao ordered the establishment of big co-operatives of a hundred to three hundred families. These collectives were 'voluntary' – though sometimes it took a peasant days or weeks in detention to become a volunteer. Mao was keen to press ahead with full collectivization, to organize the peasants so that their output could be taxed to finance the mechanization of agriculture. Other Party leaders urged that mechanization be put first. Liu Shaoqi, President of China, had seen at first hand the disastrous famine created by Lenin's overnight creation of a state grain monopoly, and warned of the danger of hasty collectivization: he called it 'false, dangerous and Utopian agrarian socialism'.[7]

Among the pioneers who came to the west after Liberation were prisoners and soldiers commanded to open up the virgin lands, including many former Guomindang soldiers. Civilian settlers came after 1954, slowly at first then in ever-increasing numbers. But in that year was created one of the most powerful and unusual entities ever seen, which was to play – as it still does – a controlling part in the sinicization of the Muslim west. The Xinjiang Production and Construction Corps (or *bingtuan*) was the result of a merger of two outfits set up to feed and supply the army, always a problem in the borderlands. Mao transferred to its care about 150,000 Guomindang and Muslim soldiers who had surrendered to the People's Liberation Army. They, their families, civil servants and others who had worked for the Nationalists (or their proxies, the warlords) were impounded in 'regiment farms'. Their task was twofold, to reclaim land for agriculture and to defend the border. Later, they would be charged with domestic riot control as well. The Corps also took in political convicts from China proper – landlords, Nationalist officials and other such 'reactionary elements' – after they had served their sentences. In its early days, the Corps sent recruitment parties to the east to bring back, more or less voluntarily, hundreds of thousands of technicians, engineers, doctors, teachers and tradesmen. A single detachment of a thousand students and staff was moved from Shanghai University, and another thousand from Beijing government offices. Altogether, at least half a million Chinese soldiers and civilians were moved to the Tarim and Dzungarian basins in the first five years of the People's Republic.

Meanwhile, Party leaders had been preparing a new administrative blueprint, a system of local government for the ethnic minorities which was designed to be sympathetic rather than substantive, cosmetic rather than representative.

When Aitchen Wu arrived in the far west he was impressed, as any mainland Chinese would be, by the sheer diversity of its inhabitants. Standing in the main street of Gulja, capital of the Ili valley region, he exclaimed that the town was a veritable museum of Asiatic types (this was in the 1930s, when race was a live issue):

At every bend of a twisting city street, at every desert halting place, beside a dung fire built upon the barren mountain, the connoisseur of anthropology must feel the urge to seize a camera or sketch-block to capture for his collection some queer cranial development, some strangeness of brow or lip or eye.

Sometimes there has passed me a type almost purely European, but olive-skinned and clad in the robes of the East; on another occasion I have seen black coat and creased trousers adorn a personality which might better have been shrouded in a lama's garb, so far from modern things was the slanted gaze.[8]

In the throng Wu counted fourteen races: Chinese, Manchus, Dongans (Chinese Muslims), Mongols, Uighurs, Kazakhs, Sibos and Solon from Manchuria, Kyrgyz, Tartars, Tajiks, Chakar Mongols, Torgut Mongols and White Russians.

The Uighurs, however, were no longer a race apart. Although borrowed from the Uighur Turks who controlled Xinjiang a thousand years before, the name was a generic applied during the rule of the warlord Sheng Shicai to the oasis Turkis in general. Until 1934 they knew each other by their provenance: they were Kashgarlik, or Khotanlik, or Keriyanese. They saw themselves as the true natives, which the Kazakhs, Kyrgyz, Tajiks and Hui were not. The generic name 'Uighur' was first proposed at a conference of émigrés from the Tarim at Tashkent in 1921, and was later endorsed by the Chinese Communist Party: 'To a certain extent the Uighurs are who they are because the Chinese state has registered them as such . . . Their identity has evolved in "dialectical" fashion.'[9]

The naming of the Uighurs had a paradoxical result. It gave these subjects of China a national as well as a religious identity of their own – one which they had not felt before – and hence another focus for their grievances against the Han. This new sense of identity was to cause the Chinese a lot of trouble in the years to come.

One of the first acts of the provincial government (temporarily designated the 'Xinjiang sub-bureau' of the Party's Central Committee) was to do what the Manchus had done after their conquest: forbid the use of insulting names for Muslims. The Party was afraid that Han chauvinist behaviour would stir up the sensitive Turkis, already enraged by their treatment at the hands of the Han during the Nationalist period. Mao called for the enlistment of more native cadres, and warned Han Chinese cadres to respect minority culture and avoid discrimination, condescension and coercion.

The edict against insults was the prelude to the Party's most important administrative programme, the creation of 'autonomous' areas. These were devised to win the hearts and minds of clan leaders, promote solidarity between 'fraternal nationalities' in the struggle against unspecified foreign imperialists, and wean the Turkis from their Soviet sympathies.

Party theorists did not have far to look for a model. They had been provided with one by the Soviet Union next door in western Turkestan. A proclamation in 1917 signed by Lenin and Stalin (who was in charge of 'nationalities') had promised the Muslims of Russia – 'all you whose mosques and places of worship have been destroyed, whose beliefs and customs have been trampled on by the tsars' – that from now on their national and cultural institutions would be 'free and inviolable'.[10]

Turki leaders in central Asia had proposed joint government with the Russians but were refused on the grounds that the Muslims were not ready. Their attitude towards the Soviet Union was 'uncertain'; they were not yet proper 'workers'; their leaders were either bourgeois or religious. Stalin gradually put a stop to all talk about the right to self-determination. 'Only those with impeccable credentials had this right, and the foremost of these credentials was unflinching loyalty to Moscow.'[11]

Muslims of western Turkestan wanted a single Soviet Turkic republic uniting all Islamic races. Instead, after a debate about the rival merits of 'fusion' and 'demarcation', the region was carved up along approximate – and sometimes invented – racial and linguistic lines. The blueprint took only three months to prepare. Anthropologists and language experts were co-opted. As one historian has said of the project, it was 'more the work of scientists studying animal or vegetable species and then assigning their location in a zoo or a botanical garden than a nation's internal rise towards self-determination'.[12]

The new entities were 'Union' republics; that is, they had the same status as the Russian Federation, with their own flags, emblems and anthems. What is more, under the constitution of 1937 they had the right to secede, each being provided with an external border to make that realizable. Of course, no Soviet republic ever did secede. But it was noticeable that when they gained their independence by default with the collapse of the

Soviet Union in 1991, four of the five new nations (Tajikistan was the exception) were quick to assert their 'national' identities.

The minorities' right to self-determination had been part of the Chinese Communist Party's agenda from its founding in 1922. The young Party envisioned a sort of United States of China, comprising the Middle Kingdom, Tibet, Mongolia and Xinjiang. A draft constitution drawn up in 1931 promised the right of self-determination – including independence if they chose it – to Mongols, Uighurs, Tibetans, Miaos, Koreans and others. After Mao took charge in 1935, however, the emphasis began to change, just as it was to change and change again up to the end of the century.

To the ethnic minorities on whom he had relied during his rise to power, Mao appeared generous. After the Long March, for example, he seemed to promise that once the Revolution had taken place, freedom would be given to the Mongols and the Hui who lived around his headquarters. Cynics observed that it was they who controlled his escape route north from the encircling Nationalist armies. Mao had nothing to lose because as yet he had nothing to give. Until the end of the Second World War, he was still writing in favour of self-determination. But once the danger from the Nationalists and the Japanese invaders was past, the Party began to talk of self-government within a united China.

Then in 1947 the Party line changed completely – and secretly. The new policy was called, confusingly enough, 'national regional autonomy'. It meant that each 'nationality' would have, in the region where it was predominant, its own government. But, as was to become clear after Liberation, these words were not meant to be taken too literally.* The new line was justified as 'combining the universal truth of Marxism-Leninism with the actual conditions in China'. Besides, the argument went, who needed self-determination now? Had it not been achieved by the Communist Revolution as a whole? Had not the people been lifted from their knees and set on their feet after long years of humiliation? Wang Enmao, the first Communist boss of Xinjiang, explained that self-determination was

---

* The history books were cooked to cover this broken promise. In Mao's *Selected Works*, published in 1953, the Chairman's 1945 report in favour of self-determination was edited to remove the embarrassing phrase.[13]

something you could aspire to while under the yoke of imperialism. In any other context, it was just separatism.

Old habits of mind played their part. For whatever Mao might say in public about the evils of Han chauvinism he, the son of a tight-fisted grain merchant and moneylender from Hunan province, was no less a Han nationalist than any other mainland Chinese. As a Communist he was able to justify it by declaring that it was the all-seeing, all-knowing Party – composed almost entirely of Han Chinese – which knew what was best for the backward races. Once the people of Xinjiang and Tibet were inside the pale, there they would remain.

The system of local government now imposed on Xinjiang was even less generous than the Soviet central Asian model. Administrative units, in ascending order of size, were the parish (a group of about ten villages, called *xiang*), the district (*chu*), the county (*xian*), the prefecture (*zhou*), and the 'region', or province. This was the pattern all over China, but in minority regions special 'autonomous' units were created in some areas. The rule was that the most docile peoples, who had not asked for autonomy, were the first to receive it.

In 1953 autonomous parishes and districts began to be set up in Xinjiang. (These two smallest units were later abolished as unworkable.) The first autonomous county was carved out for the Hui, the most co-operative and Chinese of the minorities, at Karashahr, near Korla, on 15 March 1954. Over the next six months there followed a county for the Sibo people near Gulja; a Mongol prefecture called Bayan Gol covering a large part of the eastern Tarim basin; a Kyrgyz prefecture in the Tian Shan; counties for the Kazakhs and Hui in the north; and a Tajik county in the Sarikol area of the Pamir mountains. So far, there was nothing for the Uighurs. It was not until 1 October 1955 that the Uighur presence was formally recognized when Xinjiang was renamed the Xinjiang Uighur Autonomous Region.[*]

There was no Uighur Republic, or 'Uighuristan', on the Russian model, and no right to secede. And what had been given

---

[*] Troublesome Tibet did not qualify for regionhood until 1965.

with one hand was taken with the other. The Uighurs had their name attached to the province as a whole, but the borders of the internal constituencies were so drawn as to deny them political control of areas they dominated numerically. Territories with a homogeneous populace were divided up so that in some areas the 'majority' race after which the administrative unit was named was actually in the minority. Cities and prefectures with large Uighur populations, such as Kashgar, Khotan and Aksu, were not given autonomous status at all. (Similarly, in two other autonomous regions, Inner Mongolia and Ningxia, created at about the same time, the Han outnumbered the Mongols and Muslims.)

Thus the Ili Kazakh autonomous prefecture was set up in an area where Uighurs were in the majority, and based on Gulja, a Uighur city. Korla was the capital of a Mongol autonomous prefecture whose twelve counties were mostly populated by Uighurs. Only three of the counties had a Mongol presence, and only one boasted a Mongol majority. And so on. It began to look very much like another example of the old Chinese tactic of *yiyi zhiyi*, 'using barbarians to deal with barbarians'.

Autonomy was a fig-leaf for Communist Party rule. From head to toe, the Party controlled every executive decision. It made no difference how many ethnic officials were appointed to local government. The people's delegates – including those who voted for the new policy in the first place – were Party stooges who never failed to deliver a unanimous verdict. The provincial government, headed by a chairman who was a Uighur and a congress in which minorities had half the important positions, was actually run by the Party secretary, a Han Chinese.* And although natives of the appropriate stripe were nominally in charge at lower levels, every official was shadowed by a member of the Party, and every decision could be countermanded by Beijing. A Muslim official in the highways department complained: 'I read books and newspapers in my office because I had no routine work to bother me. They let me know

---

* The chairman of the People's Congress Standing Committee of the Xinjiang Uighur Autonomous Region is the equivalent of the governor of a normal Chinese province.

only 5 per cent of the business that is done in our bureau. In fact I am deputy director in name only.' The manager of a tannery in Gulja said that his Chinese subordinates simply ignored him.[14] In the curious double-speak of Communist bureaucracy, autonomy came to mean not more freedom but less. It was self-government which depended entirely on the will of the centre.

The same 'shadow' system, copied from the Soviet Union, was applied throughout China, in councils, agencies, factories and schools. Under every native director, there was a Han Chinese deputy director or Party secretary. His Party connections made him the de facto boss. Even the courts were set up in this way. In practice, every decision or announcement had to come with a Party endorsement, or it would be ignored. The *Xinjiang Daily* held up as a model the Uighur director of the Five Star people's commune in Turfan county because he put every plan in front of local Party committees. His reward was election to the people's congress of the county, and to the people's council of the region.

Minority cadres were not altogether powerless; like the *begs* of old, they were the people through whom the Han, then still greatly outnumbered, exercised control. They had sufficient power to be objects of suspicion to one another, each being afraid that the other was currying favour with the Chinese to secure an advantage for his kinsmen. As a result, the system aggravated racial tensions: power was hard to come by, and local authority boundaries had been thoroughly gerrymandered.[15]

In fact, it was clear from the whole process that Beijing's aim at this stage was not to try and turn the Uighurs into Han, but to make them Chinese, just as the Kremlin's idea was not to Russify the Muslims, but to sovietize them.

As it happens, neither Marx nor Engels had preached self-determination, rather assuming that small nations would be swallowed up by bigger ones. So Lenin, Stalin and Mao were not doctrinally out of order in doing what they did. In stating that he was 'combining the universal truth of Marxism-Leninism with the actual conditions in China', Mao claimed that China, though composed of many nationalities, had always been a unitary state, as far back as the Qin dynasty in the third century BC. By contrast, the USSR was a federation of states. Lenin had distinguished between 'nations' (*natsiya*) and 'nationalities' (*narodnost*), between the Russians and the rest. The Chinese used the same word (*minzu*) for both concepts, as well as for 'people'. But the importance of the distinction for the Chinese was that 'nations' could have Communist parties, but 'nationalities' could not. That justified the rule of minorities by a single, Han-controlled, Party. Ultimately, of course, the idea was that all nations would disappear under Communism: first non-Han would merge with Han, and then the Han would merge with the world.[16]

Mao's deputy Zhou Enlai, in an important speech at a conference on ethnic minorities at the seaside city of Qingdao in 1957, explained retrospectively why minorities had not been given Soviet-style republics. A national republic had to be self-sufficient, compact and with a big majority of one nationality, he said. But Xinjiang had no fewer than thirteen nationalities, all overlapping, a situation 'hitherto unknown in history'. He seemed unaware that Mongolians, Uighurs and Tibetans had already had countries they called their own.

Having fought shoulder-to-shoulder for the Revolution, he added (though this was hardly the case), the minorities had to stay united with the Han after it. Secession was an open invitation to foreign imperialism – here he would have had the Ili rebellion of 1944 in mind. But Zhou's speech was important because it went on to advocate respect and equality for the Turkis, so much so that it was suppressed for the next twenty-three years.[17]

Mao and his deputy may have genuinely believed their own elaborate explanations but they were well aware of the real 'realities', which were growing antagonism with the USSR, the need for a well-defended border, and use of Xinjiang's land and minerals for an overpopulated and hungry China. Mao and his colleagues had adopted Lenin's tactic of promising freedom of choice to the old imperial colonies in order to win their support for revolution but had made sure that the promise was not honoured afterwards. One historian has called it a policy of 'studied magnanimity'.[18] Mao had the same aims as Lenin – first to woo, then to control – but he went about it rather differently. He had no intention of letting the Uighurs, Mongols, Tibetans and the rest set up their

own states, and every intention, after a suitable period of indoctrination and socialist engineering, of assimilating them altogether.
He may have realized that the Turkis would not easily become
'Chinese' of their own volition and he had to move carefully while
the Party's control was still weak. But as the Party grew stronger
and relations with the USSR deteriorated further, the freedom of
the ethnic minorities became ever more circumscribed.

Bad relations with the USSR had other consequences, among
them the choice of a new script for the Uighurs.

The original Uighur tribes, it will be remembered, had a runic
script which gave way to a form of Syriac, introduced by the
Sogdians in the ninth century, which was in turn replaced by the
Arabic script. The Communists, militant atheists, wanted to get
rid of Arabic because it was the language of the Quran. In 1956 a
conference in Urumchi decided, with the help of Soviet advisers,
to convert the Uighurs, Kazakhs and Kyrgyz to the Russian
Cyrillic alphabet. Partly this was out of homage to the USSR,
partly because some Turki intellectuals were using Cyrillic already,
but chiefly to erode the influence of the mullahs.

But as its alliance with the Soviet Union crumbled, China
wanted no more fraternization across the border. A Roman script
was decreed, based on the Latin alphabet and with a new vocabu-
lary of Chinese technical terms. It was hoped that the new script
would make a bridge between Turki and Chinese, which at the
same time got its romanized version, *pinyin*. The changes were
announced by Zhou Enlai in 1958, and took effect two years later.

The bridge was important from the Chinese point of view,
because it would help assimilate the ethnic minorities by making
Chinese more accessible to them. 'Language is the soul of a nation,'
as Maurice Druon, head of the Académie française, once said. Or, as
a former British ambassador to Tokyo replied when asked why so
few Western journalists posted there spoke Japanese: 'If you can
speak good Japanese, you *are* one.'[19] The more easily the Turkis could
study Chinese, the more quickly they would become Chinese.

In May 1956, Mao decided to mobilize the intellectuals of China
for a campaign of constructive criticism of the Party. He asked

them to speak their minds about its performance so far. The campaign slogan 'Let a hundred flowers bloom, a hundred schools of thought contend' referred to a similar event in the brief Qin dynasty of 221–206 BC. When at last people summoned up the courage to accept the invitation, the outburst of feeling was so hostile that the campaign was shut down within weeks. The Uighurs, asked by the Xinjiang Party boss Wang Enmao for 'your unreserved criticism and suggestions', were happy to oblige. They complained that they did all the hard work while the Han merely supervised; that native cadres were sycophantic; that autonomy was a farce. They demanded that all the Han be expelled from Xinjiang, or at least that immigration from the east be halted. Some asked for independence, others for a Soviet-style republic of 'Uighuristan' or Eastern Turkestan.

In the resulting purge, supervised by a six-month session of a special Party conference in Urumchi, 100,000 people were investigated, 830 were arrested and tried, and 53 cadres were executed.[20] Designated in the rest of China as an 'anti-Rightist' campaign, in Xinjiang it took the form of an anti-ethnic campaign. No longer was it so wrong to behave like a Han chauvinist: much worse to be a 'local nationality' chauvinist, a bourgeois attitude at odds with the 'world outlook of the proletariat'.[21] The peasants were warned even more strongly in propaganda carried by radio and the proliferating newspapers against the still greater sin of pan-Turkism, that bogey of a continent-wide conspiracy which still haunts the slumbers of the Chinese leadership.

Cultural freedom was out, and 'voluntary assimilation' became the order of the day. As Zhou Enlai said in his Qingdao speech, given just before the 'anti-Rightist' campaign was launched, there was nothing wrong with assimilation if it was of the right kind. Other nations – he mentioned Spain, Portugal and Britain – had 'weakened' the indigenous people when they colonized the Americas. The French, Belgians and British had done the same to the Africans in Africa. It was racist to consider one nation superior and another inferior. 'Assimilation is a reactionary thing if it means one nation destroying another by force. It is a progressive act if it means the natural merger of nations advancing towards prosperity,' he declared.[22] But as the Party's nationalities theorist explained, in this merger one nationality would of course be central – the Han. For another of the party's 'realities' was that the Han were, when all was said and done, the most civilized people and made up no less than 94 per cent of the population of China – begging the question of how extensive 'China' really was.

Either Zhou had missed the mood of the times at Qingdao, or he was attempting to moderate the impact of the purge. But in his banned speech he was still trying to reassure China's minorities. Not only was it wrong to regard one nation as superior to the others, he said, but local customs should be respected. Religious belief was not to be considered a political issue, and might still exist even when Communism was achieved. The peasants were not to be exploited, but the native élites deserved happiness too. The populations of some of the minorities should be allowed to increase, and the Muslims' refusal to eat pork should be respected. He even declared that Han dance troupes had no business modifying traditional Turki dances to suit their own taste.[23] 'Our fraternal nationalities are unhappy about this.' As has been noted earlier, the speech was not to see the light of day for over two decades.

Mao's next venture, the Great Leap Forward, began in 1958 and lasted three years. It had a devastating effect, especially on the nomadic herdsmen of the far west. The idea was to achieve the targets set by the second five-year plan in only two years, by investing massively in industry at the expense of agriculture, skipping a whole phase of development and showing the Soviet Union what 'real Socialists' could do. (By this time the Chinese Communist Party was calling the Soviet Union a 'capitalist' country, and the Great Leap Forward was a deliberate rebuke, inviting the rift that followed.)

The first stage of collectivization had been achieved with the co-operative farms. Now virtually the whole of Xinjiang's population was corralled into 450 giant communes in spite of the protests – and a few deaths – that had followed the intensification of co-operative farming in the preceding years. Much bigger than the Soviet *kolkhoz*, a Chinese commune could contain up to 20,000 people. Communes were not just a cornerstone of socialist architecture; they were a way of speeding up the fusion of races and keeping the natives under tight control. To achieve this fusion, the authorities made sure that the communes contained a broad mixture of ethnic groups. Rural industry took the form of brick kilns and mini-steel furnaces in villages all over the country.

But this accelerated collectivization not only beggared the peasants, who could not meet the quotas set for them and who had their possessions confiscated, it also had the result predicted by Liu Shaoqi and others three years before. Though bumper harvests were reported by zealous officials, and quotas set ever higher, grain yields were falling. By 1959 China was in the grip of a famine greater even than that which had ravaged the Soviet Union in the 1930s. Xinjiang coped with the famine rather better than most provinces because of its small population and dependable irrigation system. But many thousands of starving refugees trudged across its eastern border from Gansu, one of the worst affected provinces. There the Party secretary was a Mao devotee who offered to supply other provinces though he could not afford to – so he had the province's villagers tortured, hanged and robbed blind in order to fulfil his pledge.[24]

Before 1957 immigration had been moderate, but this new wave of desperate people from the east caused much resentment, even among earlier Han settlers. Many of the new immigrants were allocated land formerly used as pasture by the Kazakhs, who themselves had been reduced to beggary by collectivization. The Kazakhs had preferred to kill their flocks and herds and starve themselves rather than give up their livestock to the communes.

The Communist propaganda machine put quite a different slant on things, as the following report from the Party secretary of a Kazakh production brigade illustrates:

During the busiest days of harvest last autumn, leaders of the Toutai Production Brigade of the East Wind People's Commune decided to assign a number of able-bodied fellows, skilled carpenters and bricklayers to the task of building new houses. Meanwhile, many Kazakh members moved out of their houses and took up lodgings in hurriedly erected huts and tents . . . This was in order to welcome the new members. Mr Tehutahung, secretary of the Party branch of the brigade, went to the county government offices and brought back fifty Chinese young men and women from Kiangsi.[25]

In the year 1959, when the railway from Lanzhou reached the eastern border of Xinjiang, half a million immigrants arrived – a new record.

Such was the upheaval caused by the Great Leap Forward and the famine that Mao was forced to retreat in 1961. The rules for ethnic minorities were relaxed all over China, and especially in Xinjiang. The Panchen Lama was asked to report on the state of things in Tibet, which had been invaded and 'reclaimed' in 1959. There were riots in Xinjiang too, in the Ili valley and in Khotan where 10,000 youths were reported to have stormed the local jail, freeing 600 prisoners and killing 50 guards. Some Han Chinese were allowed to go home to districts in eastern China.

A law was promulgated giving foreign nationals the right to leave Xinjiang if they wished. About a thousand Uighurs, with more or less convincing claims to foreign citizenship, succeeded in emigrating. Many went to Afghanistan, from where they moved on to Pakistan, or further afield. Then, in 1962, there occurred the biggest exodus of modern times, still recalled with bitterness by the Chinese authorities. Huge numbers – nearly half a million by some estimates – of Kazakhs, Uighurs and even some Han crossed the north-west border to the Soviet Union, driven by the loss of land and property, or fear of being locked up as Soviet sympathizers. The Chinese claimed that they took more than 30,000 head of cattle ('national livestock') with them, and left 400,000 *mu* (67,000 acres) of land untended. The exodus was another symptom of the Sino-Soviet split: the Chinese claimed it was a Soviet plot, and there seems to be plenty of evidence to support the claim. Forty years later, a veteran of the great escape recalled that the starving people had been tempted over the border with parcels of food put out for them by Soviet border troops, like chickens lured with trails of corn.

In its version of events, published more than thirty years afterwards, the Party claimed that only 60,000 people, but including civil servants and cadres, were seduced by propaganda broadcasts promising a better life in the Soviet Union and by the distribution of literature, clothes and food. The Soviet vice-consul in Gulja, it was said, had travelled repeatedly up to Chuguchak to hand out birth certificates and residency permits to 6,000 Kazakhs with relatives on the Soviet side. Workers from collective farms had begun crossing in April, and when China closed the border the following month there had been a riot in Gulja itself, started by passengers at the city bus station who were waiting for transport to the border town of Korgas. The rioters, said the report, damaged the bus station, broke into the parliament building and Party offices, destroyed equipment and stole records. They seized weapons from the armed police and 'loudly chanted the reactionary slogans "Xinjiang belongs to us!" "The Chinese have occupied our land!" "Down with the Communist Party!" and "Destroy the Chinese!"'[26] Other reports say that one or two hundred people were killed, prompting a further wave of refugees.

The border was strengthened with the arrival of 341,500 Chinese military veterans who were formed into fifty-eight state farms; and in the following year, 1963, 100,000 young people from crowded Shanghai were dispatched to Xinjiang. Although the exodus was checked, the Soviet propaganda offensive continued. Refugees were allowed to broadcast into Xinjiang, accusing Mao of 'Great Han chauvinism'. Moscow radio gleefully took up exiles' reports that millions of Han were moving into the north-west, that local people were being driven into the lifeless deserts or punished with starvation rations, that Kazakh, Uighur and Kyrgyz girls were being taken away from their parents and forced to marry Han Chinese on pain of death. The barrage did not cease until 1983 when China and the USSR agreed to resume normal relations and re-open the border to trade.

Party theorists struggled to keep up with events. Now they said that the nationality problem had been misunderstood. It was not about cultural differences, which had in any case been exaggerated, but about class struggle. This was the bond which united Uighurs, Kazakhs and Mongols with the Han people. Native élites would never reform, and there would be no automatic cultural convergence.

It had become obvious to the province's leaders that socialism was not working in Xinjiang. The economic gap between the minorities and the Chinese was getting wider, not narrower. Party leaders in Urumchi had an impossible job. Mao was demanding communes, class struggle and purification of thought, but it was impossible to defend the border, however many tribal elders were removed and mosques closed, if the people hated the system imposed upon them. From now until Mao's death, the bosses in Urumchi were obliged to play something of a double game – especially when the Chairman returned once more to the ideological attack, with the manipulated anarchy of the Cultural Revolution.

The Great Proletarian Cultural Revolution was announced in Beijing by the Central Committee on 8 August 1966, and the infamous Red Guards were launched with a rally of a million youths in Tiananmen Square ten days later. The wheel was turning again. A week later the first Red Guards from Beijing arrived by train in Urumchi, on the new railway line from Lanzhou which had been further extended as far as the provincial capital. They were offered comfortable rooms at the university by the Party secretary, Wang Enmao. Angrily, they refused, and spread out to the city's schools. Though denounced in poster campaigns as 'the native emperor of the small kingdom of Xinjiang', Wang managed to keep the upper hand during the chaos that followed. One reason for his success was the shrewd manoeuvre of recruiting his own corps of Red Guards, who harried the radicals from Beijing and threw them into confusion by denouncing them as 'Rightist troublemakers'.[27]

Daily life became a nightmare for Mao's supposed enemies inside and outside the Party. The news films at local cinemas showed Chairman Mao, looking old and careworn, visiting factories and farms. But to comment on his appearance was to risk being 'struggled' by the zealots during organized sessions of public vilification. Uighurs with foreign connections were particularly suspect. 'It was dangerous even to admit that you had relatives over the border,' recalled one Uighur who had a grandmother in Kazakhstan. 'You might be persecuted as a spy.'[28] A Uighur cadre at the Ministry of Railways in Urumchi was imprisoned for two years, just because he had a sister living in Uzbekistan.

The Cultural Revolution was almost a civil war, dividing even the Uighurs among themselves. But not everyone sank into the mire. There were examples of neighbourliness, too. A Uighur who went to visit a commune occupied by anti-Mao 'rebels' was taken prisoner, beaten up and tied to a tree. He was rescued by a Han Chinese from the north-east, one of the Nationalist soldiers drafted into the Xinjiang Production and Construction Corps, who took him to his house and looked after him for ten days until he was fit to walk the 60 miles home. This Chinese used to visit the Uighur's family, taking them shoes, socks and jackets from eastern China where they were not so scarce.

Early in 1967, Wang was in Beijing trying to alert the leadership to the risk it was running in the west. While he was away there occurred on 26 January one of the most serious clashes between rival squads. Young radicals imported from Shanghai tried to take over a textile factory at Shihezi, a Chinese industrial city north-west of Urumchi. Wang's supporters in the paramilitary Production and Construction Corps which ran the factory were sent to deal with them. These old hands called themselves the 'Xinjiang Military Region Production and Construction Corps "August First" Field Army Swearing to Defend the Thought of Mao Zedong to the Death', surely the longest regimental name in history.

Wang's troops arrived in ten truckloads. They stopped a bus containing ten youths and shot the occupants on the spot. In the fighting that followed, scores of the young radicals were killed, as were some bystanders. Some of the survivors were packed off back to Shanghai, others ended up in detention camps.*

The message that Wang was trying to communicate to the Party leadership appears to have got through. The following month Beijing announced a 'new stage' in the Cultural Revolution in areas like Xinjiang which were vital to national defence. Virtually all revolutionary activity was halted. Zhou Enlai was put in charge of directing the ceasefire, and the People's Liberation Army took charge of the Corps.

Though victorious, Governor Wang ate humble pie. In a message to Mao he said that he had made a thorough 'self-criticism' which had been graciously accepted by his good friends the young radicals. Perhaps it was part of the deal. Reports which reached

---

*Years later, a crowd of 10,000 Shanghainese left stranded in Xinjiang by the Cultural Revolution held a demonstration in Aksu; they attacked officials and occupied buildings, demanding to be allowed to go home.

Hong Kong suggested that Wang had won the argument by playing his trump card: the Lop Nor nuclear base. He warned that the base was vulnerable to foreign agents and 'domestic opponents'. He may even have threatened, on grounds of safety, to take over the nuclear facilities himself. After a further meeting with Mao and his defence minister Lin Biao, it was announced on 25 February that the Cultural Revolution in Xinjiang would be suspended.

Riots and strikes across China forced Mao to call on the army to restore order, effectively putting an end to the national struggle he had set in motion, although its effects continued to be felt until his death in 1976. Meanwhile the government of Xinjiang was put under a revolutionary committee headed by Long Shujin, and then under a collective leadership which lasted until 1979. Wang was apparently 'struggled' in Beijing, and his name disappeared from the Xinjiang records. He was last seen in Beijing at a May Day rally in 1969, but he re-emerged in the late 1970s, rehabilitated, as a political commissar in Nanjing.

Although they were not the target of the Cultural Revolution, the Turki minorities – like the Mongols in their region – had been among its principal victims. Mosques had been attacked and scriptures burned; Muslim clerics were covered in paint and paraded through the streets. But as before, repression was followed by a period of relaxation.

In 1971, with the Uighur Saifuddin, the former minister in the Eastern Turkestan Republic, now installed as the political boss, the reins were loosened. A limited amount of 'sideline' production was permitted from private plots and herds, so long as the communes were kept intact. Free markets were allowed in rural areas, and wages were geared to work 'points'. Schools and colleges reopened, although the curriculum was still heavily loaded with political and practical subjects.

Old habits of mind seemed never to change, however. When the Gang of Four were arrested and tried after Mao's death on 6 September 1976, their opponents claimed that their tentacles had reached deep into Xinjiang. Mao's wife Jiang Qing was supposed to have said that ethnic minorities, with their 'outlandish' songs and dances, were no better than 'foreign invaders and aliens'. 'What is so special about your tiny Xinjiang? I despise you!'[29]

Perhaps she never said any such thing. But the insult attributed to her showed that in the minds of many Chinese, the Uighurs were barbarians still.

Following the death of Mao, the Party began to take more seriously the disruption suffered by the peoples of the far west. In 1978 came land reform and some debt forgiveness: land was allocated to the peasants, though not formally transferred, on the understanding that the state would not take it away again unless the peasants failed to work it. The climate grew even warmer after Hu Yaobang, the liberal who was about to become General Secretary of the Party, spent two weeks in the west in 1980 and recommended that the ethnic provinces should be given real autonomy and that Han cadres should be withdrawn. In 1982 Erkin Alptekin, the son of the nationalist Isa Yusuf, was able to revisit the country he had left as a child in 1949. He found the Chinese 'well-disposed towards the local people', particularly after the Soviet invasion of Afghanistan in 1978, but also reported widespread unemployment and poverty among Uighurs: some people were still going barefoot in midwinter.[30]

For the first time since the Manchu conquest, it was officially acknowledged that the people were of Turkic origin. They were allowed to read their own history. The Roman script was abolished and the Arabic restored. Uighur families in Kashgar whose houses had been seized for the use of 'the people' were compensated, and many were able to rebuild. In Aksu, following clashes between local people and Chinese immigrants, mosques were reopened and Islamic literature was allowed to circulate.

Article 46 of a new constitution adopted in March 1978 gave citizens the freedom to believe or not to believe (but not to proselytize – only atheism could be preached). Women were exempt from the recently introduced birth-control quotas. Following the débâcle of Kazakh emigration in 1962 and the huge loss of livestock during collectivization it was accepted that nomads could not simply be turned into state labourers. They were allowed to own animals and to lease both livestock and land. A reporter and photographer from an American magazine were taken to meet contented Uighurs and

Kazakhs. One herder in the mountains above Urumchi told them he was not sure what a commune was, but another at the afore-mentioned Commune of the East Wind was found to sing the praises of the collective system: 'We are happy. We work – but not too hard. When we are sick, there are doctors to treat us. I didn't go to school, but my daughter studies physics at Xinjiang University. Last year Chairman Hua [Guofeng] was here. This is the best of times!'[31] Deng Xiaoping, Hua's successor, visited Xinjiang in August 1981 to sort out a power struggle inside the province's politburo. He was told that the Uighurs had been planning a 'province-wide uprising', which may have encouraged him to go even further in dealing with their grievances.

By degrees, however, the shackles were replaced as Uighurs used the new climate to air demands for jobs and autonomy. The first of several anti-crime campaigns – which in Xinjiang seemed always to be directed against Uighur 'separatism' – was launched in 1983, and with it came a marked increase in the use of torture. Uighur students at the Central Nationalities Institute in Beijing took to the streets in 1985 to protest against nuclear weapons testing in the Lop desert. The same year there were riots in protest at the removal of Saifuddin, the Uighur governor of the province. Other student demonstrations were mounted against supposed racial slurs in Chinese films.

Hu Yaobang the reformer, who had been dismissed from the leadership in 1987, died in April 1989. On 19 May, Uighur students marched through the streets of Urumchi. At first the author-ities described the march as an orderly demonstration in support of the pro-democracy students then occupying Tiananmen Square in Beijing. That sit-in was terminated suddenly and violently by a massacre on 4 June 1989, halting the democracy movement in its tracks and ushering in a new period of hardline government.

The march in Urumchi, it later turned out, had been far from orderly. The Xinhua news agency reported that cars were wrecked and more than 150 police and other officers injured. An internal Party memorandum claimed the students had also attacked Communist Party headquarters. What is more, the object of the march was not, as had been supposed, to show solidarity with the students of Tiananmen. It was a march of religious protest, in which many thousands took part – replicated in other cities and probably the biggest since Liberation – against a book called *Sexual Customs* that purported to describe the sexual life of Muslims.

As far as the authorities were concerned, however, the Urumchi demonstration was 'an organized and premeditated incident devised by a handful of people who adopt a hostile attitude to the Chinese Communist Party and the socialist motherland, and oppose the reunification of the motherland and unity among all nationalities'.[32]

The demonstration of 1989 marked the beginning of a decade of violence in Xinjiang, of confrontation with the Party and the state, with consequences we shall see in the next chapter.

6

Riots and Reprisals

O N ANY ORDINARY day there is a small but steady flow of worshippers at the Id Kah mosque in Kashgar, the heart of Islam in China. Most of them are old, and none of them are women. Women must do their praying at home. The same steady attendance can be seen in secular Urumchi. At the northern limit of the Uighur quarter in Ittipak Square, opposite the old city theatre, there is a mosque above a small courtyard reached by a double staircase. Here at midday about a hundred men, young as well as old, gather to pray, led by the elders in their big white turbans and the imam in the biggest turban of all. Watching this scene from a respectful distance, the visitor is left wondering whether mosque attendance is not – at least for the younger men – as much a way of asserting their identity in an overwhelmingly Chinese city as it is of paying respect to a higher authority.*

Freedom of religious belief and 'normal religious activity' are guaranteed by the constitution of China. In practice, however, these freedoms have been tightly circumscribed according to the authorities' mood. The constant shifts in government policy towards Islam can be read between the lines of a notice for visitors posted inside the Id Kah mosque. The notice recalls that the mosque, built in 1442, was 'thoroughly renovated' in 1955, the year the Autonomous Region was created. In 1962 (that is, four years before the Cultural Revolution when the mosque was severely damaged), the regional government declared it a protected monument. In 1983 (the period when control of minorities was relaxed) washrooms were installed

---

* As it was in Catholic Poland, for example, during the years of Communist government there.

for ritual cleansing before prayers. In 1994, the budget for 'offices' was increased. All this, says the notice, shows that the government pays 'special attention to the religious and historical culture of ethnic groups, and such policies . . . are very popular'. It goes on to reiterate that religious belief is protected by the state and that the different races 'are building their own beautiful country hand in hand'.[1] Tourist brochures wax eloquent about the six or seven thousand people who attend Friday prayers, and the tens of thousands who flock to the mosque for the big festivals of Eid-Adha and Eid al-Fitr: 'the loud, exciting, soaring Nagla drum and suona music . . . bidding welfare [farewell] to the old and ushering in the new with wile [wild] dance. Jubilant crowds are dancing without restraint day and night . . . it becomes a unique horizon in the ancient city of Kashgar.'[2]

These are not the words of a hostile regime, certainly. Who, reading the notice and brochures, would guess that the mosque and its worshippers are generally kept under the strictest control? Islam is the chief obstacle to the Uighurs' assimilation, and whatever the constitution may say about the freedom of religion, officials behave as if belief in Islam and civic rights are incompatible.

In the first years of Liberation the right to religious belief, though narrowly defined, was formally protected. In 1955 the authorities even allowed the faithful to make the haj, the pilgrimage to Mecca. But the apparatus of faith was removed. It could hardly be otherwise: Islam is a religion which permeates the daily life of its adherents as few others do, and its clergy wield real authority. The Communists removed the judicial power of the imams, abolished the religious tithe (*zakrat*), and negotiated a distribution of mosque land to the poor. Later, especially during the Cultural Revolution, thousands of mosques were shut or converted into barracks, stables or slaughterhouses. Mullahs were arrested, tortured and given menial jobs, such as cleaning sewers. Those left in office were obliged to write testimonies of loyalty to the state. The mosque schools, or *madrasahs*, were closed down and with them the traditional Islamic syllabus covering theology, ritual, metaphysics, poetry, logic, arithmetic, geometry, ethics, astronomy, medicine and agriculture. All this was done in the name of removing the clergy's privileges, or abolishing 'feudal oppression'.

After the wreckage left by the Cultural Revolution and Mao's death, there was a brief respite during the 1980s, when some mosques were re-opened. But religious repression resumed in the wake of the Tiananmen Square protest and the Muslim demonstrations in Xinjiang and elsewhere. Mosques rebuilt without permission were destroyed. For example, the Khazan Bulach mosque in Uch-Turfan, near Aksu, was demolished following its use for an 'unsanctioned public meeting'– a Ramadan service. The war against religion was intensified during a nationwide anti-crime campaign in 1996. Underground Koranic schools were the target this time, and a grass-roots purge of believers ('in-depth atheist education') was conducted in the Party and in state bodies. Believers who worked in government offices or state agencies were told they would lose their jobs if they went to the mosque. Civil servants, teachers and students in Uighur areas were forbidden to pray in public, to fast, or to attend religious services. During the month of Ramadan they were watched by the police in case they stopped eating, were made to write letters undertaking not to fast, or were offered free lunches. Illegal praying could lead to expulsion from university.

Sometimes the purge took strange forms. In June 2000, a young Uighur villager called Yasin Kiver was detained for 'illegal religious activities'. After three months, having paid a fine of 3,000 yuan (approximately US$350), he was released. He returned home but was then summoned to the office of the local Communist Party secretary who forced him to drink alcohol, so breaking a religious taboo. He was warned that if he was caught praying again he would be thrown in jail.[3] Uighur workers in the northern oil town of Karamay were likewise given free alcohol from time to time in order to wean them from Islam.[4]

On 27 July 2001, two Uighur boys were arrested for secretly attending religious classes. The Han Chinese police allegedly tortured the boys to extract information about other students. As a result, eighteen more people were later detained, including 7-year-old children. All were fined between 300 and 500 yuan; the teacher was held in detention for a month and his property was confiscated.[5] During their winter holidays, according to other reports, children were made to go to school on Fridays, the Muslim Sabbath, to prevent them praying at home.[6] In state religious schools, religion is certainly on the syllabus, but it is a Marxist view of religion as a superstition held only by the lowest in society. The Xinjiang Islamic Institute, the regulatory body for religion, offers courses entitled 'Marxism against Religion' and 'The Works of Deng Xiaoping'.

No government can be sure of controlling the ideas in people's heads; but the Chinese state has gone as far as it can to undermine belief in Islam, by means of propaganda, threats and punishment. A parallel campaign has been waged against the other pillar of Uighur culture, its language.

The Uighurs are especially proud of their literature, founded (so it is said) by the eleventh-century poet Mahmut Kashgari. He is to the Uighurs what Shakespeare is to the English, or Pushkin to the Russians. He was born in the pretty oasis of Opal, south-west of the city from which he takes his name, and his walled tomb in the village cemetery is a place of homage.[7] On the short climb from the road the visitor passes a spring covered by an old poplar tree said to have been planted during the poet's lifetime. From the cemetery above there is a wonderful view of the Pamir mountains soaring over the desert 30 miles away, a great rampart of rock and ice with banners of cloud fluttering from their peaks. Mahmut Kashgari is best known for his *Divani Lughat Turk* of 1065, an encyclopaedia, gazetteer and dictionary which relates the history of the Turkic tribes, their customs and languages. The book was recently translated into Chinese for the first time by the Xinjiang Academy of Social Sciences, 'to help Chinese scholars and historians to have a better understanding of the Uighurs and Central Asia as a whole'.[8]

In spite of this conciliatory, even respectful acknowledgement of the Uighurs' culture, exiles complain that the study of their classical literature is being taken over, and manipulated, by Han scholars. So little is published in their own language – only a sixth of all books issued in Xinjiang – that they have no modern literature to speak of, no up-to-date encyclopaedia, no Uighur dictionary and no basic science books. Furthermore, they say, any Uighur who writes about his own people's past is liable to be accused of endangering the unity of China. They claim that not a single Islamic book, including the Quran, can be published in the Uighur language.

History books have been singled out for censorship. In 1991 three titles were targeted on the grounds that they were separatist, part of a campaign to create an independent Eastern Turkestan (a name abhorrent to the Chinese). The books were entitled *The Huns*, *Ancient Uighur Literature* and *The History of the Uighurs*. The author of the last, Turgun Almas, was reportedly placed under house arrest in Urumchi for linking the Uighurs to other Turki races, and was still under surveillance many years later.

The authorities have also been accused not merely of banning Uighur books but of burning them. Unconfirmed reports from Kashgar claim that in May 2002 more than 32,000 copies of a book with the innocent title *Ancient Uighur Craftsmanship* were destroyed by the state-owned Kashgar Uighur Press, along with copies of two of the books mentioned above.[9] The craft book, published in 1988, describes techniques for making paper, candles, carpets and silk. But on the first page it carries verses from the Quran. Officials made no comment on the allegation, and the local Party was sceptical. But the *Kashgar Daily* said the press had censored 330 books and halted publication of other 'problematic' volumes. A claim by the exiles' organization in Munich, Germany, that copies of the Quran had also been burned was formally denied.

A more direct, physical – and even violent – form of administrative interference has been the birth-control programme. All of China is, as is well known, subject to compulsory family planning. The one-child policy was introduced in a number of cities in the 1970s, and in 1979 it was formalized by decree for the whole of China. The rule was later relaxed in some rural areas, and ethnic minorities became – at least in theory – exempt. In 1988, however, compulsory birth control was extended to the Muslims.

The quotas may seem generous: two babies for urban couples, three for farmers and peasants. (Han immigrants to Xinjiang are also permitted two children per family.) In practice, they are less so. Furthermore, apart from the overtones of racial aggression, enforced birth control is, for Muslims, nothing less than an affront to God. In response to the imposition of compulsory birth control, the World Muslim League in Mecca immediately fired off an angry telegram to Zhao Ziyang, China's then prime minister, complaining of 'arbitrary actions' which infringed human rights and Islamic teaching. On a more pragmatic note, the telegram added that Muslims were 'a tiny minority in China, who are exposed to deadly diseases and epidemics such as hepatitis . . . not to mention the deadly effects of the atomic tests carried out in Lop Nor'. It quoted a Chinese radio report that 60,000 Muslims had died in a recent hepatitis epidemic.[10]

Even in a secular society, and even in a country as populous as China, it is ethically questionable for the state to set baby quotas and enforce them by means of compulsory sterilization, abortion and large fines. When Indira Gandhi introduced compulsory sterilization in India in 1975 the outcry spread far beyond the country's borders. While the ethical question is a serious one, and the efficiency of controls doubtful, in Xinjiang there is another issue: the justice or otherwise of using birth control against an ethnic minority. Although the Uighurs are (according to the official figures) the largest ethnic group in Xinjiang, they are only a fraction of 1 per cent of China's total population. Furthermore, anecdotal evidence suggests that – as in the case of religion – enforcement is in practice much harsher than public statements pretend.

The story of a woman called Hayrinisahan cannot be verified, and may not be believable. It is typical, however, of reports which come out of Xinjiang. According to this story Hayrinisahan was 32 years old and living in Turfan when she married a man called Ahmetjan. Each had a child from a previous marriage. The couple believed they were entitled to have another child between them; but when Hayrinisahan was five months pregnant the family planning people told her she was 'outside the plan' and must have an abortion.

An official came to the house every day. Ahmetjan was warned by his boss that he would be sacked if the pregnancy was not terminated. To save the baby and his job, the couple decided to go through the motions of divorce. Hayrinisahan went to another district to have the baby, but after a month had gone by she was discovered by the family planners and forced to return to Turfan for the abortion. Giving them the slip, she then went to the town of Toksun, 20 miles from Turfan city. There she was discovered again – by this time eight and a half months pregnant – but she escaped once more, to a remote mountain village 200 miles away. When she was on the point of giving birth the authorities caught up with her. A family planning officer, accompanied by two policemen, took her back to Turfan like a criminal. In hospital she gave birth, possibly by Caesarean, to a child which 'ended up dead'. It is not clear whether the baby was still-born, died after birth, or was killed. Whatever the case, the mother went mad, and roamed distractedly through the streets of Turfan.[11]

According to Amnesty International, some abortions have been performed by Caesarean section within days of term. The ill-treatment of women by officials includes cases where careless surgery has been the cause of permanent physical damage, and sometimes death.[12]

Birth control is managed by means of 'birth limitation contracts' between the local commission and the individual married woman. A specimen from Kashgar translated for Amnesty says that family planning is for 'financial and social development, and to raise the quality of the culture of all nationalities [that is, races] and their standard of living'. A choice of methods is offered. If an unplanned pregnancy occurs, then both sides agree to use 'a supplementary approach' – a euphemism, presumably, for abortion. Those who stick to the contract are rewarded at the end of the year. If they go for three years without a child they become an 'Honourable Family in Family Planning'. Couples who refuse an abortion are to be fined 50 yuan a month each until the abortion is carried out. If they have a baby outside the plan they pay hospital charges on top, plus 'a heavy punishment' laid down in 'the related government Article'.[13]

A document drawn up in 2000 by the Communist Party committee in the southern city of Khotan laid down that village headmen were to be fined or dismissed if surplus babies were discovered in their villages, and that large fines were to be imposed on doctors who removed contraceptive coils. More significantly, it revealed that child quotas were not individual but geographic. The local newspaper of 1 September 2000 boasted that of the 45,000 women in the area, no fewer than 30,400 had been brought under planning controls. In another, unnamed, town with a population of 180,000, only 1,000 women were allowed to give birth, and 40 civil servants were sacked because their wives became pregnant.

Not surprisingly, resentment has boiled over into violence.

On 18 July 1994, following 'family planning trials and birth control experiments' in two counties in the Aksu area intended as pilot schemes for the whole of Xinjiang, two bombs were set off. One of them hit the family planning office of a county in which a hundred women had been subjected to forced abortions that year. After the explosions, over a thousand people were arrested. The following year, a crowd attacked the family planning offices in Khotan, on the other side of the desert, and set fire to them. In 1998 Rehem Sajeden, a Uighur farmer in Aksu, killed a female family planning official who had been visiting his house to 'talk to his wife about birth control'. His execution was reported in the *Xinjiang Daily* which ran a series of articles lauding the official as a 'martyr'.[14]

The high priority given to family planning, the zealousness of local officials in carrying it out, and the violence of the methods sometimes used, all suggest to Uighur activists that there is more to birth control than 'improving the quality of life'. Add to this the higher mortality of Uighur peasants, who in rural areas often lack medical help or are too poor to afford it; add also the small absolute size of the Uighur population, and the system begins to look much more discriminatory.

Compulsory birth control not only undermines the Uighurs' faith in their doctors and nurses, it adds to their suspicion that they are being targeted by the state for a covert form of 'ethnic cleansing'. As one Uighur health official said: 'If our children are limited, we will disappear.'[15] What makes matters worse is that China's leaders are well aware that the policy has failed. Coercion has been met with resistance and evasion, and as a result the country's population has far exceeded the targets set for it. By contrast, trials conducted in a number of areas have shown that a voluntary system is effective.[16]

The Uighurs of Xinjiang cannot pretend to be unfamiliar with injustice. Their history is littered with cruel khojas, corrupt *begs*, ruthless warlords and grasping dictators. Often they have seemed (at least in the eyes of outsiders) to have fared better under Chinese administration. Today, that cannot be said. Examples of persecution by Han officialdom abound, not just in matters of religion and family life, but in the dispensation of justice itself.

A prominent Uighur exile recalled the case of a Chinese soldier who, while driving a military truck in Kashgar, ran over a Uighur and killed him. Convicted of manslaughter by a Uighur-dominated court and sentenced to death, the soldier escaped his sentence because the Han-dominated police refused to execute him and the army threatened to mutiny if they did so.[17] The sentence imposed by the Uighur majority may have been much too harsh. The point is that the Han had no need to go to appeal: he was immune. Such double standards permeate the system, from arrest and detention to trial, imprisonment and execution, as we shall see.

Many of the grievances which led the Muslims to rise in the past are finding echoes again in the present, such as forced labour, or the *corvée*, and the expropriation of land and property. But rarely in the past were direct attacks made on their religious beliefs, their clergy and rituals. Nor is there any precedent for the systematic and compulsory abortion of babies unwanted by the state.

In the past, affronts to the Turkis' sexual mores were generally avoided, but when they did occur (as in the 'oleaster rebellion' of 1765, the Hami revolt of 1931, or the publication of the book *Sexual Customs* in 1989), they provoked a violent response. Cases of molestation and rape involving Han and Turki have always been especially provocative; and when the offender is not brought to justice, the offence is compounded.

Just such a case was reported in April 1999. Five Chinese migrants were said to have raped two Uighur girls, aged 11 and 13. The girls were the daughters of Sadir Imin, who lived in a village of Fukang district, near Urumchi. The local police chief promised to investigate the case but for four days appeared to do nothing. In the meantime, Sadir Imin himself captured one of the alleged rapists and brought him to the police station. But the police arrested Sadir Imin instead for making an unauthorized arrest, and threatened him with five years in jail. The father escaped and killed the police chief and also one of the rapists. When Ainur, the older girl, died from bleeding shortly afterwards, five Uighurs took revenge on the other men said to have raped the girls, and beat them up severely. About a hundred policemen were called in to arrest the Uighurs, one of whom was killed in the course of a struggle. The others were put into detention. Friends of the families were ordered not to help, as that was considered 'giving assistance to separatist elements'.[18]

Even very minor incidents have led to violence and serious reprisals against Uighurs. One involved a Uighur woman who accidentally stepped on the foot of a child in a Chinese shop in the Khotan area. 'Despite her apologies, a Chinese man kept insulting her. Moreover, he beat the poor woman up with a metal rod until she bled. Another Chinese stood by and encouraged the assailant, saying that he would not make a move even if the woman was killed.'[19] A crowd gathered and fighting broke out between Uighurs and Chinese settlers which resulted in many injuries. Riot police then used tear gas and physical force to stop the fighting. About two hundred Uighurs were detained. Later the authorities announced the incident had been started by 'national separatists and counter-revolutionaries'. Inquiries and arrests continued for several months.

The event which marked the end of Turki co-operation, and which opened a decade of hostilities between them and their Chinese masters, was a riot in Baren, a poor town in the autonomous Kyrgyz prefecture south-west of Kashgar.

The post-Mao leadership of the early 1980s, as we have seen, had acknowledged the special hardships suffered by the minorities of the far west, and had made large concessions to them. But these had been whittled away over the years. At the end of that decade, however, the Tiananmen Square demonstrations, and the rise of political Islam in central Asia following the collapse of the Soviet Union sent the Chinese leadership into reverse. It was also a turning-point for the people of Xinjiang.

The Baren riot erupted on 5 April 1990, and its size and ferocity – more than matched by the reaction of the security forces – took the provincial government by surprise.

The government later claimed that it could only have been the work of fanatical foreign infiltrators, but local people said the immediate cause of the outburst was the closure of a mosque just before a religious festival. The previous month all mosque-building had been banned, and several weeks of protest had followed. On 4 April, groups of people gathered in village mosques to demand more freedom. The trouble started the following day when police tried to break up a crowd of several hundred who had held a public prayer meeting outside the local government offices. The riot involved about 2,000 people, almost all local peasants, with Kyrgyz and Hui (Chinese Muslims) as well as Uighurs reportedly among the leaders.

The riot was brutally put down. Some in the crowd appear to have been deliberately shot and killed although they had offered no violence. Many of those arrested were reportedly beaten in detention. The official death toll was 22, but witnesses claim that 50 protestors died, including those shot dead while running away. Others were allegedly killed in the woods and in a nearby village by mortar fire, or by troops shooting from helicopters.[20] It is also claimed that from a community of 10,000, all the males aged between 13 and 60 were initially arrested.

According to others, the trouble began with a meeting of Kyrgyz leaders in a mosque, where complaints were voiced about birth control, nuclear testing and the export of Xinjiang's natural resources to 'inland' China. A mass protest followed, at which calls were made for *jihad* or holy war, for the expulsion of the Han, and for an independent Eastern Turkestan. About a hundred police were sent to suppress the protest but they were overpowered and had their weapons stolen. In the end the riot was put down by the Public Security Bureau, armed police and – reportedly – 1,000 regular army troops. Xinjiang's Chinese-language television channel showed purported Uighur documents calling for *jihad* and an armed uprising, and the state media claimed that the rebels had been armed by mujahidin in Afghanistan.[21] In July the television station said that the courts had handled 5,000 criminal cases and 7,900 defendants arising out of the incident. During the crackdown, which involved arrests all over Xinjiang, the Politburo member responsible for security, Qiao Shi, visited the region.

A report on the Baren rising commissioned by the government, and initially for internal Party use, said the riot was 'the most serious carried out by ethnic separatists since the Liberation of Xinjiang'. It had been planned well in advance, it said, by 'a small number of reactionaries and ethnic separatists hidden in Baren' who had set up an 'Eastern Turkestan Islamic Party' and duped members of the public into taking part in a plot to destroy national unity and overthrow the government. The plan had been to set up, under the 'cloak of religion', an Eastern Turkestan Republic by armed revolt, and to eliminate non-believers (that is, the Han).

> They set up loudspeakers in mosque courtyards in the villages of Baren and Turand, and played cassettes praising *jihad*. A small number of reactionaries set knives on the ground, and forced people to take a vow, touching the Quran, to join the *jihad*. They threatened to kill those who betrayed Islam. In the early morning of 5 April 1990, a group of ruffians gathered nearly 200 people to pray in front of the local government building, seeking trouble. In the same afternoon, the ruffians tied up and beat the police officers who came to keep social order, and took away their weapons. Moreover, they trapped our Party and administrative officials, police officers and armed police officers for over ten hours in the town government courtyard by madly shooting and throwing grenades at the courtyard, obstructing the armed police officers who had come to help. They savagely killed seven armed police officers.[22]

Jihad had been fomented through private schools, the Chinese researchers claimed, by the organizer of the rebellion, one Zeydin Yusuf, and by such books as *The Biography of King Bograhan* published in 1988 by the Kashgar Uighur Publishing House. Yusuf and his friends had 'fabricated rumours' that the birth-control policy was designed to destroy the Uighur nation, and had openly shouted slogans such as 'Down with Socialism!' But the quelling of the Baren uprising, the report added, had been 'a great victory . . . a heavy blow to foreign and internal separatist forces'.[23]

The reverberations were felt right across the province. 'Everyone knew what had happened in Baren,' recalled a Uighur surgeon who at the time was working 800 miles away at the railway hospital in Urumchi. The ethnic members of staff – three Kazakhs, one Tajik and twenty-five Uighurs in a hospital of nearly 1,000 employees – were summoned to a meeting and warned that if they continued to attend the mosque they would be sacked. At about this time cameras were installed in mosques to spy on worshippers. Uighur members of the secret police would attend services while their Chinese colleagues kept watch outside. At big festivals, there would be armed police outside and films would be taken of people as they emerged. 'After the warning I stopped going to the mosque every week,' the surgeon said. 'I attended only two Muslim festivals a year, secretly, because I would have lost my job. I didn't dare go to the mosque in Urumchi as there were cameras inside and I was afraid of the secret police.'[24]

Meanwhile, thousands of cadres in 'rural work teams' were sent to the border areas, and newspaper editors from China's autonomous regions were summoned to Lhasa and told to spend more time condemning separatism and less time reporting ethnic unrest. Police and militia forces in Kashgar were reinforced; later, it was decided to recruit an extra 28,000 armed policemen, and riot units were created in Urumchi and Kashgar.

It seems that from about this time a bombing campaign began in Xinjiang. Who was behind it, and whether it was co-ordinated, is not clear. But the Chinese authorities had no doubt as to the perpetrators. The first bomb went off in February 1992, on a bus in Urumchi, injuring twenty-six people. Two more were reported, on a second bus, and in a cinema, but no one was hurt. Internal documents claim that these were followed by explosions in other towns on both sides of the Tian Shan. Martial law was instituted in Kashgar in June the following year when, according to a German news magazine, a seven-metre hole was blown in the front of a Ministry of Agriculture building.[25]

The protest now widened to other issues: in March 1993, a big anti-nuclear demonstration was held at Lop Nor, where China's nuclear warheads were being tested under the desert. A thousand people reportedly broke into the compound, setting fire to aircraft, tanks and other vehicles, and pulling down the perimeter fence. The People's Liberation Army opened fire on the crowd, killing some, and hundreds were arrested. The Hong Kong publication that reported on the demonstration also claimed that radioactive material and explosives were stolen.[26]

*

If the consequences of the Baren rising were serious, the aftermath of the Gulja riot, seven years later, was shocking and hangs over the region like a shadow to this day.

Gulja, known as Yining to the Chinese, is a small and pleasant city set in the most fertile part of the province. It has long spelled trouble for China. The city lies in a valley between two ranges of the Tian Shan mountains, close to the border with Kazakhstan, and it is more accessible from the western side than it is from the Chinese side. Subject to Russian influence during the time of the tsars, it was annexed and occupied by them between 1871 and 1882. After the Bolshevik Revolution, Soviet influence was equally pervasive, and (as we saw in Chapter 5) many valley dwellers were persuaded that they would have a better life across the border. Gulja was also the headquarters of the breakaway Eastern Turkestan Republic of 1944 (described in Chapter 4). The awkward reconciliation with China which followed that secession has not been forgotten by Beijing.

At nine o'clock on a freezing but sunny morning in February 1997, a crowd of demonstrators set out to march through the streets. Hundreds of young people (thousands by some accounts) joined the demonstration, carrying banners and shouting slogans, calling for the release of religious teachers, and demanding jobs for Uighurs.

The day before the march, 4 February, was the end of the holy month of Ramadan, and the police had chosen that day to arrest leaders of a *meshrep* which had been running for some years. A *meshrep* is a kind of religious youth club, and large numbers of them had been set up in and around the city, initially with the agreement of the authorities. Local people said they were doing good work, educating young people against drunkenness and drug abuse. But the police had been mobilized by a national 'strike hard' campaign, launched the previous year. In mainland China the campaign's target was criminals; in Xinjiang it was ethnic minority separatists, or 'splittists'. The arrests took place at a mosque when the police arrived to detain two *talibs* or religious students.[27] Worshippers intervened, fighting broke out and a number of civilians and police officers were killed. In another account, by a prominent Uighur in Turkey, the police went to the mosque and rounded up thirty women who were praying on the feast of Laylatul Qadr. Three of them were tortured to death at the police station, and their bodies were thrown on to the street. Such was the provocation that the people took to the streets with chants of *Allahu Akbar!* (God is great!), and started attacking police stations with sticks, stones and whatever else came to hand.[28]

The protest march was not allowed to last long. About two hours after it had started, the demonstrators were stopped near the Ili Hotel, formerly the Russian consulate, by a large contingent of armed police and dog-handlers. Between 300 and 500 people were arrested, some bystanders among them. One of those taken was the alleged ringleader, Abdulhelil Abdumejit, a 28-year-old married businessman and leader of the *meshrep* movement who had already been detained in 1995 when the *meshreps* were banned but who was released after 're-education'.

Whether the violence broke out then or later is not clear. But by the next day the city was full of riot police and soldiers who 'went through the streets arresting and beating people, including children'.[29] In some places the police came under attack themselves, as did Chinese residents and shopkeepers, and the security forces retaliated with firearms. Unconfirmed reports said that dogs were set on the crowd, and that police flame-throwers and rifles were used. Officials said nine people, including four policemen, had been killed. Unofficially the toll was put at thirty, or a hundred, or four hundred. A curfew was imposed, the airport and railway station were closed, and the city was sealed off for the next two weeks.

Now there were house-to-house searches resulting in further arrests, until the jails and detention centres were bursting with between 3,000 and 5,000 people. It was claimed that demonstrators arrested on 5 February were hosed down with icy water in a stadium or some other open space, or made to run barefoot in the snow. Those who suffered frostbite had to be taken to hospital where their feet, fingers or hands were amputated. Photographs of serious frost-bite injuries were shown to Amnesty International investigators.

As the search widened, a truckful of armed police called at a house in the village of Uchun on 8 or 9 February. Neighbours said they arrived to arrest a man who had organized a Quran study class. He had been detained twice before and on both occasions had been ransomed back by his father, a farmer. This time the father said his son was not at home, protesting that he had committed no crime. The police pushed him aside and went into the house, at which the father picked up an axe and followed them. He was shot dead on the spot. Hearing the screams of the women of the family, the son appeared. He launched himself at the police, injuring some of them, and was shot in the leg, but he escaped, taking refuge on the roof of another house.

Meanwhile, a youth who had been to the man's Quran class saw his teacher's escape and, snatching a machine-gun from one of the police officers, climbed on to the roof with him. The house was surrounded and, while the youth was struggling with the gun to try and fire it, both he and the teacher were shot from below. The police also shot dead the teacher's mother and sister.[30]

The repercussions continued. At the end of April a public sentencing rally was held in the city stadium, at which three Uighurs were condemned to death and the rest were given jail terms for their part in the protests. While the prisoners were being paraded through the streets in a convoy of open trucks before the rally, the police opened fire on the crowd, killing three Uighurs and wounding ten. Various official explanations were given: that the crowd had rioted, that they had tried to rescue the prisoners, or that they had tried to enter a 'no-go area'. Warning shots fired into the air had apparently been ignored. According to some witnesses, the crowd consisted of people who had been rounded up to watch the parade, and when relatives or friends approached the trucks in order to speak to the prisoners, the escort fired directly at them. Other accounts added that the accused appeared drugged, their hands and mouths had been tied with wire, and they were made to kneel as the trucks drove round the suburbs.

A crowd of 5,000 people gathered at the stadium to watch the sentencing. The three charged with 'causing injury, arson, hooliganism, smashing property and looting', Yusuf Tursun, Aishan Maimati and Ibrahim Kasim, were sentenced to death. Immediately after the rally they were taken to an execution ground on the city's outskirts, made to kneel, and shot through the base of the skull from close quarters. (This is the standard method of public execution in China.) Their bodies were not returned to their families. In July a second rally was held at the stadium and shown on television

The Taklamakan desert: the camel train of the 1993 Anglo–Chinese expedition tacks up a dune ridge. Often described as the most hostile desert on earth, the Taklamakan is as beautiful as it is intimidating, a waterless ocean of sand which echoes the great sea that filled the Tarim basin in prehistoric times.

Remains of ancient Niya: timbers of an 1,800-year-old dwelling preserved by the dry climate. Once this was an attractive riverside town inhabited by Buddhists of Indo-European descent. The shrinking of the glaciers in the mountains to the south, or a sudden change in the river's course, left the town high and dry, forcing the people to abandon it some time between the third and fifth centuries AD.

'Cherchen Man': one of the well-
preserved Taklamakan mummies,
naturally embalmed by the desert
sand. Nearly 6 feet tall, with brown
hair, beard and moustache, this
3,000-year-old body is proof that the
earliest settlers of Xinjiang had no
racial affinity with the Chinese.

The abduction of Lady Wenji: she was seized by the Xiongnu 'barbarians' from her father's house in Honan in about AD 195, and carried off to Inner Mongolia. Her captor, a nomad commander, looks back at his unhappy prize in this scene from a fourteenth-century scroll now in the Metropolitan Museum of Art, New York. Copied from a Song dynasty scroll, it illustrates the horror which the home-loving Chinese have of exile. Wenji is a national heroine because, when a delegation arrived twelve years later to ransom her, she decided to leave her barbarian husband and children and return to China.

The Fragrant Concubine: a version of the portrait by the Jesuit priest Castiglione. The legend is that Iparhan, a Kashgari girl, was taken for the imperial harem of the Emperor Qianlong in about 1760. For Uighurs she symbolizes their unwilling subjection to inner China; to the Han, however, she is evidence of the union of east and west.

The victorious Zuo Zongtang: the general whose recapture of Xinjiang from Yakub Beg in 1877 put him into the pantheon of Chinese commanders. To overcome the formidable obstacles of distance and terrain he spent six years making his military preparations: they included borrowing money from a British bank.

Soldiers of Yakub Beg's palace guard: recruited from all over central Asia, their various physiognomies delighted the British delegation from India that went to woo Yakub in 1873. But they were much resented by the local people, who were taxed heavily to pay for them.

Governor Yang Zengxin: described as having 'the greatest mind in China' he was also said to be the most absolute ruler on earth. Yang kept the peace in Xinjiang from 1911 until his assassination in 1928. A smooth mandarin who made a deep impression on the English missionary ladies who met him, he was as ruthless as a Mafia boss.

The 'Baby General' Ma Zhongying: the Chinese Muslim warlord who rampaged through Xinjiang in the 1930s. A soldier at 14 and a commander at 15, he was still only 21 when he took over leadership of the Turki revolt in Xinjiang. Vain, naïve and merciless, but also charismatic, he was worshipped by his men for his physical courage and prowess. 'A mystery to everyone, perhaps even to himself . . . his real loyalty was probably to the vision he had of himself as a new Tamerlane.'

Statue of the Great Helmsman, Mao Zedong: his ethnic chauvinism still casts a long shadow over the Turkis of Xinjiang. Mao's treatment of them after 1949 became increasingly harsh. The statue, one of the largest of him in China, dominates People's Square in Kashgar which the Chinese are trying to establish as the new centre of the city.

A border guard in fraternizing mood: a scene from the Tajik enclave in the mountainous south-west corner of the autonomous region. Han Chinese regard the minority peoples with a mixture of fear and fascination, as attractively exotic but also as primitive and 'unpatriotic'. Official policy towards them has since 1949 been mostly repressive, with only brief periods of tolerance.

Harry Wu, graduate of the gulag: his crime was to be the son of a Shanghai banker, and it took the Chinese state nineteen years to 're-educate' him from his 'rightist thinking'. His example shows how easy it was to gain admission to the labour camps, how difficult to get out again. A refugee to the US, he bravely returned three times to China to gather information on the gulag which, until recently, was the principal method of colonizing Xinjiang.

General Riza Bekin, a leader of the Uighurs in exile: a nephew of the former Emir of Khotan, he escaped Xinjiang with his family as a boy in 1934. Now retired from the Turkish army, he is prominent in the campaign for Uighur rights. The picture was taken at the small mosque in Istanbul which houses a centre for Xinjiang exiles.

Young Han migrants head west: a chance to refill the tea mug at Lanzhou railway station in Gansu. Thousands of immigrants are pouring into Xinjiang every day, especially since the railway was extended to Kashgar. They get preference in jobs and housing, putting the local people out of work. Although official census figures show the Uighurs to be the biggest racial group in Xinjiang, the Han Chinese may now be an absolute majority.

Han Chinese playing chess in Urumchi: the provincial capital, once known as 'the town in the desert where camels drown in the streets', has become a modern Chinese city, dominated by skyscrapers in fanciful postmodern style. Uighurs make up only 13 per cent of its population and are confined mainly to an area in the south of the city.

The shadow of Islam: women chatting in old Kashgar. Though religion is an important part of their culture, the Muslims of Xinjiang are not known for their zealotry. Yet the state, obsessed with the threat posed by 'splittists' and 'terrorists', regards Islam as one of the greatest obstacles to maintaining China's unity.

the next day: in the film armed soldiers can be seen lining the top of the stands, which suggests that the crowd of 4,000 may not have been entirely voluntary. On this occasion twenty-seven men were sentenced; nine of them were executed and three others were given suspended death sentences. Unusually for Xinjiang, one of those executed was a Chinese, accused of theft, and one was a Chinese Muslim, accused of drug-dealing.

Twenty days after the Gulja demonstration, three bombs went off in Urumchi, causing civilian casualties. On 7 March, another exploded on a bus in Beijing, killing two people and wounding eight. Eight Uighurs accused of planting bombs were executed, and a crackdown across the province followed. The *Xinjiang Daily* claimed that more than a thousand 'separatists' or 'terrorists' had been denounced and arrested in just three cities: Urumchi, Khotan and Aksu.[31] In July the head of the regional Communist Party, Wang Lequan, announced that 17,000 officials had been sent to villages, workplaces and farms to carry out propaganda and education against 'separatists'.

In Gulja three businessmen were arrested for talking about the demonstration to a group of foreign journalists who visited the city shortly after the march. The reporters were expelled from China. The businessmen were reportedly given prison sentences of between fifteen and eighteen years for passing 'secret' information to foreigners. In April 2002, a Chinese taxi-driver in Gulja who has lived in the city for a long time told me that the march had consisted of a lot of young unemployed Uighurs. They had posed no threat to the authorities, who had greatly overreacted. 'I have always got on with the Uighurs,' he added, 'and the demonstration made no difference to my opinion of them.'

As for the *meshrep* leader Abdulhelil Abdumejit who was arrested during the march, it is said that he was beaten, interrogated and tortured. He was held in jail without charge or trial until, in October 2000, three and a half years after the event, it was reported that he had been tortured to death in Chapchal prison, and his body taken under heavy guard to a cemetery and buried in a shallow grave. His family were not allowed to see the body or visit the grave.[32] Exiles claimed that 162 people were shot dead by Chinese security forces between February and June, several hundred were sentenced to death, thousands of young people were left crippled by bullet wounds or torture, and 1,600 were still missing. Many thousands more fled across the border to Kazakhstan.

After Gulja, there were no more marches. Instead, a new militant opposition emerged, attacking military targets, seizing weapons and occasionally detonating bombs to terrorize and kill Han Chinese settlers.

Reports of these attacks are sketchy, and largely unconfirmed. Towards the end of 1997 or early in 1998, an armaments factory at Korla was said to have been robbed of 20,000 Kalashnikovs and millions of rounds of ammunition. In August 1998, an army airbase near Kucha was attacked by Uighurs: using a tracked armoured vehicle mounted with a small gun they sabotaged 24 helicopter gunships. About a hundred and fifty people were killed on each side. The same year there were raids on police stations, arsenals and prisons. Weapons seemed to be circulating freely in the south. 'Everyone has weapons here,' a military officer admitted in 1999 to a researcher who found Khotan plastered with posters calling on people to hand in their weapons.[33] A guided missile base south of Korla was attacked in February that year and twenty-one soldiers were killed, six wounded and a large number of vehicles destroyed.[34]

A 'massive accident' causing serious casualties in a motorcade of the armed police was reported by the Xinjiang police headquarters on 20 March 1999. The accident had happened three days before in the suburbs of a city called Changji, north-west of Urumchi, while the motorcade was driving out to the Shihezi highway. At first the police blamed a mechanical failure in the steering of one of the vehicles, which sent it off the road into a ravine 130 feet deep. But six days later Wang Lequan, the Party Secretary of the province, told the victims' families that the accident was the work of separatists, that the dead were 'martyrs', and that each would get 200,000 yuan in compensation. The relatives were warned not to talk about the attack to outsiders. A Western monitoring group later said the authorities had positively identified the attack as the work of an armed nationalist organization which had planted explosives at a bend in the road, detonated either by a timer or remote control, and which destroyed the first and second vehicles in the column.[35]

An even bigger blast killed 60 people and wounded more than

300 in an Urumchi street on 9 September 2000. The authorities blamed it on a lorry which was transporting old explosives intended for destruction. Witnesses said the accident happened near a bridge being built in a district where houses were being demolished. Overseas newspapers raised the possibility of a terrorist attack.[36]

The truth about these bomb attacks is hard to establish. Explosives are generally easy to obtain in China and some of the unexplained blasts round the country were probably the work of peasants settling scores with each other. In Xinjiang they could have been due to land disputes with Han settlers. Some, like the bus bombs in Urumchi and in Beijing, plainly had a political motive. Whatever the case, after 11 September 2001, all explosions were likely to be ascribed to 'Uighur terrorism'.[37]

At times during the 1990s it looked as if the authorities were going out of their way to provoke the minorities, as if seeking to protect themselves by getting their retaliation in first. By any standards – especially by Western standards – reprisals against those who challenged the status quo were severe.

Judicial shortcuts are common, even traditional, in China. Current practice includes: arresting suspects' families, jailing suspects without trial, dispensing with defence lawyers, reaching verdicts in secret 'adjudication committees', handing down long sentences for political dissent, persecuting religious believers and hunting down pregnant women.

In Xinjiang, however, the repression goes deeper. The province has earned a reputation for vengeful treatment of dissidents which recalls Stalinist Russia at its worst. Treason can take the most trivial forms: insulting the government; using the term 'Eastern Turkestan'; planting the Eastern Turkestan flag; taking part in demonstrations; copying or distributing banned religious newspapers; organizing religious classes; possessing banned tapes of poems or songs; writing plays and poems with a political message; passing secret information to foreigners (such as journalists); publishing a history of the Uighurs in Chinese abroad; fleeing abroad; reading a banned foreign magazine; reading a newspaper; and swearing at a Han Chinese.

In order to ferret out such offences, surveillance is necessary. Informers are essential. For this the police rely on local 'security committees' which operate in every parish (*xiang*) and city block. They are the so-called 'mass line' of police work. Not even Stalin thought of this.[38] The Public Security Bureau, which is organized on military lines into brigades, regiments and battalions, has agents disguised as employees attached to every factory, school, business and government agency.

The readiness of the security forces to shoot unarmed civilians has been illustrated. What has not been described is the torture routinely inflicted on suspects. Torture is said to be widespread in China, in spite of the country's adherence to the United Nations Convention against it, but it has taken a particularly ugly form in Xinjiang and Tibet. In addition to the usual beatings and kickings, the delivery of shocks by electric batons, the shackling and suspending of victims in painful ways and the sticking of needles under nails or the extraction of nails with pliers, reports suggest that refinements peculiar to Xinjiang have been developed. They include injecting substances to induce incoherence or insanity; stuffing pepper or chilli powder into the mouth, nose and genital organs; and inserting horse hair or barbed wire into the urethra. One man tortured in Urumchi said he was made to wear a kind of metal helmet to prevent him trying to dull the pain by battering his head against the walls of the torture chamber. A former court official from Xinjiang told Amnesty that 90 per cent of defendants complained of being tortured to extract confessions. While newspaper reports of police being prosecuted for using torture are common in other provinces of China, they are strikingly absent from the Xinjiang press.[39]

Xinjiang is the only province in China known to continue executing political prisoners.[40] Between 1997 and 1999 Amnesty recorded 210 death sentences and 190 executions in the province, mainly of Uighurs convicted of political and religious 'crimes'. In succeeding years, the execution of Uighurs continued at the same rate; one historian has calculated that this makes them, per capita, ten times more vulnerable to the death penalty than the Han Chinese.[41]

Specific crimes for which the death penalty was to be used were listed in a handbook of April 2001 for one of the leadership's periodic law-and-order campaigns. In Guangdong province, for example, economic crimes – theft, fraud and corruption – were to be the primary target. In Shanghai, executions were to help clean up the city for visitors to a meeting of the Asia-Pacific Economic Council. In Xinjiang, they were to 'solve the separatist problem' in two years. Thousands more Uighurs were imprisoned on charges of nationalism, separatism and religious extremism, and the torture and disappearance of Uighurs became commonplace.

The authorities' desire for law and order in Xinjiang is understandable. But the extraordinary severity of their regime there seems to require some other explanation.

History shows that alien races make the Chinese both fearful and contemptuous. Perhaps it should not surprise us that officials, especially those new to the province, have racialist attitudes – that the bureaucracy suffers from 'institutionalized racism', to use a phrase recently fashionable in Britain. Those attitudes are engrained in the psyche of the Chinese. Nor does the structure of government help: the tone is set from the top, by people with little or no experience of the region; officials live in fear of their superiors, from the village policeman all the way up to the Party Secretary; local initiative is no more encouraged than it was in the days of the Emperor and his mandarins.

Fear of Islam is the most obvious symptom. Chinese officialdom sees behind the mask of the religious zealot the scheming traitor who seeks to 'split the motherland'. That there are some religious zealots among the 9 million Muslims of Xinjiang is certain. That there are many people who would like to see an independent 'Eastern Turkestan' is equally certain. But the picture consistently painted by the authorities is crude, and their analysis of the problem is both naïve and un-selfcritical.

Although their prose is a lot less lively, official reports are only echoing the standard Han view of the Turki Muslims passed down for generations. They are different, and therefore untrustworthy. They are religious, and therefore volatile. It is a view typified by the urbane Aitchen Wu, who wrote in the 1930s: 'To see indolent Moslem farmers, living a prosperous life in a fertile valley, with little to distress them and much to bless, change at the call of their Ahuns to wild fanatics eager for the blood of unbelievers, is to despair of the human race.' Economic pressure was not enough, he said, to explain why these shrewd, peaceful, even passive people, given to laughter and song, were so ready to follow their fiery preachers and to commit atrocities to 'stagger the imagination'. The answer, he believed, lay in their history. Their ancestors had come with sword in one hand and Quran in the other, handing down 'a terrible heritage of hate . . . When once some slight on their faith is seen or imagined they are turned to raving fanatics, capable of any deed of blood and shame.'[42]

The religious factor should not be underestimated: the history of Xinjiang teaches that. Yakub Beg used religion cynically to bolster his power; the short-lived republic which came out of Khotan in 1933 enforced it to show its hatred of the Chinese; the Gulja republic of 1944 tried hard to keep it at arm's length. Western diplomacy has often failed because diplomats – not least American diplomats – take it as an article of faith that religion should play no part in politics. How much truer that is of the Han Chinese cadre, trained to see religion as a mind-poisoning heresy, a superstitious distraction from material progress.

But to recognize the importance of religion – especially Islam, which has trouble accommodating secular authority – means understanding the psychology of believers. It means understanding, for example, that pogrom and persecution are counter-productive. Though he shared his countrymen's view of Muslims as hysterical fanatics, Aitchen Wu criticized General Zuo Zongtang's treatment of the Muslims after 1877: 'Later opinion agrees that tribes can be brought under a stable system of government without the deliberate destruction of customs they hold dear and which are probably far better suited to them than the alien precision of Chinese rule.'[43] Wu recognized that misgovernment was one of the causes of the Muslim revolt of the 1930s. Ill-chosen magistrates administered the law unfairly, and the revolt succeeded because the provincial government combined injustice with inefficiency. 'It was no upheaval of primal forces; it was the product of human folly, and human wisdom might well have avoided it,' he declared.

Communist rule, even one as non-Marxist as China's has

become, has its own peculiar inhibitions which make objective analysis difficult. It has something to do with its severely bureaucratic structure; it has something to do with the narrow mentality of the people who make it their living; it has something to do with the sanctity of dogma. Analysis is about confirming, not questioning, the Party line.

One example of this inhibition is that for many years violent protests in Xinjiang went unreported, or were disguised in vague terms as 'accidents', 'hooliganism' or 'sabotage'. Occasionally, as in the case of the Gulja riot, the protest was too large to hide and then it was broadcast – but only to disseminate an official version of events. In December 2001, two months after the terrorist attacks on the World Trade Center in New York and the Pentagon in Washington, the official line suddenly changed. The *Xinjiang Daily* published a list of terrorist acts it said had been committed in the province during the previous decade. The list included explosions, assassinations, arson, poisonings and riots.

The change was politic. With the whole world suddenly afraid of what Islamic extremists might do next, and with the American President George W. Bush declaring a 'war against terrorism' to justify a military attack on the Taliban in Afghanistan, it became conveniently easy for Beijing to justify a purge in its own backyard. Now all Muslims, and especially the majority Uighurs, were potential terrorists. Where formerly the Party had blamed separatists disguised as religious demagogues, now it blamed Islamic fundamentalists seeking to overthrow the state.

The malign influence of foreigners has been an enduring scapegoat for internal trouble. At one time the foreign enemy was 'socialist imperialism' (the Soviet Union), at another it was Uighur exiles in Turkey, and at yet another 'pan-Turkist' fanatics in other parts of central Asia; and nearly all the time it was, as the minutes of a Politburo meeting in 1996 show, 'international counter-revolutionary forces led by the United States of America'. The need to see a foreign plot behind every domestic disturbance is an old Chinese – and not only Chinese – habit. As the former British consul at Urumchi observed in 1945, the Chinese authorities refused to accept that there were 'ample causes purely internal to [Xinjiang]' to explain events.[44]

Behind the banal, off-the-peg language, there were genuine concerns. The USSR, and before it Tsarist Russia, did have enormous influence in Xinjiang; Uighur exiles did – and do – lobby for an independent 'Eastern Turkestan'; the Americans did lead the field in making an issue of human rights inside China. Some Uighurs were, indeed, found at the al-Qaeda terrorist training camps in Afghanistan. There is a 'pan-Turkist' movement – although few people take it seriously. No doubt some Islamic books, tapes and funds have been brought in from countries like Iran and Saudi Arabia. Weapons and explosives may also have been smuggled in – although there are plenty of both already inside the country.

But another question has to be asked: was the enemy without blown up to monstrous proportions in order to disguise a fundamental weakness within?

An internal research paper on separatism produced in 1993 (whose account of the Baren riot was quoted earlier), followed the usual Party logic.[45] It admitted that there were weaknesses but put those down to a failure to carry out the Party line vigorously enough. 'We had not done enough religious work, united front work and public education work.' That is, the failure was due entirely to lack of propaganda. The study gave examples of discrimination by Muslims against other Muslims – against those who did not go to the mosque, or who did not fast, or who refused to wear the veil. It had nothing to say about Han discrimination against Muslims. It talked of the Islamic 'private courts' which convicted offenders and 'arbitrarily beat them', but it made no mention of the arbitrary detentions, convictions, torture and executions practised by agents of the state.

The authors of the study observed, correctly, that what happens outside China affects the temperature of nationalism within. The obvious case in point was the sudden collapse of the Soviet Union which gave independence to the five republics of Kazakhstan, Uzbekistan, Kyrgyzstan, Tajikistan and Turkmenistan – three of them sharing a border with Xinjiang. The document's authors did not speak of domestic demands for democracy or of the peasant revolts which were occurring elsewhere in China against punitive taxation and government corruption. Nor did they consider whether the mass appeal of phenomena like the Falun Gong cult might be a symptom of spiritual frustration. The nearest the researchers came to self-criticism was to mention some 'improper restriction of interactions between people' and 'severe control of small businesses' which had upset Uighur traders in the bazaars.

Using the language of war and struggle, the analysts itemized the lessons of their research: to continue the teaching of 'Marxist ethnic theory', especially among the young; to follow Chairman Mao's guideline and make the economy the first priority; to 'firmly trust and rely on the cadres and mass of all nationalities' (that is, ethnic groups); and to 'strengthen the leadership of the Party'.

Those conclusions simply echoed the standard liturgy of the leadership. In their own, more vernacular, summary the authors took a few liberties. Collectively, the comrades were chided for being lulled into too relaxed a view of the threat. The dangers of separatism were to be borne continually in mind: not overstated in case 'we might fall into a panic and undermine the courage of the army', nor on the other hand dismissed as merely 'the naughtiness of a few kids who cannot make big waves'. Some comrades, they wrote, had been arguing thus: 'When we didn't mention the importance of ethnic unity . . . everything was fine. Now, we talk about ethnic unity every year, and we have problems every year.' That, too was a mistake. Most importantly, separatism had to be nipped in the bud, villages had to be watched as closely as the towns, and border officials had to be more vigilant.

The leaked minutes of a 1996 Politburo meeting chaired by President Jiang Zemin displayed a poverty of thinking which went a long way to explain why, in spite of all the propaganda, the riot control, the informers, the sentencing and the public spending, Xinjiang continued to be such a problem. Marked 'top secret' and written in constipated bureaucratic style, the document purported to be the record of a meeting on 19 March 1996, when the 'political-legal commission' of the Central Committee delivered a report on Xinjiang.[46]

What it showed, once again, was an exaggerated reliance on slogans ('holding high the banner of defending ethnic unity'), on training Party cadres and soldiers to be more reliable, on shutting down 'illegal organizations', on censoring the media and textbooks, and – a curious detail – on vetting school exchange programmes with foreign countries. Other sections called for better training of the police, and more efficient running of the labour camps and prisons. Special mention was made of the Xinjiang Production and Construction Corps, the Han-dominated para-military development agency whose unique status will be described in the next chapter. There was a rare piece of good general advice, however. The authorities were urged not to treat every incident as an ethnic one, nor to allow conflicts to become ethnic in character.

In June 2001, the Chinese government issued a report on popular revolts in eleven provinces, and singled out Xinjiang for special mention. Unrest was on the increase, it said, due to the growth of Islamic fundamentalism. That in turn was the fault of the Taliban regime in Afghanistan, which China accused of indoctrinating Uighurs and supplying them with arms.[47]

Missing from all these analyses, however, is any hint that the authorities in Xinjiang might be abusing their powers. There seems to be no qualm, no hesitation, no flicker of doubt within the Party about the wisdom of its own policy, which amounts to this: punish the Uighurs for the slightest sign of dissent, and when they protest, punish them harder. There is nothing to show that the Party can see what is obvious to anyone who visits Xinjiang: that the Uighurs have been reduced to second-class members of the 'great Chinese family'. Absent, too, is any recognition of the anger caused by Han Chinese immigration, a wholesale transfer of population from the east which began as exile and which now flourishes on the foundations of China's desert gulag. It is time to look at the labour camps of Xinjiang.

7

Skeletons in the Sand

IN A DEPRESSION in the sand, a few hundred yards from the desert track that winds down from the Altun Tagh mountains, across the southern edge of the Lop desert and through the ancient city of Miran, a foreign traveller recently made an unpleasant discovery.

He was an American zoologist, and when he saw a large bone lying on the sand in front of him, he knew that it belonged to no animal. Shaped like a long-tailed '7', or a roughly cut walking-stick, it was readily identifiable as a human femur. Digging with his hands, he brought up more pieces – arm bones and knuckles. Puzzled and unnerved, the American covered up the remains. A few hours later he took me to the site. Digging just below the surface we found the skeletons of perhaps a dozen bodies scattered between tamarisk mounds. One of the skulls was that of a child, and it had an earring still attached to it. Beside another skull lay two small-calibre bullet cases.

The climate of Xinjiang may be hostile to the living, but it is unusually kind to the dead – the wonderfully preserved mummies of the Taklamakan are proof of that. So these skeletons were a mystery. If they were from a graveyard, then why were the bones so clean? Had they been uncovered by the constant drifting of the sands, picked clean by animals, and buried again by the wind? But if the bones were old, it was difficult to explain the bullet cases. Perhaps a party of travellers had been set upon by bandits, robbed and shot, and left to die.

There was another possibility. About a mile to the north-west, beyond a Buddhist stupa, was a long, high fence and a belt of conifer trees. Behind the fence is a place called No. 36 Regiment

Farm, which once contained – and may still contain – a prison camp. Were these the skeletons of former prisoners, taken out of the camp and summarily executed? If so, why was the little girl with the earring among them?

In Chinese pinyin romanization, Miran is written 'Milan', an incongruous name for what must be one of the most desolate places on earth. To the east lies a bleak expanse of black gobi, upon which pointless piles of stones have been raised – make-work, perhaps, for truculent prisoners. After descending the pass from the Altun Tagh mountains, our small party had halted on this plain. To the south stretched a further barren plain with a disconsolate vista of mountains, the northern rampart of the Tibetan plateau. A few miles westwards lay the first dunes of the Taklamakan sand ocean; to the north-east could be seen the salt flats of Lop Nor, a vast shimmering mirage of the lake that was once there, and which was, until recently, China's nuclear testing ground. After half an hour a lorry appeared from the west – the first vehicle we had seen for a week – full of cheerful uniformed men carrying shovels. Some of our party said they were illicit gold-diggers, off to try their luck in the mountains; to me they looked much like any other Chinese military detail.

Miran guards a branch of the southern Silk Road which runs through desert and mountain towards Dunhuang and mainland China. Chiang Kai-shek planned to make it his grand military highway to the west. Nothing was built but a few lonely milestones in a mountain corridor. Traces of ancient Miran, a Buddhist settlement which flourished in the third century AD, are, however, plentiful. On both sides the desert track is flanked by a fine collection of yardangs, eroded remains of an ancient clay river bed; they stand as usual with their heads to the prevailing wind, like ships at anchor. Doorways have been cut in many of them, to make dwellings or byres; others were plainly used as kilns, for the sand in front of them is littered with shards of pottery, glazed and unglazed. More importantly, the site is dotted with crumbling stupas whose frescoes and statues show that the influence of Greek art reached even to Miran. The stupa to the north of the spot where the skeletons lie was identified by Aurel Stein early in 1907 as part of a *vihara* or monastery. From it he took some colossal stucco heads of the Buddha. The rounded capital of a classical column can just be seen poking through the sand piled against the eastern face. On the walls of a circular passage inside a phallic-shaped stupa by the desert track, Stein found frescoes of a beauty which astounded him. 'There was a dado formed of angels' heads, quite Graeco-Roman in style and with an Oriental tinge so slight that it might have been painted no further off than, say, Alexandria', he wrote.[1] In another he discovered a mural that had been signed with the name 'Tita'. And Miran is still dominated by the high rampart of a fort built in the eighth or ninth century during the time of the Tibetan empire. Stein excavated a rubbish dump in its back settlements, uncovering two hundred Tibetan documents.

No. 36 Regiment Farm lies across the track. Our party had been told to stay away from it, so we pitched tents for two nights near the Tibetan fort. Since the only way to reach the southern Taklamakan road was through the farm, however, on the third day we drove up to the big gates. They swung open to reveal another world.

For a moment it seemed a mirage – a Potemkin village or a film set made of painted boards propped up from behind. But it was real enough. Here, in the middle of nowhere, was a proper little township of tarmac roads and street lights, neat lines of offices and stores, with living quarters behind. It was as orderly as the army barracks at Aldershot. Near the central crossroads stood a building that looked like regimental headquarters, its roof festooned with aerials and satellite dishes. The secret of the camp's survival was revealed as we emerged on the far side: a concrete-lined canal ran beside the road, and down it rushed a torrent of water from the distant Kunlun mountains. But there was something odd about it: for mile after mile, the water appeared to be pouring uphill towards us. Was this another triumph of socialist central planning? The miracle was explained by an optical illusion: the ridge of the distant mountains sloped down to the left and gave us the impression that we were descending, rather than ascending, towards them.

Inside the wire the convoy halted while one of the Chinese jeep drivers (whom I had privately dubbed the Secret Policeman) went off, presumably to make a report. There were fields of cotton on all sides, bounded by lines of poplars. A few people cycled by. But what was most remarkable about No. 36 Regiment Farm was that nowhere, neither here in the fields, nor in the streets, was a single Uighur face to be seen. In a region where Uighurs predominate, every person, old and young, was a Han Chinese.

While we waited, an old man came down the road driving a donkey cart. I asked him where the labour camp was. He pointed vaguely behind me and passed on. It wasn't evidence of much, but in fact No. 36 Regiment Farm is the first link in a chain of former concentration camps which extends north and west along the banks of the Tarim and Yarkand rivers to Kashgar, and into the Dzungarian basin where they make a line along the former Soviet border. Like ugly beads on a necklace, this chain of 185 settlements is a vital part of China's gulag.

And that is why every face inside No. 36 Regiment Farm is Chinese. The people living here – reportedly 25,000 of them – are the children and grandchildren of exiles. Their parents or grandparents were sent here as soldiers to secure China's western borders against the threat of Soviet Russia; or they were banished as criminals; or they were among the hundreds of thousands of innocent citizens condemned for crimes of thought or speech against the revolutionary ideology of the People's Republic. From camps like these, very few were ever allowed to return. Miran, an artificial oasis in the wilderness, the remotest place of exile in China, is what their children think of as home.

Nothing is new under the Chinese sun. The Communist liberators may have raised to perfection the system of forced labour in exile, but they did not invent it. Exile to China's far west has been going on for two thousand years. The idea of banishing dissident officials started with the Qin in the third century BC: and the greater the offence, the greater the distance.

As a form of punishment, exile was doubly appealing to the earlier emperors. It made them appear benevolent by mitigating the death penalty, and it terrified their subjects into submission: for the Chinese are famous homebodies who fear exile more than death and have preferred to commit suicide rather than face it.

The pain of exile is movingly expressed in the story of Lady Wenji, whose abduction by the Xiongnu was described in

Chapter 2. The far west was regarded with particular horror by the educated classes. They passed through the Jiayuguan gate at the end of the Great Wall heaving with sobs and sighs. They stepped from the land of men to the land of ghosts and devils. Some scratched their names on the walls of the gate's narrow mouth – graffiti which were not, however, included in a recent restoration. The poet Hong Lianji, exiled under the Qing, lamented:

> For half a lifetime, never one idle stride.
> Scaling the Five Peaks left my temples hoary white.
> But now, outside the wall, for ten thousand li,
> East, west, north, south – Heaven's Mountains all I see.[2]

In those periods when the Emperor had jurisdiction over the far west, exile served a third purpose. It supported the garrisons in their job of keeping the barbarian nomads at bay. Long before the Manchu and Communist conquerors thought of it, the Han dynasty emperor Wudi in the second century BC set up military farms and created paramilitary peasants, deploying convicts to grow food for his soldiers at Hami, Turfan and Korla. Later settlers who also came by administrative fiat included herders from the Russian steppe, farmers from the Tarim and criminals from mainland China sent to repopulate Dzungaria after the Qing dynasty massacres. A colony of 10,000 Manchus whom Aitchen Wu found living on the south bank of the Ili river arrived by another kind of accident – one that strangely pre-echoed the gulag. These Manchus were descended from soldiers who had been sent by the Emperor Qianlong to guard the frontier with the promise that they would be relieved after ten years. It had taken them three years to reach Xinjiang with their wives, families and household chattels in tow. But when the decade was up, they were simply forgotten. Wu observed that these lost colonists spoke the purest Manchurian in China; everywhere else, the language had been forgotten.

Soldiers sometimes chose to stay behind in the west. Most of the voluntary emigrants, however, were Chinese merchants who, sniffing an opportunity, followed on the heels of the armies periodically sent out to impose order on the natives. It will be recalled that merchants were not allowed to fraternize with Muslims, in case they offended them, or to live in Turki townships. Chinese civil servants, likewise, were barred from holding office in the province during most of the Qing dynasty. It was not until 1830 that they, along with soldiers and farmers, were permitted to bring their families to Xinjiang and put down roots. The reasons for this change of heart foreshadowed the Communists' own logic: the more Han there were, the more control the government would have, and the weaker the Muslims would be. Even so, it was not until late in the nineteenth century that any serious attempt was made to colonize Xinjiang, and it was largely unsuccessful. Under the Republic, settlers were sent to the west with the promise of government aid, in the hope that they would alter the demographic balance. But the scheme was limited and there were few takers.

The Communists, too, tried voluntary methods at first. We have seen in Chapter 5 that in the idealistic early days of Liberation many thousands of pioneering volunteers made the journey west. But later attempts to recruit settlers were no more successful than those of previous regimes. One scheme involved transferring 433,000 people to the borderlands, with expenses: it was not long before many were trying to go home again. Another project, in the summer of 1956, saw 45,000 young men and women drafted into Xinjiang's farms, ranches and factories. A more refined programme in the late 1950s offered new homes to young, able-bodied and politically reliable migrants. Reception centres were set up for them in Xinjiang, and counsellors were sent out from the emigrants' home provinces to stiffen flagging morale.[3]

A Han doctor exiled to Jiayuguan at the start of the Cultural Revolution in 1966 explained how difficult it was to acclimatize to life in the west. He told a Western reporter fourteen years later that he and his wife had found things hard. 'But we have little choice. Doctors are needed here. We have petitioned the government to let us move; we have distinguished contacts trying to arrange a transfer, but it's an open question whether we shall ever be able to leave. Some people like it here. It doesn't rain much.'[4]

Right up to the end of the century, the Party sought opportunities to swing the racial balance in favour of the Han. In 1992, for instance, the city of Kashgar 'offered' to take up to 100,000 of the 1 million peasants who were to be flooded out by the vast Three

Gorges hydro-electric project on the Yangzi river. The news was greeted with outrage by a delegation of Muslims then on a visit from western Turkestan. Beijing withdrew the offer after a mission from Russia's president Boris Yeltsin, and the promise of a reduction in the number of Russian Federation border troops.

When all other schemes failed, exile, in its various guises, proved to be the answer.

The Manchus had anticipated the physical and ideological architecture of Mao's terrible gulag. It was they who used the refrain 'multiple ends by a single means' (*yi ju liang de*) to justify the banishment of tens of thousands of criminals and political dissidents to Xinjiang in the years after their 1759 conquest. Colonization, defence and *Lebensraum* were the ends; exile was the means.

Under the Communist government the gulag became both the prime agency of Han Chinese control and the vehicle for systematic colonization. The camp regime followed the imperial model closely, and Xinjiang continued to be a prized dumping ground. The concentration of prisoners may not have been as dense as in the bleak plateau of neighbouring Qinghai – one ex-prisoner claimed that a third of that province's population was made up of resettled prisoners and their families – but Xinjiang was strategically and economically more important.

The Communists created two kinds of labour camp. The first, run by the Public Security Bureau, are known as *laogai*, an abbreviation of *laodong gaizao*, meaning 'manual labour reform' and usually rendered 'reform through labour'. These are places for real criminals as well as for 'thought criminals', and they involve long – and often in practice indefinite – sentences handed down by a court. Prisoners who have served their sentences are then either detained for further 'reform' or are declared 'free workers' or 'free convicts' – free, that is, to stay on in the camps until they die.

During the anti-Rightist crackdown of 1957 and the Great Leap Forward of 1958, Mao introduced a second type of punishment called *laojiao*, or 're-education through labour'. The re-education camps are designed to correct 'mistakes' rather than punish socalled crimes. They are run by local authorities, and the standard sentence is supposed to be three years. *Laojiao* is a speedy way of dealing with political opponents, a form of administrative detention which has no need of courts and lawyers, charges and trials. Recently, the re-education camps have been much used against religious offenders, whether Muslim mullahs or members of the Falun Gong spiritual sect.

Reform through labour, or through education, it makes little difference. Both pervert the benign concept of rehabilitation in a cruel and arbitrary way to put people out of circulation. The sentiment behind the system, whether cynical or naïve, is reminiscent of the slogan used by the Nazis at Auschwitz: *Arbeit macht frei* ('Work makes you free'). A wrought-iron sign bearing those words hung over the main camp entrance through which Jews, Gypsies, homosexuals, political undesirables and other renegades were marched during the Second World War.

The poet of Auschwitz, Primo Levi, has unforgettably described what happens to human beings when they are reduced to the level of animals, fit only for hard labour, medical experimentation or slaughter. Zhang Xianliang, 22 years old when he was thrown into a labour camp in Ningxia, the Muslim province between Inner Mongolia and Gansu, is the poet of the Chinese gulag. He sees with the same ironical and unselfpitying eyes that Primo Levi did.

How, asks Zhang, does a dying man reduced to a diet of grass soup and weighing less than seven stone manage to carry nearly his own weight in earth clods? How does he find freedom through work? By remembering what it was like to weed the paddy field for the previous three months: standing up to the waist in water, all day and half the night, until his legs were inflamed and blistered, and itched with an itch 'that worked its way into the soul, an itch that drove men to madness'.[5]

In Western penal theory, a prison sentence is supposed to serve three purposes: deterrence, restitution and rehabilitation. The third leg of the tripod is usually the weakest, as reoffending rates show. But at least the convict's sentence is fixed, and the rules of parole are laid down.

In China, where everything is permissible in the name of rehabilitation ('reform'), sentences are prolonged at whim, according to the prison authorities' notions about the prisoner's attitude. And once released he may be re-arrested at any time. The Communist

Party, like the Manchu court, regarded the primary purpose of prison as moral regeneration – an apparently humane objective which took terrible forms in practice. There was one striking difference between them, however. The Manchus treated their prisoners according to their rank, Confucian-style, and the more educated had an easier time of it than common criminals. Under Mao, whose suspicion of intellectuals was pathological, the inverse was true: the higher the class, the harsher the punishment. Someone from the landlord class might get ten years' hard labour for stealing corn from a commune, while a poor peasant would be let off. Less adapted to hard labour, the intellectual 'Rightists', city types with no experience of farming, were regularly beaten for failing to meet their work quotas. Because of the indeterminate nature of their 'crime' they were psychologically vulnerable, and so were offered as targets to the criminal convicts.

Intellectuals got their own back on the peasant convicts by denouncing them in 'struggle' sessions: but they were also quick to denounce each other, says Zhang, himself a 'Rightist', and imprisoned for a poem. Educated prisoners were trapped by their life-long respect for words into believing the rubbish they were made to recite. They feared physical punishment too much to resist the endless probing of the leaders who were 'madly checking out each person's thoughts, sorry only that they could not reach into each brain, scrape out what was there and examine it under a microscope'. They really came to believe that men could live on grass and weeds. Like Primo Levi's 'Mussulmen', they were marked for death. 'Most of the intellectuals', writes Zhang, 'would do their utmost to "continue to be educated" until they died from the effort.'[6]

Political prisoners in China usually come eventually to believe that their thoughts are crimes through an endless process of verbal abuse, written and verbal self-denunciation, and brainwashing. Jean Pasqualini, a French citizen with a Chinese mother who was jailed in 1957 as a foreign spy, has described his instruction by the leader of a study session:

[His] calm rhetoric was tremendously persuasive for a cellful of dejected and hopeless men who knew they were utterly dependent on a bureaucratic judgement to decide their fates. Every day the prisoner was taught to believe that it was not a judicial process . . . that would mitigate his future sentence, but rather his manner – *the way he behaved.* Our relationship with the state was that of a child–parent . . . The child must put his entire trust in the parent because he has no other choice.[7]

Subservient Chinese jurists justify the system by arguing that it is the right of the working class to exercise its 'democratic dictatorship' over class enemies of socialism. But over the past fifty years, what has constituted a correct attitude has been as changeable as the autumn fashions. Many, like Deng Xiaoping, a Mao lieutenant and late ruler of China, have been disgraced and rehabilitated more than once.

The Chinese penal system, which bears comparison with that of Stalin, is as arbitrary as a Kafka nightmare. And entry is all too easy.

Wu Hongda (known in the West as Harry Wu), one of its more famous victims, was by any reckoning a small fish. The son of a Shanghai banker, he was labelled a 'Rightist' because of his bourgeois background while studying at the Geology Institute in Beijing. In 1960, at the age of 23, he was hauled in front of a kangaroo court of classmates and cadres. He was later to describe the scene:

Some people sat stiffly, while others turned awkwardly to look at me. Wang's opening words broke the silence [Wang Jian was the political education officer of Wu's department]: 'Today we meet to criticize the rightist Wu Hongda.' A chorus of allegations sprang from the audience.

'Wu Hongda still refuses to reform himself!'

'He opposes the Party, he must be expelled!'

'Down with Wu Hongda, he must now show us his true face!'

For perhaps twenty minutes the accusations continued. I stared straight ahead until Wang Jian signalled for me to stand. 'According to the request of the masses and with the full authority of the school,' he intoned, 'I now denounce, separate, and expel the rightist Wu Hongda, who has consistently refused to mould himself into a good socialist student and has chosen to remain an enemy of the revolution.'

Precisely at that moment a uniformed Public Security officer appeared at the doorway. 'Representing the people's government of Beijing,' he declared as he stepped to the front desk, 'I sentence the counterrevolutionary rightist Wu Hongda to re-education through labour.' He motioned me forward and pulled a piece of paper from his jacket pocket.[8]

Wu was told to sign the paper, which listed the charges against him, then he was led away. He did not come back for nineteen years. It took the state until 1979 to complete the 're-education' of Harry Wu, through hard labour and starvation in a series of camps.

Harry Wu's evidence is anecdotal but on his release he showed himself fearless in improving his knowledge. Armed only with an American passport, he went back to China three times to film the camps under cover. In 1995 he was caught and detained for two months. On the second visit he found himself outside the school of a prison camp near Aksu to which one of his brothers had been sent thirty-five years before – not as a prisoner but as a teacher. The brother had paid the penalty for being a member of a counter-revolutionary family. Harry Wu's driver parked outside the school, but Wu dared not go in. He later explained that he felt partly responsible for his brother's banishment and that a meeting would have put both of them in danger. 'Let's go,' he told the driver, putting on his dark glasses so that nobody would recognize his face or see his tears.[9]

Wu was a victim of the 1957 anti-Rightist campaign. During the great famine which followed, the labour camps became death camps. The number of inmates swelled again, not just with peasants who stole food, but with political enemies who were overheard complaining about a famine which officially did not exist. For once, penal exiles were no worse off than their families at home: those outside had as little to eat as those inside. Harry Wu tells of an escapee from his last but one camp, the Qinghe farm in Hebei province (where Zhang also spent time), who made his way to the capital, found nothing to eat and turned himself in to the police so that he could be sent back to the farm.

Mao's forcible collectivization of the farmers destroyed agriculture all over China, creating a famine which is estimated to have claimed at least 30 million lives. Prison camp inmates may have had to forage for toads and snakes, or rob food from rats' nests, but now many peasants outside fared even worse, especially in neighbouring Tibet, Qinghai and Gansu. In Ningxia, where the unreformed poet Zhang set a fashion for escaping occasionally in order to forage, some of the mountain people resorted to eating their own children.[10] Other starving peasants migrated to Xinjiang. For by comparison with most regions of China, Xinjiang was fortunate: its oases were fertile, it was underpopulated and it was protected by its irrigation system.

During the Cultural Revolution the labour camps flourished again. At the height of Chairman Mao's war against revolutionary backsliders and real or perceived enemies, the gulag contained 10 million political prisoners, according to Harry Wu. Other estimates at the time gave as many as 20 million. These figures may be too high. The former inmate Jean Pasqualini described the population of the *laogai* as 'colossal',[11] but the real figure is not known.

Until the very recent past, penal exile was a mainstay of the colonization programme. In Xinjiang, moral reform took second place to economic development or 'supporting the borderlands' (*zhi bian*): 'Xinjiang is one of the provinces where our country's *laogai* system plays a comparatively important role,' explained the *Xinjiang Legal Journal* in 1990. 'They [the prisoners] opened desert to make farmland, planted trees to make forests, built roads and bridges, made bricks for buildings, explored mines to extract coal, and manufactured goods.'[12]

The Chinese leadership is shy about the present size of China's gulag. Government sources suggested in early 1995 that 10 million people had been held in prison camps since 1949. Harry Wu estimated between 30 and 40 million people were convicted of political crimes throughout China between 1949 and 1989.[13] Even if government figures are far too low, Wu's are considered too high by scholars, who believe the gulag today has shrunk to fewer than 2 million inmates.

Uighur exiles say the current prison population of Xinjiang, including both labour camps and jails, is 250,000, of whom three-fifths are Uighur political prisoners. Counting is made difficult by the fact that, as in other parts of China, many prisons have a double identity. For instance, the camp near Merket on the western edge of the Taklamakan desert calls itself Pailou Farm but is better known to the authorities as Pailou Labour Reform Detachment. The sign over a factory gate in Urumchi which reads 'Xinjiang No. 3 Machine Tool Works' is code for Autonomous Region No. 1 Prison. The factory probably does make machine tools, but its workers do not go home when the hooter sounds.

On the west bank of the Keriya river, about 20 miles north of Keriya town, is a place described on the map as 'Yutian *xian* agriculture-grass 1 farm'. When in 1993 a group of British army adventurers drove up to the gates of a place in the same locality, seeking help after one of their vehicles had got bogged down, they found high walls, watch-towers and armed guards, and men in the fields wearing leg-irons. It was a *laogai* camp. Yet the prison governor was happy to lend them a bulldozer and 200 of his prisoners to dig the vehicle out.[14]

Two years later, the group of which I was part encountered a *laogai* after a 100-mile walk across the desert. We had been picked up by jeeps and were driving on a narrow rutted track near the junction of the Khotan and Tarim rivers, heading for Aksu. The Secret Policeman was once again in the lead. The track took us past huts of reed and mud, then a small building with bars on the window, until it reached a checkpoint where three policemen stood guard. The place had an abandoned, depressed look; the barrack blocks were cracked and stained, large areas of ground were churned up and littered with building debris; even the fields in which women picked cotton looked exhausted. Lorries plied back and forth, to no apparent purpose, but the central building was decked out in brightly coloured tiles, and two satellite dishes pointed skywards from its roof. The Chinese accompanying us confirmed that this was indeed a *laogai*. But whether it was still taking prisoners, or was housing 'free' workers, was not clear.

As well as the two kinds of camp already described, Xinjiang has a variety of other penal institutions: detention centres, city prisons, prison farms and factories, not to mention – or so it is rumoured – special camps for those with serious diseases, handicaps and deformities.

One thing seems reasonably certain: although the population of

Uighurs and Han Chinese in Xinjiang is about equal, the great majority of prisoners held in the province today are Uighurs. The labour camps built to house exiles from inner China have developed into Han colonies, and in their place has grown up another network of camps and jails whose customers are mainly local people. For it is they, the Muslims, who are now the chief suspects in the crime of counter-revolutionary thinking.

Regiment farms like Miran, described at the beginning of the chapter, show how the penal system has mutated during the half century since Liberation, following the savage twists and turns of Chinese policy. Originally built as concentration camps for defeated Nationalist troops, they were later populated with civilian prisoners from the east, such as landlords and Guomindang officials, who had served their time – the so-called 'free workers' whose only release was death. The job of these former soldiers and convicts was to reclaim the land and provide a ready-made militia in the event of an invasion from the Soviet Union. When the Soviet threat receded in the 1980s, the regiment farms were given a new paramilitary role: domestic riot control.

The regiment farms and prison camps are operated by one of the most powerful and peculiar organizations in China, the Xinjiang Production and Construction Corps. Founded in 1954, the Corps was the chief agency for Han Chinese immigration (see Chapter 5). Today it is the province's biggest economic enterprise and landowner, its largest employer, and a powerful instrument for controlling the Uighurs. It is a state within a state, run by the People's Liberation Army, independent of the provincial government and reporting directly to Beijing. It employs – if that is the right word – between 2 and 3 million workers, a seventh of Xinjiang's population. The tentacles of the Corps spread everywhere. Its capital is the industrial city of Shihezi, north-west of Urumchi. It runs whole cities, such as Korla – an important hub for transport and the oil industry – it farms a third of the arable land in Xinjiang, and it produces 40 per cent of its cotton.[15]

Like any Western agro-industrial conglomerate, the Corps operates farms, forests, mines, factories, canals, reservoirs and transport.

But it is also a welfare state, with its own schools, hospitals, laboratories, pension funds, police force, courts, prisons – and, of course, labour camps. Yet its structure is a military one: it has fourteen divisions, each with their own regiments and companies.

China makes no secret of the purpose of the Corps. In 1977, the Xinhua news agency described it as 'shock brigade in building socialism' whose workers stand 'with rifle in one hand and hoe in the other'. These days, the hoe has been joined by the engineering lathe, and the rifle that used to be aimed at Soviet border troops is used to shoot down Uighur demonstrators. Like the gun-toting Jewish settlers on the Palestinian West Bank, the role of these workers is politically strategic. But unlike the settlers, they are rarely volunteers.

Over the years, Muslims originally impounded in the Corps were replaced with Han immigrants, creating 'an army of Han Chinese colonists'.[16] This army – which still includes a few Uighur farmers – is supplied with weapons and paid a soldier's wage by the government. Corps members are generally better off than the Uighurs around them.

Many of the old *laogai* of Xinjiang are still run by the Corps, though the number of detainees – mainland Chinese and a few Tibetans – seems to have fallen steeply, to 100,000 in 1995 and perhaps half that two years later. The Corps's deputy political commissar, Wang Guizhen, conceded in 1999 that the organization still ran prisons and a few labour camps but claimed that most of the inmates were the Corps' own members who had committed minor crimes like theft. He acknowledged that occasionally the Corps would be instructed by Beijing to take prisoners from other parts of China.[17] One draft of 2,000 'free' prisoners (officially described as 'forced job placement personnel') was reportedly dispatched from a single labour camp near Beijing in 1965.[18] The last publicized mass transfer took place in 1983 when, according to a Chinese magazine, no fewer than 100,000 prisoners from the east coast were sent to the Corps for detention and forced labour. If that was true, Harry Wu noted, it was one of the largest prison transfers in history.[19]

By some yardsticks, the Corps could claim to be the biggest company in the world.[20] Certainly its priorities have shifted, from land reclamation and border defence to farming and manufacture. Commissar Wang even boasted that prison labour had been made profitable. Yet the organization's Jekyll-and-Hyde identity persists, for it still doubles as a reservist army and police force. Can so unwieldy and schizophrenic an organization ever be called a company, or make a genuine profit? Beijing, at least, thinks so, because in the late 1990s the Corps was renamed 'Corporation'.

Partly this was the result of some bad publicity arising from a project funded by the World Bank. The Bank had been underwriting a large irrigation scheme on the western margins of the Taklamakan, designed to improve the lot of poor Uighur farmers. Now it came under fire for allegedly subsidizing labour camps. According to Harry Wu's lobbying organization, the Laogai Research Foundation, the Bank had failed to mention in its prospectus that within the project area lay at least twenty *laogai* camps and twenty-eight regiment farms – all full of Han Chinese. A project intended to benefit the Uighurs was, it said, propping up a regime of state and paramilitary forced labour. It noted that the Chinese themselves had claimed, back in 1983, that prisoners produced a quarter of the Corps' grain, a seventh of its cotton, and a tenth of its 'profit'.[21]

The World Bank conducted a six-week inquiry 'down to the village and household level' which seemed, at first sight, to acquit it of the charges. No evidence was found of any connection between the irrigation project and forced labour, the Bank said. State farms had won some civil works contracts, but there was no sign that prison labour had been used to carry them out. And the beneficiaries were overwhelmingly Uighur people living in two river basins. However, the Bank went on to make a number of admissions which contradicted its own virtuous conclusions. The implementing body, the Xinjiang State Farms Organization, turned out to be another name for the Corps, which, the Bank admitted, did run 'some prisons and adjacent farms' for the Ministry of Justice. A number of the farms being provided with a water supply and sanitation were 'in close proximity to prisons and prison farm areas'. The Bank said it accepted Chinese assurances that there was no management connection between the state farms and the army, but in future the Bank would not employ the state farms organization unless it separated its commercial and penal functions 'to avoid even the appearance of a link to forced labour'.[22] In other words, the Corps should develop what, in the City of London, are called 'Chinese walls'.

If nothing else, the controversy proved that the Corps' association with forced labour was a political Achilles heel. In 2002 China achieved its ambition to join the World Trade Organization. Membership conferred respectability: the country could now call itself a mature member of the world trading system. But WTO membership also brings obligations, ethical and commercial; and using forced labour to gain a competitive edge in export markets is one of the things members are not supposed to do.

There is nothing in international law to prevent prisoners working, provided they are paid and the conditions in which they work are reasonable. And as Amnesty International has pointed out, many prisoners prefer to work rather than do nothing. Some also choose to stay in the area of their detention, making it hard to determine who has been freed and who has not.[23] Compulsory labour and slavery are not the same thing, although some campaigners use the terms interchangeably. Slavery implies that a person has an 'owner'. Many countries require convicts to work as a matter of course.

The International Labour Organization (under its Convention No. 105) specifically forbids the use of forced labour for 'political coercion or education'; as a punishment for political dissent; or for economic development. At the time of writing China has not signed this Convention.

However, human rights activists claim that China is well known for forcing prisoners – convicted or not – to work in conditions which violate international standards. According to Anti-Slavery International, prisoners do not generally receive any kind of remuneration for their work. And much of their work involves making goods for export, even though the export of labour camp produce is technically illegal in China itself. Activists say that Western companies often collude in the trade.[24]

A visit to any Western supermarket or DIY store at the beginning of the twenty-first century will confirm that China's export sales are booming. But also booming are the activities of the human rights lobbies. They, at least, are preparing to make sure that China obeys international law and honours its obligations to the World Trade Organization. At the same time, Western companies are under scrutiny for any sign that they are conniving at, or profiting from, forced labour or inhumane working conditions.

As we shall see in the next chapter, China is trying hard to attract foreign investment to the impoverished western provinces. It cannot therefore avoid also attracting inspection by foreign companies, consumers and pressure groups.

False identities and fudged numbers will not hide the desert gulag for much longer, nor the repressive penal regime against the Uighurs who now mainly inhabit it. There are a lot of skeletons in the sands of Xinjiang.

8

The Great Leap West

DAHEYAN, 40 MILES from Turfan, is not much of a place: a small Chinese town in the middle of the desert which happened to find itself on a railway. But this is not any railway. It is the line which ties a continent together. Coming up from inner China via Xian to Lanzhou, it crosses the desert to Urumchi, runs up and over the border into Kazakhstan where it joins the Turk-Sib railway, then the Trans-Siberian railway, and so reaches Moscow and Europe.

Daheyan matters because it is the entry port for southern Xinjiang. It is from here that a branch line was built over the mountains to Korla, a painfully slow nine-hour journey away, to help turn what was a small oasis on the north-east edge of the Taklamakan desert into the industrial hub of the Tarim basin. From Korla the line was driven on to Kashgar in the far west, where it arrived in May 1999.

One chill April evening, the downstairs hall of Daheyan station was packed with Chinese. Nearly all were men, standing or squatting, jostling each other and arguing, tying and retying their bundles and boxes. They looked small and undernourished, and they seemed confused, flinching at the shouted orders of the stocky female station officer who boomed at them through a loud-hailer. Shortly before the train was due, more women guards ranged themselves on either flank of the mob, hustling them, like collie dogs nipping sheep, through the doors and out on to the platform. There they were marshalled into an agitated zigzag to await the arrival of the train. When the silvery locomotive drew in, the crowd, ignoring the screams of the platform gauleiters, broke ranks, scrambled for the doors and hurled their bundles through the open windows.

These people, travelling together like some outlandish package tour, were peasants who had come up by rail from some impoverished region of China – Gansu or Sichuan, perhaps – and were taking the train from Urumchi down the branch line to Kashgar.

Such scenes occur every day. The scurrying throng at Daheyan was a sliver of the great shoal of migrants which floats back and forth across China in search of work and which every day leaves some 7,000 settlers on the shores of Xinjiang.

They are just one manifestation of the 'Great Leap West', a programme of economic development sponsored by Beijing which is every bit as ambitious as Mao's infamous Great Leap Forward of 1958, and which is designed finally to transform ethnic regions into Han Chinese provinces.[1]

For another, more startling, manifestation of the Great Leap West, one need only take the main line north to Shihezi, a Chinese city 120 miles beyond Urumchi in the bleak Dzungarian basin. Founded in the same year as the Great Leap Forward, Shihezi is the headquarters of the *bingtuan*, the paramilitary Xinjiang Production and Construction Corporation, flagship of the development fleet, and the model of sinicization. The visitor who arrives by car turns off a new stretch of motorway (financed with World Bank help) to be greeted by an outsize poster of a uniformed youth saluting the future, a dreamlike drawing of a Utopian city rising in the distance. Everything at Shihezi is on a gargantuan scale. On either side of the road stretch broad fields under intensive cultivation and, more unexpectedly, the vineyards of the Shihezi wineries. The main approach road is a triumphal avenue of gleaming factory buildings – a sugar refinery, a tomato paste processing works, a power station. Across the top storey of a newly completed mansion block, with balconied windows and mansard roofs that would do credit to London's fashionable Docklands, a banner advertises three-bedroomed flats for sale at 120,000 yuan ($15,000) – an enormous sum for this part of China. A building at one of the city's main intersections proclaims, in giant letters, the spirit of Shihezi: 'The Finance Hotel'.

This new town in the middle of nowhere, with its face to the north slopes of the Tian Shan and its back to the blasts of Siberia, is overtaking even itself. In 1997 more than 70,000 migrants arrived to work its factories and farms, and the city continued to expand at the rate of 10,000 people a year. Among its intake were reported to be peasants dislodged by the Three Gorges hydro-electric project on the Yangzi River.[2] For the first time in Xinjiang's history, the people of the northern basin outnumbered those of the southern.

The gold fever which drew explorers like the Russian Nikolai Prejevalsky to Chinese Turkestan in the nineteenth century was as nothing compared to the development fever which gripped China's leaders at the end of the twentieth.[3] Their ambition to make the wild west a Chinese California reached its fulfilment in the 'Great Western Development Plan' launched by President Jiang Zemin on 17 June 1999 in Xian, ancient capital of inner China.

Fifteen years in preparation and involving 300 researchers in working parties on every aspect of the economy, the blueprint set a budget – of about 100 billion yuan ($13 billion) in the first year – and listed 78 projects for an area covering more than half the land mass of China: ten provinces, autonomous regions and cities in all, with Xinjiang as a focal point. The Chinese press could hardly contain its enthusiasm. The editor of the *People's Daily*, prefacing a report by a delegation of journalists sent to Xinjiang the following year, wrote:

> People of various ethnic groups in Xinjiang cherish an extremely strong desire for stability, unity, development and prosperity. Local people at the upper and lower levels, united as one, and in high spirit and with soaring working enthusiasm, have thrown themselves into the tidal wave of massive development.[4]

The name chosen for the campaign, *xibu da kaifa*, was seen by some Western analysts, however, as a give-away: they pointed out that the word *kaifa*, 'development', was more accurately translated as 'exploitation'.[5]

Xinjiang had certainly been exploited in the past – notably by its trio of pre-Liberation governors – but it was never systematically developed before the Communists took over. Stories were told, however, of the secret richness and fertility of this barren-seeming land. A traveller in Manchu times, for example, reported that giant grains of rice were grown in the Aksu oasis, and a visitor to Sheng Shicai's headquarters in the 1940s claimed to have seen a lump of coal so large that it took two men to carry it.[6] A joke told earlier in the century concerned a man called Ma who set out to visit the iron bridge built by the Americans over the Yellow River at Lanzhou. Stopping for a cup of tea in the Gansu corridor he met another Ma coming the other way to see the famous melons of Hami.

'Tell me about your iron bridge,' said the first Ma.

'Well,' replied the second Ma, 'it's so high that a year ago a man fell off it and his body still hadn't reached the water by the time I left.'

'Amazing!' exclaimed the first Ma. 'But let me warn you it's not worth your going all the way to Hami to see our melons. They grow so big that by this time next year you'll be able to see them from Lanzhou.'[7]

The Qing dynasty emperors wanted Xinjiang because they thought it made China secure, not because they thought it could be profitable; the usual extortion was practised by local *begs* and Chinese moneylenders, but little thought was given to digging out its mineral wealth, except for the ever-popular jade, or developing it as a market, except for tea.[8]

A 29-year-old clerk called Gong Zizhen working in the Grand Secretariat seems to have been the first formally to propose colonization of Xinjiang. In a remarkably prescient essay written in 1820, he said the old policy of using barbarians to control barbarians was wrong. China should invest in the west – build canals and windbreaks and populate it with unemployed Han peasants and Manchu bannermen, or soldiers. In a passage which might equally well have come from an adviser on the 'Great Leap West' he declared that the centre would give up people to help the west, and the west would give up wealth to help the centre. The project would take twenty years, wrote Gong, but was worth the wait. Nine years later, Gong passed the mandarin examination and was able to campaign openly. Xinjiang had been annexed, he declared, and so could never be let go again. He drew up a blueprint of prefectures, districts and counties, complete with sinicized names to replace Turki and Mongol ones.[9]

He was supported by Wei Yuan, a member of the so-called 'statecraft movement' who invoked Mencius' equation of wilderness with misrule, declaring: 'It is Heaven's wish that the thorny thicket be transformed into busy highroads, the canyon's gloom into brilliant daylight, the teeming jungle into [crowds wearing] caps and robes, the felt tent into village and well.' He called on the government to 'turn this rich loam into China proper', a project which would make governance easier, and be profitable too. 'Some day', he added, 'this idea will have to be implemented.'[10] Because the Qing court had considered Muslims 'subjects beyond assimilation', Chinese civilization had not been imposed on them.[11] But Wei's ideas influenced General Zuo, who, as we have seen after his reconquest of Xinjiang, set about trying to make the region irreversibly Chinese, believing the native people would naturally adopt the language and customs of the Han.

In his memoir of the 1930s, the mandarin Aitchen Wu recorded his own vision of Xinjiang's future. Although he warned against harsh treatment of the natives, who should be placed 'on an equal footing', he went on to advocate the transfer of millions of Chinese from the overcrowded mainland. The frontiers of Xinjiang should be strengthened, roads improved, the capital redeveloped, a railway driven to the north-west border, new cities planted and the Muslim ones allowed to decay. He called for the gold, silver, coal and iron to be worked, the irrigation system improved and oil deposits surveyed. '[Xinjiang] is like California before 1849, and Altai like Alaska before 1867, when it was in the hands of the Russians,' he wrote. 'We must start work immediately in [Xinjiang] to save this vast province for, like a piece of natural jade, once polished and shown to the world, it will prove our most valuable possession.'[12]

During the Republic it was Moscow, not Nanjing, which showed the most interest in and, by clever manipulation of weak governments, exercised the most influence over the economy of Xinjiang. The province became a virtual colony of the USSR. Soviet geologists mapped deposits of manganese, copper, lead, tin, wolfram and oil in the mid-1930s, and the oilwells they drilled in the Dzungarian basin were particularly useful when Russia had her back to the wall during the Nazi invasion in 1941.[13]

The Nationalist leader Chiang Kai-shek launched his own 'Northwest Development Movement' in 1942, involving the resettlement of poor Chinese peasants on Uighur land, a measure which was extremely unpopular and which reminded people of the expropriation that had provoked the Hami rebellion ten years before. The Nationalist troops who lived off the land were described as 'human-faced locusts'.

Xinjiang's industry was heavily concentrated in the north, especially following the discovery of oil at Karamay, and after the Communist victory it was to the north that most of the Han settlers came to work the factories and state farms around Urumchi and Shihezi. Mao himself recognized the potential of the region. 'We say China is a country vast in territory, rich in resources and large in population; as a matter of fact it is the Han nationality whose population is large and the minority nationalities whose territory is vast and whose resources are rich.'[14]

In the early days after Liberation, the USSR was both the model and the prop for Chinese industry, but all co-operation stopped for twenty years with the ideological split in the 1960s. Yet the Party claimed that the value of industrial output in Xinjiang rose by twenty times in the first twenty-five years of its administration, and an English-language propaganda bulletin of the period asked its readers to believe that Kazakh herders were riding about singing songs to express 'the joy of the people of all nationalities at the rapid development of industry'.

> Our village is making a leap
> Forty horses can't match it.
> Factories going up on the grassland,
> Shepherds learning to make steel,
> Machines to churn the butter.
> Tracks drive right up to our mountain village.[15]

In reality, as the Party well knew, the grasslands stayed pastoral and the oases agricultural: as early as 1962, the central planners had privately recognized that development had done little or nothing for the ethnic minorities, and that socialist construction had failed to turn them into a proletariat.[16]

In the 1990s, Xinjiang began to receive enormous central subsidies in order to make it a 'regional powerhouse'.[17] This powerhouse was to be supported by two pillars, oil and cotton, 'one black, one white'. These were to be the locomotive industries, pulling the economy up and drawing in the migrants. Oil production came to the south with the discovery of deposits beneath the Taklamakan desert – which did not live up to expectations. However, the province did become the largest grower of cotton in China, contributing a quarter of national output, and spinning mills were transported from Shanghai to process it – even though imported cotton was cheaper and the country was stockpiling its own produce.[18]

When the leadership gave up the state monopoly of industry and sold off the smaller businesses, Xinjiang remained heavily dependent on Beijing to make up its budget deficits, and the promised tax rebates did not arrive. Central government had 'cheated', and far from relaxing, its financial grip actually increased.[19] Nor, in spite of the inducements, did the province become any more attractive to foreign investors.

Meanwhile, tremendous efforts were made to overcome the tyrannies of distance and terrain which had deterred Chinese administrators, migrants and armies for centuries. The railway was extended, as we have seen, to the north-west border, with a branch to Korla and along the southern slopes of the Tian Shan to Kashgar. A secondary line was proposed, swerving south from Korla around the desert's eastern edge, through the Lop desert, over the Kunlun mountains and into Qinghai province. A 300-mile motorway from Turfan city to Urumchi was extended with the help of World Bank loans to Kuitun, on its way to the Kazakhstan border. New airports were planned and existing airport terminals rebuilt. Chinese hotels and office blocks appeared on broad avenues, as did restaurants with clean floors.

Soon backpackers and tour groups were 'travelling the Silk Road', flying in to Urumchi and being ferried by bus or air-conditioned jeep from the frescoed caves at Dunhuang in Gansu along the north Tarim road to Hami, Turfan and Kashgar. Hong Kong money was mobilized and five-star hotels appeared to tempt the traveller. Pagodas and rest-houses sprang up in scenic mountain areas, and Kazakh and Kyrgyz families were encouraged to put up summer yurts offering bed-and-breakfast and a slice of nomad life to passing tourists. Officials set about recapturing a Chinese past which Xinjiang had never really had. A heritage agency in Urumchi announced in 1999 that the city was founded not a couple of hundred years before, as everyone thought, but in AD 650. No evidence was offered, but the deputy director of the Urumchi Cultural Bureau was reported as saying that the discovery 'would make the residents proud and help tourism'. He may have been referring to ancient Beshbalik, a former Uighur capital outside the city which was now earmarked for development as a Chinese theme park. Meanwhile plans were drawn up for a Buddhist Chinese recreation centre with museums and guesthouses at the ancient site of Loulan, and for an enlarged wild camel reserve in the Kumtagh desert, overlapping the Lop Nor nuclear testing ground made redundant by the moratorium of 1996.

Most impressive of all was the completion in 1995 of a highway which cut through the high dunes of the Taklamakan desert from Luntai, near Korla in the north, to Niya on the south road. The sand was held back in high banks either side by means of nets and plantings. Squads of roadsweepers were continuously employed to keep the highway clear: though claiming to be migrants from Sichuan, many wore Uighur caps, which suggested they might have been prisoners from local labour camps.[20] The desert road's immediate purpose was to give access to the new oil production wells of Tazhong. Later it was opened to tourist traffic. But its strategic function was to accelerate the modernization of the rebellious southern oasis Uighur towns, providing rapid transport in an emergency. Military and police reinforcements could now be sent down from the north in a matter of hours.

The desert road could stand as a symbol, because the grand projects, the huge subsidies, the frantic pace of construction are all an economic means to a political end. The real aim of the Great Leap West is internal security – what the Party calls 'stability'. The Party is trying to prevent the break-up of China and its own disintegration by narrowing a yawning gap between the rich east and the poor west. If Xinjiang were to secede, so it believes, others would follow and China would dissolve as the Soviet Union did in 1991 after the Baltic states were allowed to leave the Union.[21] And it was, after all, the failure of the system to improve the people's lot which did as much as anything to bring the Soviet Union crashing down.

In Xinjiang a hostile populace and an insecure border – the same problems which confronted the Nationalists in the 1940s and the Communists in the 1960s – have returned to haunt the new pragmatists in Beijing. Formerly, the Soviet Union was the threat. Now it is militant Islam in the post-Soviet central Asian republics. It was no accident that the Great Leap West was launched after NATO had intervened on the Muslims' side following the break-up of Yugoslavia, bombing the Serbs to prevent them reclaiming separatist Kosovo. Chen Dongshen, a member of the Chinese economic team for the Great Leap West, warned in 2000 that Uighur nationalism could create 'a Kosovo in Asia', while an economist at the Chinese Academy of Sciences, Hu Angang, was quoted as saying: 'The worst case scenario – and what we're trying to avoid – is China fragmenting like Yugoslavia . . . Already, regional [economic] disparity is equal to, or worse than, what we saw in Yugoslavia before it split.'[22] Other painful precedents were Indonesia, which lost East Timor, and Chechnya in the Caucasus, where Russia fought a brutal war against secession.

The investment boom is designed, in other words, to 'solve the nationalities problem', as was spelled out by Li Dezhu, Minister of the State Ethnic Affairs Commission, a year after the campaign was announced.[23] It was hardly a new concern. In 1996 the Party reported that only by making the minorities better off could it counter the evil influence of 'hostile Western forces' – that is, America – and Islamic zealots who were duping the simple masses. Only then would the minorities be persuaded to 'follow the path of building socialism with Chinese characteristics and take the initiative in resisting and combating national separatism and all sorts of sabotage activities'.[24] Earlier still, the Party Secretary in Xinjiang had told ethnic cadres after a bomb attack in Kashgar that the region was 'rich in underground resources, and our main task . . . is to maintain stability so that other parts of China can develop smoothly'.[25]

The country's accession to the World Trade Organization has

intensified what some Western observers see as China's paranoia about separatism, because it makes the future more cloudy still.[26] The greatest danger is that 100 million small farmers will be put out of business by foreign competition, leading to a wave of peasant revolts across China.

Beijing's triple tactic in Xinjiang, therefore, is to exploit the land and the natural resources on which the Uighurs live for the benefit of inner China; to overwhelm the Uighurs numerically by means of huge population transfers; and to pacify them and win their loyalty with a better standard of living. If these aims sound contradictory, it is because, in practice, they are.

On 28 February 2001, President Jiang Zemin signed a number of amendments to the 1984 law which defines the autonomy of the ethnic minority regions and enclaves. In an official account of the changes little was said about autonomy, but a good deal about the state's priorities, central planning and 'market demand'. It talked of the support the state was offering to ethnic regions, in the form of subsidies, bank loans and special waivers, and it repeated many of the aims set out by the Great Western Development Plan, including that of 'promoting national solidarity'.[27] To some foreign analysts, this plainly meant that the state was removing those parts of the law which gave local people a say in their own development, and awarding itself still greater powers over the use of land and resources in their regions.[28] There was, however, a positive note: the promise of financial compensation at 'a certain level' for areas which supplied natural resources and contributed to the country's 'ecological equilibrium'. The right to compensation is not recognized in China's constitution.[29]

From the leadership's point of view, these measures must have seemed not only necessary but also just – and even generous. After all, the ethnic minorities constitute less than 10 per cent of the total population, but the autonomous areas account for 60 per cent of the land; and the minorities of Xinjiang are a scant sixtieth of China's population living on a sixth of its territory. What is more, Xinjiang contains – by some estimates – three-quarters of China's mineral wealth. According to the Constitution of the People's Republic of China, all the land and the resources beneath it belong to the state. 'There is a feeling that the Chinese government has given and given to Xinjiang, and all they get is criticism,' an American scholar commented. 'Now they have abandoned that tactic and are studying how America settled the West and decimated the Indians. They risk making the same mistakes we made.'[30]

If Xinjiang is part of China, then Xinjiang's wealth is China's too. And if, as the Party believes, Xinjiang has been part of China for two millennia, then its title to the property looks unquestionable. Even if both propositions are doubtful – indeed dubious – the Party can fall back on another justification, hallowed by time: that the Great Leap West is part of China's manifest destiny.

For twenty-five centuries, from the time of Confucius and Mencius onwards, China's destiny has been elaborated in one way or another: sometimes it was said that the Han had a mission to civilize and absorb the barbarians; sometimes that the minorities were genetically Chinese; sometimes that the Han were destined to rule all Asia, and the world. A seventeenth-century philosopher, Wang Fuxi, wrote: 'It is no injustice to conquer the lands of the barbarians. It is not inhuman to kill barbarians. It is not dishonest to deceive barbarians.'[31] Manifest destiny was invoked in the poems of that great empire-builder, the Emperor Qianlong, written to stiffen morale for the conquest of the west. The 'statecraft' thinkers of the early nineteenth century put an economic gloss on the vision, while the Nationalists of the twentieth interpreted it in Fascist terms, as a kind of genetic imperative.

Manifest destiny was not, of course, solely the prerogative of the Chinese. The Russian adventurers who opened up the 'eastern treasure-house' of Siberia never doubted that the land belonged to them by right, however strange and uncongenial they found it.[32] According to N.M. Yadrintsev, writing in 1882, the natives of Siberia were 'disposed of callously and unceremoniously'. 'It was quite usual for armed bands of Russians to kill natives whom they encountered and divide the booty, and it has been said that in the first stages of the conquest the natives were hunted like animals.'[33] Soviet writers liked to contrast the bloody annexation of the American West with the peaceful assimilation of the Russian East. They said the Russian colonists merely 'flowed around' the natives, who were drawn into friendship with the 'simple, unassuming representatives of the working Russian people.'[34] The truth, not admitted until *glasnost* in the 1980s, was rather different. Like the American Indians, the Siberian tribes fell into debt, mortgaged their land, became dependent on the invaders for supplies and were ground down by smallpox, influenza and syphilis. After the Revolution, the Bolsheviks, like the Chinese Communists in Xinjiang, were comradely. They sent grain to feed the starving tribespeople, set up health clinics, cancelled debts and forbade the sale of alcohol. Within a generation, however, the land had been stripped and poisoned by vast projects controlled from Moscow and carried out by transient workers, a process likened by post-Soviet critics to the colonial rape of Africa or the destruction of the Amazon rainforest. In 1989 a member of the Congress of People's Deputies went so far as to say that the Siberian tribes had been treated no better than the native Americans.[35]

American pioneers believed even more strongly in a God-given destiny. Some forty years after Wei Yuan had waxed lyrical about the 'rich loam' of China's far west, his words found an echo in the Rocky Mountains. The *Cheyenne Daily Leader* explained the position to its readers:

> The rich and beautiful valleys of Wyoming are destined for the occupancy and sustenance of the Anglo-Saxon race. The wealth that for untold ages has lain hidden beneath the snow-capped summits of our mountains has been placed there by Providence to reward the brave spirits whose lot it is to compose the advance-guard of civilization . . . The Indians must stand aside or be overwhelmed by the ever advancing and ever increasing tide of emigration . . . The same inscrutable Arbiter that decreed the downfall of Rome has pronounced the doom of extinction upon the red men of America.[36]

Colonialism finds the same old excuses. Thomas Jefferson had preached the moral correctness of war against the Indians so long as they refused to become civilized and assimilated. For him, Americans were one big family, just as for Mao and Zhou Enlai China was one big family of nationalities.[37] When it came to slaves and natives Jefferson was, surprisingly, less tolerant than that other great imperialist with a civilizing mission, Great Britain. It was 'the natural progress of things', he said, that Indians be required to give up hunting and turn to farming and manufacture. They would then need less land, while the whites certainly needed more. Anticipating General Zuo after his conquest of Xinjiang, Jefferson agreed with a suggestion that the civilizing process should be started by means of village schools. It was 'desirable but not essential' that the Indians convert to Christianity; fluency in Latin and Greek would not be necessary, he thought, but an ability to speak English would be. All this would save America 'the pain and expense of expelling and destroying them'.[38]

Jefferson and his friends well understood that the real motor of colonization of native lands was an economic one – the Virginian was himself an investor – but they felt obliged to find a moral, and then a political, justification: it was the patriotic duty of white Americans to defy the British Crown, which had refused to reallocate to them the territory gained from the natives.

China's answer to the native problem, as we have seen, is somewhat more sophisticated in theory, if almost as ruthless in practice. But it is far from clear that the means it has chosen – the Great Leap West – is any more sustainable than was Mao's Great Leap Forward. Doubts were soon expressed about the country's ability to afford the subventions promised to the west when it had 300 million unemployed and 100 million migrant workers drifting across the land; when it was running a record budget deficit and spending cuts were being imposed; when state industries (upon which the west was heavily dependent) were bankrupt, and the people's savings banks were having to be bailed out to prevent their collapse; when local administrations were profligate and corrupt, and the peasantry was being taxed beyond endurance. The boomtown appearance of Urumchi, Kashgar, even distant Gulja, is impressive at first sight; a second glance is less reassuring. The west was not immune to the economic recession which overtook China at the turn of the century: many of the skyscraper office blocks were untenanted, and there were few customers in the smart boutiques and grand department stores.

Critics of the plan said the emphasis on physical assets was misplaced. In 2002 the Asian Development Bank told China, its biggest customer, that the next round of loans would have to be as much for poverty relief as for infrastructure – implying not only that the programme was already top heavy, but also that the interests of the native people were being overlooked. The planners had not entirely overlooked them: the new autonomy law recognized a need to build primary and middle schools in pastoral and mountain areas. However, that item was not costed; it was for local authorities, not central government, to find the money. Such discrepancies only reinforced the sceptical reaction of outsiders. 'The emphasis on hard infrastructure betrays China's colonizing instincts,' commented one Beijing correspondent. 'Roads and railways make it easier for troops to be dispatched in times of popular unrest, and for the centre to control its empire. That, in short, is what the "Go West" campaign is all about.'[39]

To make the campaign work, China will need private-sector and foreign – even Muslim foreign – investment. Apart from a few multinational companies in oil, power and telecommunications, outside interest in the far west has been meagre.[40] Companies are deterred by the distances involved and the area's remoteness (and lack of infrastructure), but principally by the effort required in dealing with state bureaucracies and the whimsicality of their rules. They have also to make some judgement about the likelihood of sabotage and rioting – not an easy thing to do when the government is ambiguous on the subject, playing down the risk when talking to Western investors, playing it up when talking to Western diplomats. In the long term, the Great Leap West may bring the social stability that Beijing desires, but in the short run, as one Xinjiang-watcher argues, stability will have to be 'enforced' by repressive measures. The government cannot attract foreign capital if there is danger, nor will companies be eager to sign contracts in places where China is using 'strong-arm tactics to bring the ethnic peoples of the region under control'.[41]

Less quantifiable still is the risk of being caught up in the kind of political controversy which rattled the World Bank when, as described in Chapter 7, it was accused of supporting labour camps along the Tarim river. The protest had its effect. The Bank stiffened its conditions for supporting a subsequent project, the resettlement of Han Chinese farmers in an ethnically Tibetan part of Qinghai province, with the result that China refused the new terms and the project was suspended. The ethical dimensions of foreign investment can no longer be ignored.

One of the biggest projects in the Great Leap West is a proposed 2,600-mile pipeline to carry natural gas from the Tarim basin to Shanghai. The so-called 'West–East' pipeline, with its attendant wells, pumps and distribution network for houses, factories and power stations in Shanghai, is expected to cost $18 billion (at 2001 prices), more than the budgeted cost of the whole Great Western Development Plan in its first year. To the critics, the Shanghai pipeline illustrates everything that is wrong with the strategy. Xinjiang's wealth will be consumed on the eastern seaboard; there is no 'development' for the Uighurs contained within it; and the whole operation is to be carried out regardless of their concerns.

Because of the enormous cost, foreign companies were invited to bid for shares in the project; and it was not long before they were getting protest letters from Uighur exiles. BP, one of the oil companies invited to join the venture, was urged in October 2000 to pull out. It did so, not on humanitarian grounds, but because it felt there was not enough in it for the company. Another protest went to Shell, which a few years earlier had suffered a public relations crisis due to its involvement in Nigeria, warning of 'political tensions and bloody conflicts' in Xinjiang.[42]

For the ethnic minorities in Xinjiang, however, the skewed economics of the Great Leap West are not the main concern. Their real worry, the thing that affects their lives, the everyday reminder of Chinese domination, is immigration.

In 1949, there were about 300,000 Han Chinese in Xinjiang in a population of 4 to 5 million, or about 1 in 15. For many years the number of Han was a 'state secret', for fear of provoking the Uighurs.[43] A census in 2000 showed 7.5 million Han in a population of 19.25 million, or more than 1 in 3. According to the official figures, the Uighurs were the largest group, with 8 million, the Han next, and the other minorities – Mongols, Hui, Kazakhs, Kyrgyz – made up the rest. But the census did not count as residents the million or so members of the armed forces (soldiers and police), nor the professional advisers, nor – more importantly – the 2.5 million Han Chinese living under the umbrella of the Xinjiang Production and Construction Corporation. If these are added, the number of resident Han is nearer to 12 million, making them not only the largest ethnic group but close to becoming an absolute majority in the Xinjiang Uighur Autonomous Region.

Settlers and migrant workers are pouring in from the east at such a rate – 7,000 a day is the figure usually quoted – that Uighurs are beginning to feel like strangers in their own land. It is the largest colonization Xinjiang has seen. One Western historian has called it a demographic change 'unparalleled in the modern history of central Asia'.[44] Uighur nationalists have another term for it: demographic genocide.

However, the picture is not clear-cut. The number of Uighurs may be much greater than the census showed. The Han worry that their lower birth rate will reduce their presence from a half to a quarter by the year 2030.[45] That would help explain why tougher birth-control rules were introduced for minorities (described in Chapter 6), and why ever greater numbers of Han are being accommodated. From the beginning of the Cultural Revolution until the death of Mao, nearly 5 million outsiders arrived. By 1984 immigration had pushed the population of Xinjiang to 13.5 million, making it the fastest-growing province after Heilongjiang. The then General Secretary, Hu Yaobang, thought that the north-west could easily take 200 million of China's people; and a confidential plan to move 5 million to Xinjiang by the end of the century was later disclosed.[46] Other reports suggest that a target population of 20 million Han – nearly three times the present official number – has secretly been set for the year 2010.

When the railway came to Korla, people joked that the noise made by the freight train as it drew in was *chi, chi, chi* ('eat, eat, eat'), and as it drew out again, *chibaole, chibaole, chibaole* ('I'm full, full, full'). What the local people see as the theft of their riches – oil, uranium, wool for carpets – is epitomized by the natural gas export pipeline. Exiles complain that only 2 per cent of the value of Xinjiang's oil stays in the province, for education, and that when a Uighur government leader asked for the rate to be raised to 7 per cent, he was summoned to Beijing and put under house arrest. Western critics have wondered how, in a place of such natural wealth, the Turkis could find themselves living 'at a level scarcely above subsistence'.[47]

Few of the benefits of the Great Leap West seem to be going to the native people. What is not transported to the rich east coast is handed first to the Chinese inside the province, whether it be land, housing or jobs.

Farmland is made cheap for the Han. A small advertisement appeared on the front page of the *Xinjiang Daily* on 15 July 1998 offering 830 acres of land, rent-free for the first two years, at Luyin Farm, Cherchen. 'High quality reclaimed land,' it said, 'irrigated, abundant in water, with sunny warm weather.' Since Cherchen is right on the edge of the Taklamakan desert, the promise of fine weather was perhaps superfluous. What the advertisement failed to mention, however, was that this is still very much a Uighur area, where cultivable land is already scarce and people have less than half an acre per head to live on.[48] Competition for land and water had already led to conflict between the Uighurs and the few Han Chinese who live there. Cherchen began drying up rapidly after 1971 when watercourses were dammed upstream to make reservoirs for incoming Han farmers, according to a Uighur scientist.[49] The state's own field studies have shown that water shortages are the biggest complaint of native farmers, and a common cause of conflict. Competition comes not only from new immigrants but from the mighty Xinjiang Corporation which has grown to control nearly half the viable territory of the province and is given automatic priority over small farmers. Again, the Party is aware of the problem. A report to the Politburo in 1996 referred to 'conflicts and confrontation' between the Corporation and 'local farmers and nomadic peoples concerning grasslands, water and other natural resources'.[50]

Nearly every small farmer in Xinjiang is Uighur, and most of the Uighurs are farmers. Like peasants throughout China they complain of extortion by corrupt officials, high rents and miserably low incomes. In the far west farmers were ordered to give up their traditional crops and to grow cotton in accordance with the central plan. Not only has the state reduced the price it pays for cotton, but the farmers well know that the whole purpose of the programme is to reclaim land: not for their use, but for the use of immigrants from the east.[51]

Even older Han residents are unhappy. Those who migrated voluntarily during the Mao era, responding to the Chairman's call to go out and build Xinjiang, now think of themselves as 'old Xinjiang people' and complain that mass immigration has ruined their good relations with the Uighurs and made life harder for everybody. Retired Han farmers and veterans of the Corporation 'who have spent a harsh life of self-sacrifice, resent the newcomers who are granted free individual plots of land'.[52]

Pressure of population has inevitably upset the delicate balance of Xinjiang's unusual ecology. Every spring, the alarm is raised as a mantle of desert dust descends on the already polluted mega-cities of northern China. In Xinjiang the fine loess of the desert edges is whipped up by the winds that scour the Tarim basin, covering the wilderness in a thick haze and piling up into angry clouds which hang over the oasis towns for days on end like a November fog. The grey dust settles on every ledge and windowsill, dripping like hoar frost from trees, telephone wires and washing lines.

In the past 2,500 years the Taklamakan desert has crept southward some 60 miles. Chinese scientists estimate that almost a third of the desert area of Xinjiang has been created in the past hundred years alone. The mountain glaciers are in retreat once more – the latest recession began in the mid-seventeenth century – but this time the desiccation is accelerated by human greed. Developers seem to be fighting a losing battle: one survey discovered that in the time it took to reclaim 15,000 square miles of desert for cultivation, the desert itself grew by 19,000 square miles. China's environment ministry has observed that the desert has spread in 53 of Xinjiang's 87 administrative districts and that many lakes are drying up, especially around the Tarim river.[53] Other reports say the grasslands, too, are degenerating from over-use and that the forests are shrinking.

Land reclamation is seen by Western economists as a dubious development option. Better, they say, to help people off poor land by giving them education and city skills than to make vain efforts to turn the desert green by subsidizing plantations in the wilderness. Certainly the desert can be made fertile if there is water to spare. But an environmental disaster in Soviet central Asia was caused by intensive cotton-farming in Uzbekistan and Kazakhstan: unreal targets, profligate use of chemical fertilizers and rampant corruption combined to deplete the Amu Darya and Syr Darya, shrink the Aral Sea, ruin the land and destroy the health of thousands of poor families.

China's central planners may be more inclined in future to heed their technicians who since the mid-1990s have been aware of environmental dangers and bureaucratic malpractice – existing forests and pastures let out as 'reclaimed' land, pet projects started without approval. Wen Jiabao, head of economic planning in the 'fourth generation' of leaders appointed in November 2002, has said the Great Western Development Plan should be slowed down to control air and water pollution.[54]

Hardship in the villages is not always visible. To the outsider, the life of the peasant farmer seems picturesque, if a little primitive: a life of rustic contentment under the poplar trees, a stream rippling past his door, his wife and daughters picking cotton in the yard, half-naked infants playing in the dust and the donkey braying in its pen. Only in the cities does the segregation, the economic discrimination against the Uighurs, become obvious.

In a field on the outskirts of Kashgar, not far from the mausoleum of the Khoja Apakh, men wearing hard hats are peering through theodolites and taking measurements. Others, bare-headed, are digging trenches and carting the earth away in wheelbarrows. They are watched at a distance by a goatherd. He is a Uighur. Every one of the hundred or so building workers, surveyors and foremen is Han. Like the scrambling mob at Daheyan railway station, these people are migrant workers, brought in from a neighbouring province to build multi-storey flats on the edge of the city. A new tarmac road has been driven up from the bazaar; crossing the old city boundary, it runs alongside the building site, past a row of condemned houses, and into a village whose centre consists of little more than a teahouse, a police station, some council offices and a few small shops and stalls. There, abruptly, the highway ends.

This place will become home to hundreds of Uighur families who are to be moved out from the city centre. The flats in the field are for them, and their own houses in the lanes around the Id Kah mosque are to be demolished. The families will be compensated – about half the market value of their houses – but they have not been consulted. All they know is that they stand in the way of modernization: their houses are insanitary, and fire engines have no access. What they have not been told is that the secret courtyards and alleyways of Kashgar are a threat to the Chinese, for they hide nests of troublemakers – 'nationalists', 'splittists', perhaps even terrorists.

Some are happy to give up their spartan courtyard houses for the amenities – running water, central heating and flush lavatories – of a modern flat. Others have exploited a traditional Uighur flair for trade, jumping into the newly free market to become successful entrepreneurs.

Not all Uighurs are doing badly from the Great Leap West. So much at least is evident from the smart new villas among the cherry orchards and vineyards of the old quarter of Gulja, or from the neo-classical mansion which a Uighur export-import millionaire has built nearby to feed, clothe and educate poor Muslim children. Home improvements are to be found down every poplar-shaded lane. Outside Kashgar, an old house in an orchard, hidden behind a mudbrick wall, has been expensively renovated, with a brick extension, elegantly fretted doors and window-frames, and a cavernous basement for summer shade.

One of the most successful Uighur entrepreneurs has been a woman. Rebiya Kadeer started work in a laundry and built up a trading company which made her reputedly the richest woman in Xinjiang. Its headquarters are on South Jiefan Street in Urumchi, not far from the Uighur Bazaar. Mrs Kadeer was politically active, founding a movement to help other women follow her example. She was a member of the National People's Consultative Conference, and a delegate to the UN world conference on women held in Beijing in 1995. But two years after that conference her passport was confiscated, seemingly as a reprisal against her husband, a campaigner for Uighur independence who had sought asylum in the United States the previous year. Then, while on her way to meet a visiting US human rights delegation in August 1999, Mrs Kadeer was arrested and accused of giving secret information to foreigners. She was tried in secret and sentenced in March 2000 to eight years' imprisonment. The verdict disclosed that the 'secret information' she was alleged to have passed consisted of copies of Chinese newspapers from Ili, Kashgar and Urumchi which she had been about to send to her husband in America.

Mrs Kadeer's son and her male secretary were arrested soon after her and sentenced, without trial, to two and three years respectively of 're-education through labour'. Both reportedly were beaten or tortured, while she herself was said to have fallen seriously ill in jail. Her conviction was greeted with demonstrations in Kazakhstan and Kyrgyzstan, and prompted a resolution in the US Congress and a question in the European Parliament.

For most Uighurs, life is neither so dizzy nor so dangerous, for they never get on the first rung of the ladder. The rate of unemployment among Uighurs in 2000 was estimated by a Chinese agency to be 15 per cent.[55] It may have been very much higher. The invariable favouritism in the job market, which seems so natural to the Han, is one of the most provocative features of China's colonization programme.

Uighurs are not employed even to put up the buildings which are supposed to be part of their own development. Contracts arising from the Great Leap West are awarded to industrial and commercial companies from China's inland provinces. Meanwhile, unrestricted immigration means that the city streets are filled with out-of-work Muslim men trying to scratch a living: if not unemployed, they are certainly underemployed. Many have set up outdoor barbecues or kiosk restaurants – so many, indeed, that the price of a meal has fallen although the cost of meat has risen.

The plight of those trying to make their way can be pitiful. One young woman, hardly out of her teens, had found a job in a restaurant at night to pay for her studies. She told me she came from a village outside Kashgar. Both her parents were dead and she had worked on the farm all her life. Now she was not only supporting herself but was also trying to pay for the schooling of a younger sister and brother. As she told her story, the girl burst into tears and held out her hands by way of explanation: their backs were pale and soft, the palms hard and brown as old leather.

A woman radiologist who has left the country described the poverty of Uighurs seeking medical help: 'Every day people came from other towns and every day there was something sad happening in my office. People were not getting government help. A couple came from Khotan, for example. She had cancer of the womb. She had sold her house and had five kids, and had to pay for treatment. She was very angry and upset.' Anyone working for the government enjoyed free medical treatment, the doctor explained, but few Uighurs now worked for the government.[56]

For people like these, the failure of the Great Leap West to include provision for schools and training that might equip them for a more competitive and urban society looks perverse indeed.

Meanwhile, the modicum of 'positive discrimination' that used to apply – the system of job quotas for minority people – appears to have been abandoned. All pretence that Uighurs are in charge of their own affairs has been given up. Now it is the ethnic origin of the work unit leader which counts – and that usually means Han. Whole sectors, such as the oil industry and the People's Liberation Army, seem to be reserved for them. Uighurs in government jobs find their path to promotion blocked, while less well-qualified Han are put in over their heads. Ethnic managers of small state-owned companies have been removed in order to make way for Chinese, leading the Uighurs to believe that in any run-down or lay-off they will be the first to get dismissal notices.[57] The Han have the pick of the high-paid jobs; they can readily get the permits which allow them to run private businesses; they are treated preferentially when it comes to raising a bank loan; and they can obtain a city residency permit, while a Uighur who may have lived in the city for years is refused.

To complain of discrimination is merely to invite the sack. 'Just holding on to your job is the main thing now,' said a middle-aged Uighur manager. Silence is the price the minorities pay to work. For some, like the former secret policeman whom I met on a train outside Korla, that price is too high. He resigned.[58]

Worthwhile employment is also impossible without fluent Chinese. In that respect, nothing much has changed. Back in 1957, when the Hundred Flowers campaign briefly bloomed and people were given licence to complain, a Uighur post office manager spoke up:

There has existed a prejudice in our office. A national minority cadre must be able to understand and speak Chinese if he wants to have something done. We are confronted with a lot of trouble because we lack such ability. Why should the national minority cadres be required to speak Chinese while they are living in, and working for, their own autonomous region?[59]

The postmaster had a point. But for today's young hopefuls, things have got worse. Not even a university degree and fluency in Chinese are a guarantee of employment. Graduates from ethnic minorities are not automatically allocated jobs as others are, and if they do get a job they are posted to the poorest and most remote areas.[60] The Han students get the best jobs.

The Han monopoly of the job market in what is supposed to be a burgeoning economy is more than frustrating. To the Uighurs, the Great Leap West looks not so much like the promise of a better future but an artificial boom in support of a Han takeover which will break up their communities and destroy their way of life.

The official doctrine of respect for minority cultures is honoured almost entirely in the breach. In most countries, it is the immigrants who start at the bottom of the pile and struggle to raise themselves up. In Xinjiang it is not the newcomers but the natives who are struggling to climb the ladder. But the ladder is slippery and its upper rungs have been sawn off.

It is no wonder that so many educated, Chinese-speaking Uighurs, the people most able to contribute to modernization, the people most adaptable to Chinese rule, have decided that the only way up is out.

9

The Diaspora

IT WAS A hot and breezy June afternoon in the year 2000 and I was walking westwards along the main thoroughfare of old Constantinople. Bounded by the Golden Horn on one side and the Sea of Marmara on the other, the original quarter of the city is a peninsula shaped like the head of a dog looking eastwards into Asia, with the Topkapi Palace resting on its nose.

As I reached Sinan's great Mosque of the Prince, I noticed a cluster of ecclesiastical buildings down a side street, and decided to ask there for directions. I was looking for a small mosque somewhere near Beyazit Square that was said to house the offices of the Eastern Turkestan Foundation, whose head was the leader of the Uighurs in exile, a man I knew only as 'the General'.

I had heard of the General the previous month thanks to a touring troupe of Uighur musicians who were performing at the Purcell Room on London's South Bank. As I stood surveying the audience in the lobby before the concert, I noticed two men handing out leaflets. One was small and dark, the other big and sturdy with a Mongolian cast to his face. They told me they were Uighur refugees from China, and that they were trying to draw the concertgoers' attention to their fear that Uighur culture was being annihilated by the Han. Anxious to learn more, I invited the older of the two for lunch the following day, and there he told me about the General.

Now, stepping through a low gateway, I found myself in a small courtyard with buildings all round it and a mosque on the right-hand side. It looked like – and proved to be – a former *madrasah* or religious school. In the porch of the mosque a man was taking off his shoes to pray. I asked if he spoke English and he waved a hand towards the other side of the yard from which a glass veranda projected. At the far end was an open door, from which another man emerged. I began again to ask directions. He pointed in turn to a third, much older man, sitting at the far end of the glass veranda. Small and dapper in a green jacket and blue shirt, he sat behind a desk which almost filled the width of the room, protected from the sun by net curtains and by the shadows of leaves that danced on the desk and walls. As I approached he rose from his chair and came round the desk, addressing me in English and making a small bow. I knew immediately who he was. 'You must be the General,' I said.

Mehmet Riza Bekin, retired Turkish army general, Korean war veteran and former assistant chief of staff of Cento, the Central Treaty Organization, was born in Khotan in 1925 and left Xinjiang when he was 9 years old. For the last five years he had been the symbolic head of the Uighurs in exile. The foundation which he ran occupied two sides of the courtyard of the eighteenth-century Damat Ibrahim Pasha mosque in which we were standing. Loaned by the Turkish government, the premises comprised an office for the secretary, a classroom for lessons in the Uighur language and history, a library and a kitchen. The General's own office, hardly bigger than a cubbyhole and set in the old stone wall, was stuffed with mementoes. Outside it hung a picture of Mahmut Kashgari, the eleventh-century father of Uighur literature, along with photographs of modern Uighur heroes. Here was Ali Khan Ture, head of the independent republic created by the Ili rebellion in 1944, who had disappeared without trace; here the twice-exiled Isa Yusuf Alptekin, who died in Istanbul at the age of 94 and was venerated as patriarch of the Uighur diaspora. Beside them a grainy picture from 1932 showed a parade in Khotan of the guns and flags of the short-lived Turkish-Islamic Republic of Eastern Turkestan which sprang up during the great Muslim rebellion. The faces of Sabit Damullah, the regime's prime minister, and Mahmud Muhiti, military commander of Khoja Niyas's forces, stared out from the wall. But the most compelling of all was the image of the breakaway movement's mastermind, the hawk-eyed Emir of Khotan, Mehmet Emin Bughra.

'He was my uncle,' the General said. He went on to describe how, in 1934, his family had joined the Emir in his dramatic escape from the Dongan army over the Kunlun and Karakoram mountains to Ladakh. From there, the refugees moved on to Srinagar in British

India and thence to Afghanistan where the Emir was given a stipend by the ruler, and his young nephew was sent to primary school.

In 1938, the General's family moved on to Turkey where Bekin was enlisted at a military academy. Graduating in 1946, he served in the Korean War as a second lieutenant. After the war he was sent on courses in military intelligence and artillery in Germany and the United States, and was posted as military attaché to Tehran. Following a spell at staff college he was promoted to general, headed a UN mission to Afghanistan and represented Turkey in Cento.

Bekin's pursuit of what he sees as justice for the land of his birth may seem surprising: after all, he has spent all his adult life in another country, has sworn allegiance to another flag and has represented his adopted nation at a high level. When I asked him why he had chosen to devote his last years to the cause he said he found it impossible to ignore the Uighurs' plight. 'The people of Turkey can never forget their national land. They know we are brothers, of the same blood, of the same religion, the same ethnicity, going back to 3,000 years before Christ.'

Perhaps, too, he felt he had inherited the obligation from his uncle the Emir. The latter lived for some years under an assumed name in Afghanistan. There he tried to interest the Shah in a scheme to invite the Japanese to take over Eastern Turkestan as a sort of protectorate along the lines of their puppet state Manchukuo in north-east China, a wild plan which seemed designed to antagonize everybody, including his own countrymen. In 1943 the Emir returned to China, to the Guomindang capital of Chongqing, hoping to persuade Chiang Kai-shek to give Eastern Turkestan its autonomy. In the capital he teamed up with Isa Yusuf Alptekin, a Kashgari intellectual who had fled from the dictator Sheng Shicai in 1932, and the two of them published Uighur nationalist journals such as *Turkistan Avazi*, *Tian Shan* and *Altai*. They returned together to Xinjiang in 1945 after the truce had been signed with the Ili republic, to become ministers in the coalition government of the appeaser Zhang Zhizhong. When the Communists took over in 1949, both had to flee again. With a party of several hundred they crossed the Karakoram in midwinter, where the dreadful conditions on the high passes caused the death of Alptekin's daughter. Reaching Leh, the two leaders were flown on to Srinagar, following the same route that the Emir had taken years before, and were given shelter by Sheikh Abdullah of Kashmir. Settling eventually in Turkey, they continued to challenge the Chinese occupation of Eastern Turkestan. The Emir remained the father figure of Uighur nationalists in exile until his death in 1965.

His mantle then passed to Alptekin, who in 1970 visited America to lobby the US government and the United Nations for an independent Turkestan embracing both sides of the Pamir mountains. According to one Uighur exile, the Soviet Union was keener still to detach Xinjiang from China; he claimed that in 1972 the USSR offered Alptekin ten divisions of troops and tanks, including two of expatriate Uighurs, for a takeover of Xinjiang. Alptekin smelled a rat and declined the invitation to fly to Moscow to discuss the invasion proposal. He remained in Istanbul until his death in 1995. All across Turkey, parks and streets are named after him.

Another survivor of those turbulent decades was the man who could take some of the credit for making them so: Yolbas Khan, the Tiger Prince, vizier to the ruler of Hami. He it was who had spread the Muslim revolt by inviting the Baby General Ma Zhongying and his rebel Dongan army into the province. When the revolt petered out Yolbas fled to Nanjing. The Guomindang made him 'special executive commissioner' and sent him back to Xinjiang in 1946. Though a senior member of the Nationalist command, he, like the Kazakh chief Osman Batur, refused to join in the general surrender to the Communists, and took to the hills with a force of Chinese Muslim cavalry and White Russians. His former employers, now safely ensconced in Taiwan, were impressed by this show of resistance and nominated him governor of Xinjiang. But the Tiger Prince soon found himself short of supplies, and on the run. The last straw came when his Dongan soldiers defected. With less than a hundred supporters left, he set out for Tibet, hoping to reach Taiwan via India. The party crossed the Tibetan plateau in midwinter and, as Alptekin had lost his daughter on the Karakoram pass, so Yolbas now lost his wife. Arriving in Lhasa, most of the refugees were arrested by the Dalai Lama, but Yolbas and a few others were allowed to continue into India, and reached Taiwan on May Day, 1951.

The Tiger Prince had two sons by his first wife, named Yakub Beg and Niyas after his heroes. Though now in his sixties, he married a 19-year-old girl in Taiwan and settled down to enjoy retirement as the honorary governor of Xinjiang in exile. He is thought to have died in his late eighties.[1]

The few characters in the Xinjiang drama who managed to escape sudden death at the hands of their enemies could count, it seems, on living to a grand old age. Sadly for him, the colourful Kazakh leader Osman Batur was not one of them. He never made it abroad. Refusing to accept the Soviet-imposed coalition government in 1946, he retired with his cavalry and tents (his train was said to consist of 4,000 yurts and 15,000 people) to the northern slopes of Mount Bogda where he 'lived like a potentate'.[2] When the Communists took control he maintained his defiance, joining other resistance fighters who had trekked south across the Lop desert and taken refuge in the wastes of the Qaidam plateau. Osman was captured during a PLA attack early in 1951, taken to Urumchi and executed as a counter-revolutionary. Harried by aircraft and Communist patrols the remnants of his train, some 3,000 people, struggled over the Kunlun mountains and across the Tibetan plateau to reach India. Many died on the way. Osman's son Sherdirman continued to hold out in the mountains until 1953, when he gave up in order to be 're-educated' as a cadre.[3]

The first wave of émigrés, therefore, were prominent people who found themselves on the losing side during the political upheavals of the 1930s and 1940s. As so often in Xinjiang's volatile history, flight was the only way to save one's skin. But whereas in the past it had been possible to slip over the mountains for a while until things quietened down, now there was no prospect of going home again – not at least for Uighur nationalists and Guomindang supporters whom the Communists regarded as ideological enemies. For them, exile was to be lifelong, like the internal exile imposed on Chinese dissidents transported from the east to populate the Xinjiang gulag. Thus, while Chinese counter-revolutionaries were being locked in, Turki and Muslim counter-revolutionaries were being locked out: they became exiles from the land of exile.

Once Communism was established, these exiled veterans of civil war were joined by dissidents of another kind, intellectuals who feared imprisonment and herdsmen who faced ruin from the seizure of their lands and livestock. Most of them had to leave secretly. Occasionally, they would be let go. In 1961, as we have seen, a window was opened when the Party allowed Uighurs and other ethnic minority people with foreign connections to emigrate. However, the 1962 mass exodus of Kazakhs and others (described in Chapter 5) resulted in that door being slammed shut again.

Among those who left while they had the chance was Ziya Samedi, a popular novelist who was described on his death in 2000 as 'the most influential Uighur writer of the twentieth century'.[4] Born and educated in Soviet Kazakhstan, Samedi had an eventful career. As a teenager he moved to Gulja where he helped set up many Uighur primary schools. He then fell foul of the warlord governor Sheng Shicai, was arrested in 1937 and spent seven years in jail. He was set free by the Ili rebellion, joined the army of the Eastern Turkestan Republic, and was promoted to colonel. He survived Liberation, enjoying high official positions until the Great Leap Forward in 1958 when, in common with many other Uighurs, he was denounced as an ethnic nationalist and sentenced to 're-education through labour'. On his second release from jail, Samedi took his family back to Kazakhstan where he spent the next forty years campaigning for the freedom of Eastern Turkestan.

During the Cultural Revolution which began in 1966, the erratic compass of nationalities policy swung in the opposite direction, as we have seen. Foreign family connections which in the early 1960s had been a passport to emigration were now a dreadful liability, a ticket to jail. The border was shut tight – so far as was possible in that mountainous terrain – and stayed shut for more than a decade. Cross-border visits were allowed after 1983 when China and the USSR restored diplomatic relations, but the mountain passes were not fully reopened until after the outbreak of Muslim militancy which followed the collapse of the Soviet Union in 1991 had abated. The Khunjerab pass leading to Pakistan, for example, was reopened on 1 May 1993 (though it was closed again during the hunt for al-Qaeda terrorists in 2002). In 1994 Chinese Kazakhs were allowed to settle in the newly independent

Kazakhstan if they wished; this was in exchange for an undertaking by the republic's president Nursultan Nazarbayev to keep his separatist agitators under control.

The emigration of Ziya Samedi could be said to mark the beginning of what has since become a brain drain. Although there are political dissidents among the latest asylum seekers, many of them are educated younger people trying to escape racial abuse and the kind of job discrimination described in the previous chapter. China does little to stop them leaving now: their problem, latterly, has been to find a country willing to take them.

A former cancer surgeon at the Urumchi Railway Hospital is an example of the second generation of refugees. He left China in 1997 complaining of persistent discrimination. The final straw, he said, was when an examination paper was rigged in order to block his promotion at the hospital. He went to Turkey, from where he helped a British television crew make a documentary in Xinjiang about birth deformities caused by radioactive fall-out from the Lop Nor nuclear testing ground, thereby making himself *persona non grata* with the Chinese. After the programme was broadcast, and fearing that he was no longer safe in Turkey, he decided in 1999 to go to London and seek political asylum.

Another doctor, a woman radiologist, had the same difficulty in getting advancement after she graduated from medical college. Coming from a highly educated family in the small Tartar community in Urumchi, she found the system weighted heavily against her. This woman described how she had passed a test which would have qualified her to study in Japan, but was not allowed to go; she then applied for the United States, with the same results; and again for Germany, but was not allowed to take the test. She was even turned down for a scholarship programme set up especially for Tartar students by the Australian government. 'I suspect the Chinese clerk in the Australian embassy was giving the places out to his Han Chinese friends,' she said. Lack of opportunity was her first reason for leaving. Her second was the lack of freedom. 'I could not speak,' she said. 'I felt something pressing on my head all the time. Every day I went to work I felt miserable. I didn't like the hospital, and I didn't like the boss constantly mocking me.'

A university lecturer who graduated from a Beijing university –

a rare distinction for a Uighur – at the time of the student demonstrations in Tiananmen Square went back to teach in Xinjiang
where he talked enthusiastically to friends about the prospects for
democracy in China. That was enough, he quickly discovered, to
put him under suspicion and to put an end to his prospects of
advancement. He obtained permission to leave the country in
order to visit his Kazakh grandmother, but on arrival in Tashkent
he took the train on to Moscow. He had no Russian, no contacts
and very little money. A kind Muscovite couple took him in while
he made the rounds of the Western embassies in search of a visa,
which the British eventually granted. After two attempts to cross
Europe by rail he finally reached London.[5]

Of the estimated million or more Turkis who have fled, some have
migrated as far afield as Sweden and Australia, but the great majority are to be found, not surprisingly, in the neighbouring republics
of the former Soviet Union, particularly Kazakhstan. Pakistan is
sympathetic to Muslim émigrés, though many refugees have been
marooned in camps there. Saudi Arabia has had a small Uighur
community since the 1930s, consisting mainly of rich merchants
who arrived as pilgrims to Mecca and who stayed on. Though its
Uighur community of 40,000 is much smaller than Kazakhstan's,
Turkey has been especially welcoming to the hardship cases,
including families who were barred from the former Soviet Union
and who crossed the mountains to India and Pakistan and became
stuck, like the pitiful remnants of Osman Batur's Kazakh caravan.
It was Turkey which in 1952, yielding to the pleas of Mehmet
Emin Bughra and Isa Yusuf Alptekin, gave political asylum to dissidents whom Egypt and Saudi Arabia would not accept.[6]

The first Uighurs settled in the Zeytinburnu district of Istanbul,
later arrivals in Kayseri, the principal city of central Anatolia,
where they recreated a home from home in the small suburb of
Yesevi. It has been described by the scholar Frédérique-Jeanne
Besson: 'two avenues and four cross-streets lined with one-storey
houses surrounded by gardens, all built to the same pattern . . .
allowing the exiles to continue a way of life much like that at home,
maintaining their own dress and diet, and even growing in their

plots the vegetables of Eastern Turkestan which they cannot get in Turkey'.[7] Although some of the younger generation have moved out into the wider community, their sense of identity remains remarkably strong. A group who left Kayseri for Istanbul, for example, were approached by no fewer than three different Uighur associations. They refused to join any of them, but instead set up their own Association of Kayseri Uighurs in Istanbul. As Besson observed, Uighurs are good at seeing themselves as Turkis when they are with Europeans, as Uighurs when with Turkis, and as Kashgaris, Keriyanese or Khotanese when they are with other Uighurs.

In recent years Uighur exiles have moved into western Europe, the United States, Canada and Australia. But it was a quirk of history that brought some to Scandinavia. They were taken to Sweden in the 1920s by Lutheran missionaries who for a hundred years were particularly active – though not, it seems, very successful – in western China. The Swedish connection, reforged by the explorer Sven Hedin and continued in a long chain of Turkestan enthusiasts, is today represented by an immigrant club in Stockholm, the East Turkestan Society, which runs a women's dance troupe and an all-Uighur football team.

It is easier to account for the Uighurs in Germany, most of whom live in and around Munich. They followed the migration of 'guest workers' from Turkey who went to seek their fortune during West Germany's economic boom after the Second World War and settled down there. Like their Turkish cousins, the Uighurs were hardly assimilated, preferring to work for Turkish employers where they could. In Germany the scope for political activity was less restricted than in Istanbul or Ankara – though Chinese intelligence agents kept a close watch on activists wherever they were. Some of them, including Erkin Alptekin, son of Isa Yusuf the patriarch of the diaspora, went to work for Radio Free Europe, the anti-Communist station which had been founded in Munich in 1950 to broadcast behind the Iron Curtain. Munich later emerged as the base of the Uighur liberation movement in Europe.

Adelaide in Australia became an improbable refuge when the Australian government agreed with the United Nations after the Second World War to take a number of Uighurs permitted to leave Xinjiang if they could show that they belonged ethnically to one of the Soviet central Asian 'races'. Some of them moved on to Melbourne and Sydney, like the journalist Ahmet Igamberdi who was born in Tashkent, spent eleven years in a Chinese jail, and was (at the time of writing) president of the Sydney association.

Only a handful of Uighurs had arrived in Great Britain by the end of the twentieth century, to form a small enclave in an area of north London already popular with Turks. A benign immigration regime – benign, at least, until the terrorist attacks on America in 2001 – attracted many more to the United States, where the Uyghur American Association found ready-made support from university academics and human rights groups. Some of the richer émigrés went to Canada, whose doors at that time were open to any Chinese who brought enough capital with them.

In these western enclaves, the Uighurs tend to maintain their traditions. Only in central Asia have they become assimilated, adopting Russian dress and speaking Russian among themselves. The wider diaspora is new enough for most of the exiles to have clear memories of home, and the younger ones who have no political record are easily able to visit their families in Xinjiang. For this reason, Uighur communities in the western world continue to run on traditional – that is to say, hierarchical – lines.[8] Authority lies in the hands of an *aksakal* (greybeard) or family head whose own experience, though it might make him a committed nationalist, has also taught him the price of protest. He may have done time in jail, in solitary confinement and in the torture chamber. He cannot with an easy conscience support the hotheads of the younger generation. As a result those who enjoy prestige in their communities are not always the ones who lead the political struggle. For that reason, among others, the Uighur diaspora, already small and scattered, is riven with faction and suspicion, and has failed to create anything like a credible government-in-exile. As Besson writes: 'The problem for the Uighurs in exile is . . . not so much to preserve their identity as to overcome their differences sufficiently to form a homogeneous community.'

Which is not to say that they have not tried. In the autumn of 2001, a month after the terrorist atrocities in the United States, I found myself sitting in a basement meeting room of the Europa Hotel in Brussels for the opening of the grandly titled General Assembly of the East Turkestan National Congress.

Among the grey-haired elders on the top table I recognized immediately the General, Riza Bekin. Above him hung a large flag showing a white crescent and star on a background of peacock blue, a design derived not from Islam but from an ancient Buddhist motif of sickle moon, stars and doves. Around the remaining three tables, arranged to form a rectangle, sat sixty delegates, graded by age, with the older ones placed nearest to the top table. The variety of their features was striking: the flat wide faces of Mongols, the square heads and thick necks of Slavic Europeans, the aquiline profiles of Iranian Turks and even, in the furthest corner, a pale Japanese. The men wore suits or leather jackets and carried cameras or video recorders. The women, in place of the usual skirt, waistcoat and leggings of Xinjiang, wore dresses of pale lilac and purple stripes decorated with sequins, with short Russian boots on their feet. Against one wall sat an old Kyrgyz woman in a coloured headscarf with a flat wrinkled face, looking every inch the Russian *babushka*. Opposite her was a dark, almond-eyed beauty in her early twenties who gazed around with unselfconscious admiration at the expensive hotel furnishings.

As they waited for the proceedings to begin, the delegates talked amongst themselves. It was clear that the majority were from the central Asian republics, for it was Russian that they spoke, not Uighur. Later, I was told that twenty delegates from Xinjiang had applied for permission to attend the conference but had – not surprisingly – been refused. More striking was the absence (with the exception of the Congress organizers and one man from London) of delegates from western Europe and the US. The second oddity was the clumsy wording of the banner over the top table: 'East Turkestan (Uyghuristan) National Congress'. The meaning of the parenthesis was soon to be explained.

The congress opened with a prayer chanted by a tall and handsome old man. This was Haji Yakup Anat, a poet and historian who had taken refuge in Ankara after being jailed under Sheng Shicai for five years, and under the Communists for twenty-six years. His prayer was for the repose of the soul of Dilbirim Samsakova, a fellow member of the organization's committee, who had been found drowned in suspicious circumstances in Kazakhstan five months before. The delegates joined in, bowing their heads and holding their palms open before them. At the end of the prayer they brought their hands together over their eyes and made the customary gesture of wiping the hands down the face and over the chin. Each delegate was then introduced in turn, rising from his or her seat and making a small bow of acknowledgement.

The first political organization of Uighur exiles was set up in Almaty (then Alma Ata) in 1963, and called the Free Eastern Turkestan Movement. It claimed to control a 'liberation army' of 50,000 refugees, many of whom had served in the forces of the independent republic in the 1940s. The liberation committee was headed by the novelist Ziya Samedi whose career we have briefly noted earlier, and the 'army' by Zunun Taipov, another Uighur from the days of the Ili rebellion. But attempts to formalize the struggle for freedom did not get under way until the 1990s. A Uighur Liberation Organization in Kazakhstan registered itself as a political party in 1991 and the following year an International Uighur Union was created in Almaty, followed by a Free Uighuristan party in Kyrgyzstan. In December 1992, after the fall of the Soviet Union, a congress was called in Istanbul with the aim of setting up an international umbrella body. It failed because of poor organization and shortage of funds, but also because of political rivalry among the forty delegates from eighteen countries. For when their Turkish hosts unveiled their own agenda, for an independent Turkestan with themselves in charge, the visitors baulked. Each delegation head saw himself as the natural first president of the new state, and the project collapsed.

In 1998, however, spurred on by the Gulja riot and its savage aftermath, refugee associations from central Asia, Turkey and Germany meeting in Ankara succeeded in creating an East Turkestan National Centre. This became the National Congress at a meeting in Munich the following year, when a fifteen-person governing body was elected, and a secretariat was established in the city. Claiming the active support of thirteen refugee associations, the ETNC listed its principal aims as broadcasting the plight of Uighurs in China, mobilizing world opinion and putting pressure on the Chinese leadership through multinational agencies such as the European Parliament, the Arab League, the Islamic Conference and, of course, the United Nations. It hoped to be recognized as the authentic medium for expressing Uighur demands for the right to self-determination, and to become – if ever that day should arrive – the interlocutor in negotiations with the Chinese for autonomy.

How far short of achieving those ambitions the ETNC still was, the most casual observer at its Brussels congress could not have failed to see. Within minutes of the opening, General Bekin was chastizing his compatriots for their laziness in advancing the cause, and their constant in-fighting. 'The Chinese intelligence police have spies in our organization and are trying to divide it and create a split with the leadership,' he declared. His complaint was echoed by the politically experienced Erkin Alptekin, who said that laziness and lack of education were the two enemies of progress:

> The struggle must be fought with intelligence, and in peace. We have too many leaders. Don't promise more than you can deliver. If you can't do something, don't pretend that you can. Study the language of the country you live in, because without it you can neither explain nor persuade. Remember that there are more than 6,000 peoples in the world fighting for their independence.[9]

Its lack of an uncontested leader is perhaps the single greatest weakness of the Uighur diaspora. After the death of Isa Yusuf Alptekin, there was no obvious successor. The Uighurs had no Dalai Lama as the Tibetans had, no one with the diplomatic skills, let alone the authority, to speak for them. (The status of the Dalai Lama had, of course, been consecrated by centuries of theocratic government which made him the only possible leader of the government-in-exile set up at Dharamsala in northern India after his flight over the Himalayas in 1959.)

The first weakness leads to the second, a deep disagreement over tactics. The ETNC condemns terrorism and proclaims a policy of non-violence in pursuit of independence for Xinjiang. But many exiles, especially in central Asia (not to mention young militants inside Xinjiang itself), see violence as the only recourse left to them, and for this reason they refuse to join the Munich organization. One such group is the East Turkestan National Liberation Front, apparently based in central Asia, whose leader has claimed to have ordered a series of bus bombings and attacks on military bases in Xinjiang. The Front's leader is said to be a man called Yusup, an octogenarian former officer in the army of the 1944 Eastern Turkestan Republic who became deputy director of the Xinjiang Museum under the Communists and fled to the Soviet Union in 1957.[10] Erkin Alptekin has acknowledged the division, but adds that if some Uighurs in their desperation are using violence, that does not mean that millions of Uighurs are terrorists. 'The vast majority want to achieve their goals by peaceful means, but they have been victims of state terrorism for the last 125 years' (that is, since the reconquest of Xinjiang by General Zuo Zongtang).[11]

Even within the ETNC there is disagreement about what a future independent Xinjiang should be called. Some want it to be named 'Eastern Turkestan', to imply a multi-ethnic republic, others 'Uighuristan' to assert Uighur hegemony. And so the organization is forced to adopt the clumsily ambiguous title proclaimed on its banner. As the poet Yakub Anat said, the argument is a waste of time. 'The solution is simple,' he told the congress delegates. 'When we have our freedom, we will let the people decide what name to use.'

Missing from the debate is what a Western human rights specialist has called an 'ethic of activism', to promote trust and put an end to 'the perennial squabbles over ephemeral titles, leadership turf and media status'.[12] Privately, one Uighur delegate was even more severe. He complained that leaders in exile were chosen for their wealth rather than their education, and that all wanted to be chief. 'Uighurs are stupid,' he said, 'and I wish someone would write this.' Why did he say Uighurs were stupid? 'Because they have inherited from the Chinese the idea that they are superior to everyone else. They all argue about who is to be president, even before they have won independence for our country.'[13]

As a propaganda outfit, the ETNC has shown itself somewhat more effective. Like dissident bodies of all kinds, it has found in the Internet a cheap and easy outlet for its message. As the Hawaii university professor Dru Gladney put it, 'They don't have a separatist movement; they have a cyber-separatist movement;' though he qualified the implied criticism by adding, 'which doesn't mean it should be taken any less seriously. But it lacks organization, leadership and a headquarters.'[14] The Internet, however, has its own constitutional weakness. Unlike television channels, radio stations, newspapers and journals, it employs no intermediary, no reporter or editor, to verify what is disseminated over it. The reader has no means of judging the reliability of claims. While the Internet makes it exhilaratingly easy for Uighur exiles and their supporters to mount attacks on China's behaviour in Xinjiang, it is equally easy for Chinese spokesmen to dismiss the claims as the false propaganda of an unrepresentative minority of politically, or religiously, motivated misfits and zealots. Investigators for bodies such as Amnesty International, which rely for their efficacy on the credibility of their reports, find the ETNC somewhat amateurish, careless of its own internal security, and not particularly reliable because of its lack of a proper network of informants inside China. Amnesty remains confident, however, of the reliability of its own dossiers on the violation of human rights in Xinjiang – indeed, they are endorsements without which the voices of the Uighur diaspora might not have been heard.

Although at the turn of the millennium few people in the West – even those who were aware of the persecution in Tibet – knew much about Xinjiang, the plight of the Uighurs was beginning to make an impression. One or two members of the US Congress spoke up for them, and the White House was kept informed. A former president of Ireland, Mary Robinson, became the UN High Commissioner for Human Rights – a newly created post – and visited China with the treatment of the Uighurs among the items on her agenda.

A small, but for Uighur exiles important, propaganda coup was achieved in the autumn of 2001, when the ETNC was invited to stage a seminar in the European Parliament building in Brussels on the day before its own congress. The venue was controversial, since it implied European Union approval for the seminar's theme: 'The Situation in East Turkestan after Half a Century of Chinese Communist Occupation'. For the Chinese government, the title and venue were both slaps in the face. Not only is 'East Turkestan' a banned phrase in China, but the word 'occupation' was an open challenge to the legitimacy of Beijing's rule.

The European Parliament had already, on 10 April 1997, passed a resolution outlining the grievances of the Uighurs and calling on the Chinese government to negotiate a settlement of them. However, the host of this conference was not the Parliament but one of its smallest constituents: the Transnational Radical Party, an alliance of political mavericks which included seven members of the Parliament and a member of the European Commission.[15]

When he heard of the invitation, the Chinese ambassador in Brussels naturally made every effort to get the conference stopped. In terms of valuable publicity, the ensuing fracas suited the organizers well, and Olivier Dupuis, secretary-general of the TRP, made the most of it. He promptly sent an open letter to the president of the European Parliament, Nicole Fontaine, full of indignation at this attempt to muzzle his guests.

When the doors opened on the day, an official from the Chinese embassy in Brussels and a young reporter from the state-run *People's Daily* were seen sitting in the row reserved for the Press, where they had to endure the occasional barb flung in their direction. Among the speakers from the platform was the chairman of the European Parliamentary delegation to China, Per Gahrton, who, after reminding his audience that it was official EU policy to support 'one China', added: 'But we cannot rule the future.' Other speakers were much less diplomatic, demanding independence for Eastern Turkestan and accusing the Chinese government of itself using terror tactics to stifle such demands. To sit and listen to such things cannot have been a pleasant experience for the two Chinese. In the interval I asked the *People's Daily* reporter whether he would be filing a story for his newspaper. 'No,' he replied. 'It is not interesting.'

Not interesting in public, perhaps. But in private, China's reaction to the separatist agitation of Xinjiang exiles has been fierce, and sometimes fearful. A clue to the leadership's real feelings is provided by the minutes of a Chinese Communist Party Politburo meeting early in 1996, which were circulated to top brass in the government and army.

This document, which somehow found its way into the hands of

Uighur activists, calls for a combination of diplomacy, co-operation and pressure on Kazakhstan, Kyrgyzstan and Turkey, 'taking full advantage of our political superiority', in order to keep the separatists under control. 'Be especially vigilant,' it tells its select audience, 'and prevent, by every possible means, outside separatists from internationalizing the problem of so-called "Eastern Turkestan". Divide the separatists, win over the majority, and alienate and fight the small number that remain.' And employing a phrase which counter-espionage adepts may appreciate, it adds: 'Establish home bases in the regions or cities with large Chinese and overseas Chinese populations.'[16] (It is worth recalling that the old habit of seeing a foreign agent behind every internal upheaval had been revived by that seminal event, the Baren riot of 1990. As recently as 1986, the Party's leader Hu Yaobang had regarded alien influence as negligible.)

Surveillance of individual exiles and diplomatic pressure on their host governments are the two prongs of Chinese security policy – though exiles claim that political assassinations have also been carried out. So the General's reference at the ETNC congress to spies and infiltrators was not idle rhetoric. Emigrés who have returned to Xinjiang to conduct academic research have been met by friendly plainclothes police, invited out to dinner and lectured on the folly of writing or speaking ill of Chinese government policy. Such pep talks seem to carry the implication of serious consequences if they are ignored. Meanwhile, Uighur activists abroad have been made uncomfortably aware that the 'friends' who seek them out are not always what they seem – they may be Muslim militants, trained terrorists, or employees of the Chinese intelligence service.

The goal of China's diplomatic pressure in central Asia is nothing less than to liquidate the Uighur resistance movement.

In its dying years, the Soviet Union was positively helpful to Beijing in suppressing the anti-Chinese activists in its Asian republics. When it collapsed, emancipating the five republics overnight, life for political refugees should have become easier. Instead, it became very much harder, thanks to Chinese pressure. Bringing her considerable diplomatic and economic weight to bear, China had within a few years secured a border and extradition treaty with three of the states – Kazakhstan, Kyrgyzstan and Tajikistan – and with

Russia. Signed in Shanghai in 1996, the treaty allows its signatories to extradite 'criminals', a term which, as we have seen, has a broad designation in China. The treaty created an 80-mile-deep cordon sanitaire along mutual borders, to be patrolled by joint military units. The central Asian states helped by closing Uighur publications and offices, arresting Uighurs who criticized China, and keeping an eye open for the export of propaganda, money and guns.[17]

Even before the creation of the 'Shanghai Five' President Nursultan Nazarbayev of Kazakhstan promised to keep a close watch on his Uighur refugees in return for greater freedom for Xinjiang's Kazakhs. That promise was more than honoured in the aftermath of the Gulja riot in 1997, when the Chinese claimed to have found two secret dynamite factories and a military training base in Kashgar, and to have captured four trucks carrying weapons into Xinjiang, including machine guns, pistols, remote detonators, anti-tank grenades and temperature-controlled bombs.

Nazarbayev's Kazakh police hunted down those who had fled across the Chinese border seeking political asylum. Uighur leaders complained that their societies were infiltrated, their mosques and imams put under state supervision and public meetings strictly policed.[18] In general, it should be said, central Asians do not much like suppressing their own kinsmen in this way and, in spite of the Shanghai treaty, spokesmen for separatists in Kazakhstan have been able to speak quite freely to the Western press.

An indeterminate number of asylum-seekers have been sent back to China – 'illegally deported' according to the human rights people – where they have usually been executed. For example, in January 1999, Kazakhstan returned three young Uighurs who had sought asylum after serving two-year jail terms in their own country. In March 2001, a Chinese court found them guilty of illegally crossing the border and attempting to 'split the country'. They were sentenced to death. The same month the Kyrgyzstan government, now running a joint counter-terrorism centre in the capital Bishkek, put four Uighur youths on trial for complicity in planting a bomb on a bus in the city of Osh, even though local officers and a regional court had ruled the accusations groundless. In the absence of defence counsel, three of the youths were sentenced to death and one to twenty-five years' imprisonment. A human rights investigator claimed that he had been told informally by an official that the young men had nothing to do with the bombing, but that the authorities had acted under great pressure from China.[19] According to a human rights worker in Kyrgyzstan, no fewer than 80,000 Uighurs were arrested following the treaty, of whom nearly three-quarters were sent to prison camps.

More sinister forces have been blamed for the sudden deaths of a number of prominent Uighur exiles in Kazakhstan and Kyrgyzstan. In May 2001 the body of Dilbirim Samsakova, the mother of two adopted children, was found in Kapshghay lake about 70 miles from Almaty. Uighurs believe the 44-year-old political activist and charity worker was abducted and killed. The parents of the adopted children had been suspected of murdering a Kazakh policeman and had themselves been killed in a shoot-out in the city.[20] Two years earlier, the leader of the 'Uighuristan Liberation Organization' was beaten up in his apartment and died of his injuries; the representative of a Uighur newspaper in Kazakhstan was also killed. In Bishkek, the head of another Uighur movement, *Ittipak* ('Solidarity'), was shot and killed outside his house in March 2000.[21]

Although not one of the original Shanghai Five, the state of Uzbekistan signed up in 2001, by which time trade and investment had been added to the security agenda. The country has been beset by militants and has replied in kind: to wear a beard can be enough to earn a jail sentence in Uzbekistan, whose prisons are said to hold 7,000 political detainees.[22] The main opposition comes from the Islamic Movement of Uzbekistan, an avowedly revolutionary body which seeks to overthrow the government and set up a theocratic state under shariah law. The IMU has recruited a number of Uighurs, some of them veterans of the Afghan war against Russia, others graduates of the Pakistan *madrasahs* or of the Taliban training camps in Afghanistan.

Quite apart from their instinctive aversion to political opposition (most are former Communist apparatchiks wearing nationalist hats), the leaders of the five central Asian republics have every incentive to comply with China's programme. The positive incentives include the promise of valuable export contracts and help in curbing their own troublemakers; the negative, fear of China's military power and economic aggrandizement. As for the intended victims of this double squeeze, the Uighur exiles, their sense of a common cause can only be enhanced by the attention they are receiving.

Among the cities which the Chinese Politburo wants monitored, Istanbul must come high on the list. Turkey's leaders have not been shy in declaring their solidarity with the Uighurs. For Suleyman Demirel, a former prime minister, they were 'ethnic brothers' whose assimilation by the Chinese was an issue for the United Nations. Turgut Ozal, his successor, said after being presented with a Uighur coat, skullcap and flag by the elder Alptekin: 'I have taken delivery of the Eastern Turkestani cause . . . It is our desire to see the ancient homeland of the Turkic peoples a free country.'[23] In Beijing this was interpreted to mean that Ozal envisioned a Turki homeland stretching from the Balkans to the Great Wall of China.[24] The bogey of pan-Turkism was thus revived – the prospect, as the Chinese see it, of a hostile, multinational alliance of Turkic-speakers, from the Ottomans on the Aegean Sea to the Yakuts on the Siberian Pacific. They have not forgotten Yakub Beg's appeals to Istanbul in the nineteenth century, or the proselytizing mission organized by Turkey in the early twentieth century when an envoy of the Sultan arrived in Kashgar to modernize the school syllabus and teach the children to regard the Sultan as their leader.

Twice in recent years China has sent senior leaders to confront the Turkish authorities with evidence of anti-Chinese activity in their country. In the year 2000 it was President Jiang Zemin, whose message was not entirely well received. There were public protests against China's treatment of the Uighurs, whom Turkish ministers advised Jiang to regard not as an enemy but as an asset, a 'friendship bridge' to Turkey and central Asia. Two years later it was the turn of Zhu Rongji, the prime minister, who extracted (according to Chinese television) a promise from Bulent Ecevit to curb the Uighur 'terrorists' in his country. At these summit meetings the Chinese would not only have reminded their Turkish friends of mutual military and trade exchanges, but would also have drawn the obvious parallel between their problems in Xinjiang and Turkey's long war against Kurdish separatism in eastern Anatolia.

China's suspicions of Turkey are understandable. In October

1999, Istanbul police arrested ten members of a group called the East Turkestan Liberation Organization, after one of their number admitted killing two Chinese restaurant owners, throwing a petrol bomb at the Chinese consulate and attempting to assassinate the consul. Though born in Turkey, the 22-year-old youth was the son of a Uighur from Xinjiang and said he had acted in reprisal for the Chinese testing of nuclear and chemical weapons in his father's homeland.[25] A month later another group, 'The Home of the Youth', claimed to have 2,000 members in Turkey, among them young tank commanders and fighter pilots in the armed forces who were itching to fight the Chinese. A leader of this 'Xinjiang Hamas', which consciously models itself on the Palestinian terrorist group, told a reporter from Taiwan: 'Every one of us is a bomb.'[26] (That it was a Taiwanese visitor for whom this display of bravado was put on was no coincidence. Uighur nationalists have often said that a Chinese attack on the island fortress of the former Guomindang would be the signal for a general uprising in Xinjiang, observing that Chinese military forays abroad have often in the past been the trigger for internal rebellions.) Given that such claims are being made on its soil, it is politic for Turkey's leaders to give China minimum cause for complaint.

Closer to home, the Chinese know that private money from Saudi Arabia and Iran has been reaching the Uighurs in Xinjiang, mainly to subsidize mosques and schools. But neither government has been implicated in providing funds for, let alone encouraging, terrorism. Saudi Arabia does not allow its Uighurs to form their own societies but there is nothing to stop them supporting exiles in other countries, including the United States.[27] A certain complicity has been suspected, however, not because Osama bin Laden and a number of the September 11 hijackers were Saudis but because the royal family is alleged to have paid bin Laden and his Taliban hosts at least $300 million in protection money to stop further attacks on American targets in the country.[28] Furthermore, the enthusiasm with which Saudi Arabia exports Wahhabism, the revivalist version of Islam which its people practise, has found outlets in the inflammatory sermons of mullahs whose mosques – in Europe as well as Asia – harbour disaffected young men eager to respond to the summons to *jihad*.

Pakistan and Afghanistan, with which Xinjiang shares a narrow border, had become a worry to Beijing well before the terrorist attacks on New York and Washington. Chinese diplomats told their ally Pakistan to use its influence with the Taliban to stop training Uighurs in their military bases, and to hand over suspects who had taken refuge in Pakistan itself.[29] A mass expulsion of young Uighurs studying at Pakistani colleges occurred in 2000 and police closed down the Kashgar Rabat and Khotan Rabat refugee hostels in Islamabad. Thirteen religious students who had fled to Pakistan seeking asylum after the Gulja riot of 1997 were handed back; twelve of them were summarily executed just inside the Chinese border. And two Uighurs reportedly trained in Pakistan were captured by Russian troops in the breakaway Caucasian republic of Chechyna, and handed over.

Like many Western analysts, the Chinese saw the *madrasahs* of Pakistan as the real breeding-ground of Muslim fanaticism, the al-Qaeda camps as merely the finishing schools. That did not stop them from discreetly supporting the Taliban government in Afghanistan, however, while at the same time keeping lines open to their opponents. Erkin Alptekin, son of the famous exile, claims that the Chinese used the Taliban to destabilize oil-rich countries of the Middle East, hoping thereby to increase their own influence, and that they had had a defence agreement with the Taliban since 1998 that promised China access to any unexploded cruise missiles the Americans might drop on Afghanistan.[30]

China's suspicions of an organized terrorist threat seemed to be confirmed by early reports of enemy casualties in the Americans' retaliatory assault on al-Qaeda terrorist bases in Afghanistan in the autumn of 2001. The reports mentioned a number of 'Chinese' who were, in fact, Uighurs. American troops certainly captured a number of Uighurs during operations against the Taliban. Beijing's estimate that 1,000 Xinjiang Muslims had been drilled at Osama bin Laden's camps was, however, considered too high. Whether they were being trained for operations inside China, or elsewhere, is another question.

Exiles accused the Chinese leadership of using President Bush's retaliatory 'war against terrorism' as a pretext for further repressing the Uighurs inside Xinjiang. After September 11, thousands more people were reportedly detained, and a number of them were given long jail sentences or were executed. There were renewed complaints of extrajudicial killings and torture, while in some areas restrictions were imposed on religious and folk traditions – not only weddings, funerals and circumcision ceremonies, but also house-moving rituals and the wearing of earrings.[31]

An official rebuttal published in January 2002 emphasized that the large show of military force in the border areas was aimed only at 'criminal activities', and that no particular ethnic group or religion was being targeted. 'The Chinese government has not taken advantage of any opportunity to institute "suppression", nor does it deem it necessary to do so,' the statement said.[32]

This view of things was about to receive the kind of endorsement of which China's leaders could only have dreamed: it came from the United States itself. After years of criticizing China's record on human rights, and in spite of recent American warnings against victimizing Uighurs, the US announced at the end of August 2002 that it would freeze the financial assets of a group called the East Turkistan Islamic Movement.

That few people had heard of this body did not seem to matter. The Movement was added to a United Nations list of terrorist organizations because, in the words of the US State Department, it was 'believed responsible for committing numerous acts of terrorism in China', including assassinations, arson attacks, and bombings of buses, cinemas, department stores, markets and hotels.[33]

The announcement appeared to vindicate, at a stroke, all the protestations that China was fighting a dangerous adversary in Xinjiang. Uighur leaders in exile were dismayed, for the statement seemed to nullify their efforts to convince the world that violence in Xinjiang was rarely due to terrorism – that is, random killing to secure political ends – but was in almost every case a spontaneous reaction to Chinese oppression. It was, said the Munich-based East Turkestan National Congress, 'a green light for China to step up its campaign of repression', and 'a victory for their propaganda machine that has tarred and feathered the Uighurs as terrorists'.[34]

Sceptics suggested that the US move, coming as it did so long after the attacks on New York and Washington, was based not so much on hard evidence against the group (the Chinese had blamed many differently named groups in the past) but more on the Administration's need to win China's support for a quite unrelated venture: the war against Iraq which President Bush was already planning.

Western commentators continue to believe that China exaggerates the number of terrorists in Xinjiang in order to disarm foreign criticism of the way it treats the Uighurs. An American authority on China's Muslims has made the point rather differently: 'People always ask, will the Uighurs go get training from the Taliban? Sure, if there's money there. These people don't have much of an alternative and they're pretty disillusioned. But if someone offers them a scholarship to Harvard, they'd take that, too.'[35]

The impotence of exile can easily mutate into frustration and discord, as the experience of the Uighur diaspora has demonstrated. Frustration magnifies the refugee's hatred of the regime he has escaped, and inflates his sense of what realistically can be achieved politically. It can even poison his attitude to the host who has sheltered him, as it poisoned the feelings of Alexander Solzhenitsyn, the Soviet Union's most celebrated refugee, while he was living in the United States. One of the few things that the Xinjiang exiles truly have in common is this shared helplessness and sense of alienation.

Some, however, refuse to become involved in political agitation on the grounds that the agitators are pursuing the wrong goal. As one of them has said: 'All this talk of an independent Eastern Turkestan is a waste of time. The exiles' agenda is not realistic after fifty years of occupation. If the people there were treated only half as well as the Chinese, they would be content.' Yet few regret their decision to leave, and when they go back they find ample justification for their decision in the despair of the people they have left behind. Friends and family who doubted the advantages of leaving are now frankly envious. An exile who returned to Urumchi in 2001 after ten years abroad had dinner with friends from his student days and was told by one of them: 'You did well to get out when you did.'[36]

In a sense the machinations of the separatists outside Xinjiang have rebounded on their friends and families inside: the more alarmed Beijing becomes at the prospect of 'another Kashmir', or a 'Kosovo in Asia', the more harshly it treats its Uighur citizens. Uighurs may be allowed to speak their own language and maintain something of their culture, but their function as a social and political force is becoming ever more feeble, their identity ever more shadowy. It is becoming, as one described it, a 'fairytale identity' constructed by others, the Han Chinese occupiers who appear to have abandoned all pretence of sharing their colony with the people they have colonized. This segregation of Xinjiang will be examined in the final chapter.

10

Separate Tables

LIKE ALL INDUSTRIAL workers in Communist China, the employees of the Maralbashi cotton-packing plant, on the northwest edge of the Taklamakan desert, lived according to the Soviet model – at the factory. Unlike their Soviet counterparts, however, they lived in two separate compounds, one for the Chinese, another for the Uighurs.

To get to the factory each morning, the Chinese had to walk through the Uighur compound, where they ran the gauntlet of the Uighurs' dogs who would chase after them and bite them. To get to the town centre and market, on the other hand, the Uighurs had to cross the Chinese compound – where they would in turn be attacked by the Chinese dogs. The children of each compound would, as a matter of course, throw stones – or balls of hard clay – at each other, and sometimes heads were bloodied. Both lots of children, naturally, threw stones at the children of the sack factory next door.

The children of the two races lived in separate areas, and went to separate schools. An exception was made for the family of the factory's deputy Party secretary, a Uighur, who was allowed to live in the Chinese compound; and occasionally the Chinese factory manager would cross over to pay a social call on *his* Uighur deputy. 'In a way, it was worse than Northern Ireland,' recalled one of those Uighur children many years later. 'There was no communication at all, not even a common language.'[1]

In those days, the 1970s, the Chinese children got the worst of the mudball fights. There were far fewer of them. Today the position is reversed. There are (probably) more Han Chinese than Uighurs living in Xinjiang now; and in the factories they greatly outnumber them. For example, of the 12,800 workers at a textile mill in the Uighur-dominated area of Kashgar, only 800 are Uighurs.

The Maralbashi cotton plant has closed – or, rather, it has been moved into the Chinese new town about a half a mile away. The factory wall remains and most of the buildings: the manager's offices opposite the gatehouse, the storage sheds and a large asphalt yard, rutted and crumbling. A few of those Uighur children, grown up now, still live in the compound, though most of it has been turned into a timber yard. The wall over which the stones used to fly is there too, standing at right angles to a section of the mudbrick wall that used to encircle the whole of Maralbashi.

Maralbashi ('Stag's head') has seen many changes. At the top of the road leading down to the cotton plant there used to be a transit depot for prisoners from inner China on their way to the labour camps of Xinjiang. The site was being redeveloped when I saw it in 2002, apparently for flats. What was once the town centre, a short bicycle ride away from the plant, was now a poor outlying suburb where only Uighurs lived. Branching from a single paved road were the dusty lanes of traditional Uighur houses made of baked earth and mud plaster, some rebuilt in brick. The tall arch of the main mosque was in disrepair. The street outside was thronged with market stalls, donkey carts and horse-drawn trailers, through which the mopeds swerved at speed. The poverty was apparent. An old peasant man was selling a few miserable chives laid on a cloth in front of him. Two women, one carrying a long knife, flew at each other, screaming, in a dispute over a cabbage.

Beyond the market, the road runs down to a stream. Formerly it was a broad river which lapped the high green banks. The factory children used to swim here after school in the summer heat to get rid of the dust that caked them, ignoring their parents' warnings that several children had drowned. Now the stream was barely deep enough to drown a chicken; it had dwindled to a series of paddling pools choked with weeds, plastic bags and other household rubbish.

Nowhere in this quarter is a Chinese face to be seen. The Han, like the cotton factory, have moved up to the new town where multi-storey flats and offices stand along broad, empty boulevards. These great avenues, radiating away into the surrounding desert, are built to a scale which dwarfs the few pedestrians and even fewer cars that use them. They are the ground plan of a city to come. There is no sound of the muezzin up here, only the blast of the loudspeaker outside Party headquarters trumpeting the good news. Already, Maralbashi county has grown from 40,000 inhabitants to 240,000 in thirty years; the town is being physically stretched to make room for immigrants from the east. But older inhabitants look at their feeble river and shake their heads. They ask how much further the city can grow before the water dries up and nature herself calls a halt.

The Chinese are stamping their own vision of the future on Xinjiang. Maralbashi is not exceptional. Everywhere new towns have sprung up alongside or on top of the old Uighur areas, reducing them to depressed suburbs where the people sell kebabs and bric-à-brac to one another. The towns are largely segregated, the villages are almost exclusively Uighur. But the separation is never total: Uighur cadres and their families share apartment blocks with Han colleagues, and many of the poorest Han migrants have settled in Uighur areas where they do the most menial tasks and are accepted by their neighbours.[2]

Kucha, east of Maralbashi and close to the Tian Shan mountains, is typical. Uighurs live mainly in the old city, a warren of lanes lined with the ubiquitous white poplars which extend down to the river bed, where livestock are bought and sold during the long dry season. Beside the bridge stands the mosque, the bazaar and a straggling parade of shops and stalls on an unmade road. The lanes wind up to the main road above, a tarmac highway lined with modern offices and hotels behind gated entrances, which runs directly into the Chinese town.

Kashgar, the ancient Muslim city under the Pamir mountains, is being turned into a mini-metropolis: the earthern ramparts and great gateways have all but disappeared, as at Maralbashi, to make way for highways which slice through the old town. The Han are trying to shift Kashgar's centre of gravity to People's Square, a smaller version of Beijing's Tiananmen Square, built on what used to be playing fields. Where Tiananmen has its outsize portrait of

Chairman Mao fixed to the front of the imperial palace, People's Square is overlooked by one of the biggest statues of the Great Helmsman still standing in China. Tourist brochures insist that this place is Kashgar's number one attraction, since it is 'the regional base for patriotism education'. The square is decorated with characteristic stone bridges, dragons and Chinese lions – 'cats' as the local wags call them – and along its flanks are hung lanterns in the shape of giant red pumpkins. East of the square, down People's Street, stands a big Ferris wheel looking out over an artificial lake studded with islands and pagodas. On the south side is a shady park of poplars where families congregate for Sunday picnics and groups of Uighur men sing, get drunk on beer and fight.

You would never guess from its downtown architecture that fewer than a quarter of Kashgar's inhabitants are Chinese. The city is designed to look as if it has always been theirs. Yet it is the Han who seek shelter, in their own section of town at the western end of People's Street, where they have their own shops, market and eating places. The old city may be under siege but it has not surrendered. Under its shiny modern carapace, the dusty Uighur town still breathes. Mudbrick is giving way to brick, and many of the balconied houses have fallen into decay; yet the streets are lined with the booths of metalworkers and wood turners, bakers and barbers, with restaurants and tea houses. And the true heart of the town is not Pumpkin Square, but the old concourse outside the Id Kah mosque where people gather to buy and sell shoes and clothes, to drink tea and gossip in groups, or crowd into wooden booths to watch television.

Turfan city, in the east of the province, also has a new Chinese centre, lit up at night by flashing neon signs and festoons of fairy lights that wink from the trees in perpetual Christmas festivity. The buildings are in the style which appears all over Xinjiang, and is best described as gaudy postmodern vernacular. Pastel colours are the rage, with blue-tinted glass and white tiles a dominant motif. It is naïve enough – some would say false enough – to be almost charming. Despite its occasional references to Islamic design, the architecture is strangely out of place and obviously paying unintentional homage to America, as if to reinforce Beijing's vision of Xinjiang as the new California. Turfan is a little

Las Vegas, Kashgar is pretending to be Denver, and Urumchi aspires to be Los Angeles.

The provincial capital was once so prone to flooding that it was known in the 1930s as 'the town in the desert where camels drown in the streets'.[3] In the 1980s it was still a small city. Today all but a handful of the public buildings of the 1930s have been swept away and Urumchi has soared upwards to form an erratic skyline which – when not obscured by a fog of dust and pollution – is as exuberant as anything in Asia. Each slabsided skyscraper is topped off with a different coloured motif, like the plastic shapes which infants are given to fit into holes: here a pyramid, there a pagoda, a wheel or a set of turrets, none making the slightest stylistic concession to its neighbour. The new government house behind the Tian Shan department store is a neo-classical palace of white marble and stucco. Round it still runs the wall over which the cowardly governor Jin Shuren climbed in 1933 to make his getaway. Here, as in other Xinjiang cities, modernization is going ahead at a tremendous rate: you can drink real coffee at five-star hotels, buy designer suits from Germany, visit Internet cafés, or have a foot massage in a private clinic. Urumchi's Uighurs are confined to a few blocks off South Jiefang Street where there are mosques, markets and a covered bazaar. They are a minority in the city (some 13 per cent of a population of one and a quarter million), many of them having been moved out from what was originally a Manchu (Qing dynasty) foundation called Tihwa and which is now the magnet for Chinese colonization.

Phsyical segregation is nothing new in Xinjiang. We have seen how the Manchus built their own enclaves from which to supervise the conquered peoples, and forbade civilian Chinese settlement in the new territory. Following the 'oleaster revolt' of 1765 at Ush Turfan, Chinese traders were ordered to live apart from native merchants, and soldiers were banned from Turki areas out of deference to native feelings. Today's separation of communities is partly the consequence of that history, but the deference to Uighur sensitivities has been forgotten.

In the smaller oasis towns on the south side of the Taklamakan, however, the Han presence is a thin façade. Communist Party officials drive about in Toyota Landcruisers, blaring their horns at the donkey-cart drivers, brushing past as close as they can. These cadres, the priviligentsia of China, put up in shiny new hotels and hold endless meetings to discuss the modernization which is gradually turning the towns from mudbrick to concrete.

A few hundred yards away, life goes on as it has for centuries. The unpaved road, raised on a levee above the irrigation channels and lined with white poplars planted six or ten deep as protection against the encroaching sand, runs between fields of cotton, wheat and maize. On either side are low houses of mudbrick or timber and wattle, each with a fenced-in yard for firewood and animals – a donkey, chickens, a goat or a small herd of sheep.

Turn up towards the desert, following the course of one of the rivers that flow vainly north to expire in the sand, and you reach places where few Chinese – perhaps the occasional archaeologist or oil prospector – have been seen. One small settlement I visited on the banks of the Keriya river, although typical, identified itself as an oddity: it was called 'The place where the Chinese came'. Presided over by two old brothers and their wives, it consisted of a few huts made of poplar saplings lashed together and padded inside against the winter cold. Meals were cooked on an open fire in the largest of the four rooms. The cotton-stuffed bedrolls, blankets and other furnishings were probably made in Pakistani factories; the huts themselves, like others on the very margins of the open desert, seemed not to have changed for two thousand years. They were made of the same poplar wood, to the same floor plan and scale, as the Buddhist dwellings in the buried cities of the Taklamakan.

Customs, too, remain unchanged. About 100 miles down-river, I watched a ceremony in progress. A crowd of women, dressed in their best skirts and wearing the ceremonial *doppa*, a cup-sized hat to hold their white veils in place, was gathered round the door of a hut. Outside the surrounding fence the men – all wearing brown sheepskin hats – stood watching or talking in groups. There was an air of anticipation. After some minutes, the knot of women at the door parted and out came a heavy object carried in a carpet. From the edge of the crowd it was just possible to see that the bearers were carrying a young woman curled up in the rug like a baby. She looked as if she was in pain and could not walk. The girl was loaded into a jeep and driven off to another settlement further down-river. My attempts to find out from one of the bystanders what was happening were in vain: I guessed that she was a bride on the first leg of her wedding.

At the point where the Keriya river disappears into the sand, 120 miles from the south road, in the heart of the Taklamakan, lies what must surely be one of the remotest villages on earth. The fifty villagers of Tongguzbasti ('The invading boar') live in a thicket behind a stockade which protects them from the wind and sand. Though far from civilization these Keriyanese (as they call themselves) are as well housed as anyone can be: their poplar-wood dwellings are strongly built and ornately decorated with carved beams, friezes and ceilings. When the river is dry, the villagers depend on a single well, about 10 foot deep and reached by a pole into which notches have been carved for steps. The well is guarded by the village policeman, who also sells baby food, old radios and moth-eaten hats from a lean-to behind his house. His credentials for the job are provided by the souvenir poster of the Kremlin by moonlight pinned to his bedroom wall. The main industry of Tongguzbasti appears to be camel-herding; the village camel-drivers conduct occasional parties of archaeologists who come to explore the buried city of Karadong a day's march to the north, or the tourists who are beginning to find their way here for trips into the desert.

Tongguzbasti is too small and remote to have excited the attention of the Chinese authorities. Yawatongguz ('Boar's bank') seems to have been less lucky. According to the *Times Atlas of China*, published in 1974, the only village of this name is situated on the south desert road between Endere and Niya. When I visited it in 1995, however, it was not there at all, but 50 miles further north at the end of the Yawatongguz river, in a charmed desert delta beside a silver lagoon.

The mystery was explained to me by a curator of the ethnographic museum in Stockholm, where the explorer Sven Hedin's collection is displayed. It seems that during one of the more zealous periods of socialist integration, the authorities visited the villagers on their delta site and decided they were being denied the benefits of Communist liberation. They were told to pack up their belongings and move down to the road – a two-day trek with camels – where they could be integrated into society. Gradually, however, they drifted back to their homes at the river's end. There they remain, subsisting on the proceeds of their cotton harvest, and their own corn, fruit and vegetables, a reservoir of water for the dry season, and whatever supplies can be brought by the single lorry making the weekly trip to the nearest shops. Perhaps to save the authorities' face, a Communist Party secretary was appointed in 1993 to look after the villagers' ideological welfare. At the time of my visit, two years later, this official was a worldly-wise character, a former accountant in a smart blue shirt with a flashy watch on his wrist. His presence did not stop one of the village elders, a man with permanently raised eyebrows and a goitre under his ear, from observing that 'before the Party we were free here'.* So free, indeed, that occasionally escaped prisoners from nearby labour camps would turn up at Yawatongguz seeking refuge. A young Chinese, the son of a landlord, who escaped from Kashgar was sheltered there for many years until the villagers regretfully raised the money to repatriate him to Guangxi province.

The villagers are not against progress. But their idea of progress – at least at the time I met them – was to get the authorities to build them a road joining them to the new trans-Taklamakan highway which was being driven through the sand dunes 12 miles north of the village. The doctor, who described himself as self-taught, wore a souvenir hat with 'World Cup' stamped on it which he had bought in the bazaar at Endere; the head man had a son living in Urumchi. The villagers had acquired two imams, which seemed somewhat surplus to requirements, who operated from a small mudbrick mosque built in 1989 beside the reservoir and containing a few threadbare carpets and a handsome print of Mecca. Despite their efforts, the clerics seemed not to have made much impression on the moral laxity of their flock: divorce is easy in Islam, but marriage is more informal still in Yawatongguz, where

---

* The prevalence of goitres in the southern Taklamakan has been noted by visitors for centuries. They are attributed to lime and magnesia salts in the mountain waters.

the women outnumber the men, and the many children appear all to be related to each other.

The wandering village of Yawatongguz will, no doubt, one day be lost altogether, joining the other buried cities of the desert. Even if the villagers continue to reject the temptations of life on the main road, modernization and the growth of population mean that the thirst of the southern oases is bound to intensify. More water will be siphoned off before the river even begins its suicidal journey into the desert. Or, as has happened so many times in the past, the river will change course on a whim, leaving the village high and dry with nothing but black and desiccated sticks to mark the place where orchards and people once flourished.

Although these settlements in the desert – flashbacks to ancient Xinjiang – seem doomed, the way of life and culture of the Uighurs which they represent in its most original form is by no means extinct. Indeed, it is startlingly and evidently present, even in the sinicized metropolitan areas, where, in spite of everything, it is hard for the visitor to believe that he is in China at all.

Uighurs and Han live in parallel universes. Their cultures are as contradictory as the landscape that surrounds them: great ramparts of rock and snow on one side; on the other, a torrid and dusty desert.

For the Han Chinese, the Uighurs' way of life is a problem. On the one hand, they have been taught to see Uighurs as primitive, superstitious, reactionary, treacherous – and dangerous. On the other, they find them exotic, amusing and attractive. The latter characterization is illustrated by a set of postcards designed for foreign visitors depicting the Uighurs as happy, smiling natives who like nothing better than to break off from the harvest to sing, dance and play their strange musical instruments. 'Happy songs on the cart', says the caption to one picture. 'In ancient time, there was a king of cart in the Western Region. Now on the country road near the desert in south Xinjiang, you'll see this ancient-styled cart and cheerful and humourous [*sic*] Uygurs.' It is perfectly true that Uighurs like nothing better than to play, sing and dance; but it is a truth which the Han find it convenient to overemphasize.

For their part the Uighurs regard their culture as superior to the

Han – at least to the materialist, morally vacuous culture of the post-Liberation generation – while being at the same time conscious of their own more primitive way of life. Their feelings about their own people can be confused. A Uighur academic who was escorting a British party into Xinjiang, for example, started behaving strangely the moment he crossed the border from mainland China into his homeland. He was later heard boasting that he had taken his group to a low-grade, Uighur, restaurant in the hope that they would get food poisoning. What was he trying to prove? That his sympathies were not with Westerners, nor even with his own people, but with the Chinese motherland, to which he was loyal?[4] On the other hand, there is nothing that alarms Uighur parents more than the prospect that their children will develop a 'Chinese temperament' (*mijaz*) by attending a Han school or playing with Han children.[5]

Han Chinese and Uighurs have strong and hostile stereotypes of each other. Yet it is not always easy, even for them, to tell each other apart by appearance alone. A story told to a Western anthropologist illustrates the point. A Uighur married a woman from another town, believing her to be a true Uighur. He had not met his parents-in-law because, according to the wife, her mother was dead and her father was in prison. One day, the husband came home to find a strange man, whom he guessed to be his father-in-law, sitting at the table eating spicy noodles. He noticed, however, that the man was eating the noodles from one bowl and the meat and vegetable sauce from another. That told him instantly that the man was not a Uighur but a Han. The couple were soon divorced.[6]

In Xinjiang, food is high politics. Han Chinese will eat in Uighur restaurants – they like the food – but Uighurs will rarely, if ever, eat in Chinese restaurants. Partly, of course, this is a matter of religious taboo: the fact that pork, a staple of the Chinese diet, is forbidden to Muslims. Some will refuse to eat anything that might have been touched by a Han. City Uighurs will consent to eat in Hui restaurants, if sometimes reluctantly. But many Uighurs refuse to enter a Chinese restaurant on principle, even to drink a cup of tea, because they feel that to do so would in some way imply their acceptance of Chinese rule. In all ages and all places food has been the sign of hospitality, and Uighurs take this obligation particularly seriously. You cannot visit a Uighur house without being offered food, whatever the time of day, and even a short sightseeing excursion is certain to end in a restaurant. By entering a Chinese restaurant, therefore, a Uighur feels himself to be a guest in his own land, accepting the hospitality of a Chinese 'host'. Whereas in fact he regards the Han as unwelcome guests in *his* home, guests who have stayed too long and who refuse to depart.

By the same logic, you will see Chinese waiters working in Uighur restaurants, but not the reverse. They will even dress up as Uighurs in order to do so, as they do in the 'Uighur street' in Beijing, built to amuse tourists like the 'Wild West saloon' bars in English pubs.* Menus are confusing, too. Both races drink tea, though the Uighurs prefer black tea from India to green tea from China. For both, noodles (probably a Chinese invention) are a staple, and both use chopsticks. The difference is that Uighur noodles are always made on the spot, to order, and Chinese noodles usually come out of a packet. Uighurs eat their noodles with large quantities of mutton – the more fat, the better – as well as spicy vegetables. Typical central Asian dishes such as *polo* – pilaff rice with mutton and yellow carrots – and lamb kebabs are sold on almost every street in the Uighur districts. In every parade of shops there is a shack where nan bread is baked in spherical stone ovens heated by sticks of poplar. The Chinese diet, on the other hand, relies far more on vegetables, although it includes beef, pork, chicken and fish, and the bread is usually steamed or processed. Hygiene worries the Han, too: they refuse to buy the local sun-dried apricots from Uighur orchards, and pay more for chemically coloured apricots, believing them to be cleaner.[7]

Cooking has become a symptom of inequality. The little eating-house or open-air brazier is a sign of poverty, an outlet for the displaced city dweller who cannot find a job. Every town has its barbecue corners where twice a day, at noon and dusk, the Uighurs set up their stalls. One such place is the junction of two main roads beside a park in Gulja. Each evening, the pavement is crowded with vendors cheerfully importuning passers-by. They

---

* Meanwhile, the genuine Uighur quarter of Beijing is being cleared away.

are illuminated by swinging bulbs which give a peculiar animation to their faces and an infernal tinge to the smoke that swirls up from their charcoal fires. Above them looms the blind glass façade of a brand-new furniture store, seven storeys high – a reminder that some people in this town, at least, have money to burn.

A few hundred yards away is the place where the Gulja demonstration was halted, the front entrance of the Ili Hotel, formerly the Russian consulate and now the resort of government and Party officials. Through its gate and past the bust of Lenin on its plinth flows a stream of shiny new Japanese 4-wheel-drive vehicles and Chinese-built Volkswagen saloons. Behind tinted windows can be glimpsed members of the priviligentsia on their way to and from interminable conferences where they sit for hours like well-behaved schoolchildren at their desks, dutifully making notes of long-winded speeches on topics such as 'Strengthening the Party role in building race unity in the Ili Kazakh prefecture'. In the grounds of the hotel, as if to underline the message of ethnic unity, a concrete meeting room has been built in the form of an outsize Kazakh yurt.

Beside the gate is an open-air barbecue restaurant. At night its glaring lamps create a chiaroscuro scene that would have appealed to Caravaggio or Joseph Wright of Derby. Set out on trestle tables are bowls of sheep's offal: soft and grainy slabs of yellow lung, grey sausages bursting from their skins, and chequered slices of tripe. Chickens, trussed and naked, are propped in artistic poses like porn stars to catch the customer's eye. Skewers of mutton and liver lie on the racks of gutter-shaped braziers supplied with hot coals from a pot at one end. Behind every brazier stands a cook, usually with his wife, fanning the flames with a paddle and calling out to the hesitant client. The stallholders are in competition. But when a gap-toothed salesman who has been beckoning from the back of the den shouts to the others, 'They won't eat anything here, you'll see!', they all laugh.

Rarely do Uighur and Han marry. Chinese law forbade mixed marriages until 1979. Muslim law still does. A greater deterrent than the law, however, is the couple's probable ostracism by the Uighur partner's family, especially in a village community. For a people so enmeshed in family ties, the threat of severance is enough. So the state encourages mixed marriages with a subsidy of 1,000 yuan, or $126, per union (at the time of writing). Young Chinese women born in Xinjiang may be sent to poor villages with a state dowry of 3,000 yuan in order to attract a Uighur mate, and young Uighur men may get better jobs if they marry Chinese girls.[8] The children are considered Chinese and brought up as such.

Han men are sometimes said to make better husbands than Uighurs, being more helpful around the house and less prone to beat their wives – but, for those same reasons, they are seen by Uighur women as less 'manly'. There can be trouble in a Uighur marriage where one of the partners has been brought up speaking Chinese. Such Chinese-educated Uighurs are often the object of suspicion, sometimes mocked as 'half-Uighurs' or labelled 'four-teenth nationality' (officially, there are thirteen nationalities or races in Xinjiang).[9]

The culture gap is exaggerated by religion – or the lack of it. The natives of Xinjiang belong to a tolerant wing of Sunni Islam and describe themselves, for the most part, as lukewarm observers. As in secularized Judaeo-Christian Europe, no one can easily say how far customs and morality derive from a pervasive religious creed, or how far they descend from broader cultural traditions. The Muslim children of Xinjiang cannot help but start life with a different set of ideas and values to the Han. However accommo-dating their strain of Islam, Uighurs imbibe a religious tradition which is designed to infuse every aspect of life. The Han, mean-while, have for half a century been reared on a diet of mandatory state atheism which denies China's own history and condemns all spiritual ideas as medieval superstition.

The races are divided, of course, by language and script. Uighur is the official regional language of the Turki minorities. All, however, must study Chinese at secondary school. Many of the poorest chil-dren never get to school, and those who do come up against the peculiar difficulties, familiar to Westerners, of a non-alphabetical, tonal and uninflected language, with 30,000 different characters in general use. Few children at Uighur schools learn sufficient Chinese (3,000 characters, say) to read and write it, and fewer still achieve the standard needed to get to university. In 2001, for example, 180 students at the Xinjiang Finance College in Urumchi were failed or made to resit their exams because of their poor Chinese. Uighurs abroad blamed Beijing's 'political' decision not to allow the students to use their first language. A recent edict has laid down that all major subjects at the University of Urumchi are to be taught in Chinese only. The decision, which was the subject of a question in the European Parliament in August 2002, was apparently made 'partly because students have asked for it', partly to meet 'the growing needs of economic and social development'.[10] The government, on the other hand, is proud of its programme of minority education and claims big improvements in literacy.[11]

Because of the high hurdles which their children have to surmount, many parents – putting their children's future before their own consciences – send their children to Chinese schools instead. But Uighur children at Chinese schools find themselves a class apart.

Enver Tohti, the son of a cadre in Urumchi, was one of them. He became aware of his difference while still at infant school in the 1960s. He recalled the nursery teacher pointing to him while she warned another child, 'Don't cry or the *chalowe* will take you away.' (*Chalowe* is a derogatory name which combines the Chinese words for 'Kazakh' and 'Uighur'.) At the age of 14, now a keen Communist, a good student and still the only Uighur in the class, he was invited to a classmate's house for Chinese New Year. He was offered pork but refused, explaining that he was a Muslim. The teacher later told the laughing pupils that Uighurs 'cannot eat pork because their ancestors are pigs'.[12]

Like other children, Enver Tohti was taught an entirely Chinese version of Xinjiang's history. Only by accident did he learn from a teacher that Uighurs had once had their own country. He went home and asked his father what this country had been called but he was discouraged from asking further questions. His mother, however, told him that it was called Eastern Turkestan and made him promise not to talk about it.

The silence about Uighur history extends to television. Infants can be seen sitting over a bowl of spicy noodles with their eyes glued to the adventures of a Turki-speaking Donald Duck on the Uighur-language TV channel. But a popular historical drama series for adults was banned recently because it contradicted 'correct history' by mentioning the conquest of Xinjiang, so casting doubt on the official line that Xinjiang has always been part of China.

In the early days of Liberation, Chinese cadres were encouraged to learn Uighur. There are signs of that happening again as the free-market climate encourages business to woo customers. Bank staff in Gulja, for example, are being urged to learn the language. But the number of Chinese who bother to learn Uighur is very small – I met one Han driver, working for a Uighur boss, who had 'gone native' and was fluent in it. The Hui, on the other hand, are frequently bilingual.

To add to the Uighurs' difficulties, their script has been changed twice in the past fifty years. As we have seen, the Arabic script which had been used for centuries was jettisoned in 1960 in favour of the Roman script but was reinstated twenty years later. A perverse result of this is that in many families there are different generations who cannot write to each other – except in Chinese – leading some Uighur nationalists to argue that the change was made, not as a concession, but deliberately to undermine their language. To confuse matters further, Uighur scholars have been considering whether the script should be romanized again, in order to make it computer-friendly.

I have talked of parallel universes, but this observation is strictly true only of the countryside where the Uighurs (and the Kazakhs and Kyrgyz in the mountains) make up the great majority. City life and schooling are beginning to bring Chinese and Uighurs face to face. Though they live in different quarters, or different apartment blocks, they find their public lives converging, their habits changing. An exile who returned to Urumchi after eight years in the West was shocked to discover that his university friends were in the habit of leaving their wives at home and going out to dinner together, where they felt feel free to chat up other women. Formerly, a Uighur's guest would always be entertained at his home.

Country aunts and uncles visiting town are shocked, though probably not surprised, to find their young Uighur nieces wearing tight jeans or mini-skirts, touring the boutiques looking for the latest blouses and shoes, or dressed to kill for a night in the disco – though showing a lot less flesh than their Western sisters. With their aquiline features and olive skin, Uighur girls are considered to be very pretty, and have always been found so by the Han. The Emperor Qianlong was besotted with his Fragrant Concubine in the eighteenth century, and in the twentieth, the dictator Sheng Shicai rhapsodized about Uighur girls' eyelashes which he found 'sharp and distinct and inclined upwards slightly in order to attract men'.

In general, however, Uighur women are careful not to breach the Muslim dress code. They wear thick leggings under their skirts, jackets over decorated waistcoats, and scarves on their heads. Only in a few places, such as old Kashgar, are they orthodox enough to wear the full Muslim veil, a heavy brown cloth lacking even eye-holes.[13]

Younger men wear the drab uniform of central Asia: grey trousers and a grey jacket over a pullover, and a flat cap. If middle-aged they often put on a four-cornered, conical green skullcap, the badge of Islam. The grandfathers are even more picturesque, in long coats and boots, with grey beards flowing under white or brown sheepskin hats.

Nomads are leaving the mountains to become city traders. Kazakh boys who a generation ago would have been herding cattle or sheep on horseback – as their fathers still do – roar about the empty streets on low-powered motorcycles. Out in the oasis villages, however, etiquette remains elaborate and distinct. People greet one another with the Arabic phrase *Salaam alecum*, placing the right hand over the heart and making a small bow as they say it. In town, the everyday '*Yahximu siz!*' will do. Yet conversational courtesies are observed, each speaker keeping his remarks short to make room for the other's. In the country, Uighur hospitality continues as travellers for centuries have described it. Guests are treated like visiting royalty for two or three days; after that, they are expected to help with the chores, or take their leave.

In village or town, the typical Uighur house is built around a courtyard. Along one side there may be a raised veranda with pillars supporting a decorated roof: here the family eats and sleeps in summer. Washing and food preparation are done in the yard, from a pump or tap, the cooking inside on a wood fire or, these days, a gas cylinder. Indoors, the high-ceilinged rooms are covered with carpets, on walls as well as floors. Uighurs sleep not on a Chinese *kang*, the earthern platform warmed by a fire underneath, but on a wall-to-wall carpeted dais upon which mattresses and eiderdowns of satin stuffed with wool or cotton are unrolled each evening.

Nightlife can narrow the culture gap. Chinese are sometimes to be seen among the guests in Uighur restaurants, performing the rituals of the round-table banquet and swapping toasts with their Muslim hosts. Uighur folk music is famous throughout central Asia for its driving rhythm of drums and the wail of the shawn, which evokes the wild steppe of the ancient Turks rather than the peaceful oasis of the Uighurs.[14] These days, however, Uighurs, like the rest of the world, have discovered the preprogrammed electronic keyboard. So these city nightspots usually feature a keyboard player and singer belting out pop versions of Turkic ballads at an amplification that batters the eardrums. Sometimes there are exotic dancers, spangled girls in clouds of chiffon who race about the parquet stage, but who avoid inflaming their audience with the sinuous wriggling and gesturing of belly dancers in Turkey. When the show is over, everyone takes to the floor. Uighurs dancing, whether they are women or men, are graceful rather than energetic. They hold their bodies erect and their arms out sideways like the Scots or the Caucasians, their fingers extended while their hands make balletic twists and turns, their feet moving in a gentle jiving pattern.

At Chinese parties the same keyboards and amplifiers are used, but the music is invariably Western. Ballads, old pop songs, even nursery rhymes are what they dance to – except that nobody appears to have been to dancing class for years. Such simple social graces, along with so much else, seem to have been snuffed out by the Cultural Revolution. Far from learning from the Uighurs, the Han have brought with them the habits of the east. When China was beginning to open up in the early 1980s, there was a certain dance hall in central Beijing where young couples would jog about to the sound of 'Jingle Bells'. The crooners of Xinjiang have hardly progressed further. As for traditional Chinese music, that is something reserved for the concert hall or the arts programmes on state television.

Chinese are sometimes invited to Uighur weddings, even if it means sitting at separate tables. Better-educated Uighurs will take their girlfriends to Chinese dance halls to avoid the heavy drinking, brawling and prostitution that have been complained of in Uighur nightspots. The Han would never go there: it would be assumed that they were preying on Uighur girls, and there would be trouble.[15] Only the strictest Muslims refuse alcohol entirely, and at parties the Uighurs are not backward when it comes to uncorking the rice wine or spirits. Although the Muslims like to blame the Han for importing alcohol into their lives – stories of tee-totallers being forced to drink are common – they seem to have learned to hold their liquor better than the Chinese, who soon begin to stumble, roar and go red in the face.

The two peoples might see more of each other if only they could agree on what time of day it is. The most glaring example of official inflexibility, because it is so trivial, is Beijing's insistence that everyone, however far they live from the capital, should observe Beijing time. The idea was presumably copied from the Soviet railways which lived on Moscow time: at mid-day on a remote railway station in far eastern Siberia the station clock would insist that it was still breakfast time. In Xinjiang all bus and railway stations, airlines and offices, and most of the Han Chinese, work and live to the Beijing clock, two hours ahead of local solar time. In the small oasis of Keriya on the south road I was woken before dawn by martial music blaring from loudspeakers hung about the town centre, to see men in their worksuits and flat caps and women made up with bright red lipstick and thick white powder arriving for work on sit-up-and-beg bicycles.* As a concession to common sense, opening and closing hours of offices and banks are often readjusted so that workers do not have to get up in the dark and can eat their lunch more or less in the middle of the day. Uighurs set their watches to

---

* Uighur women use a lot of powder because as children they are taught that they are 'yellow' like the Han and they want to be different from them.[16] But this make-up was also popular with Han girls when, in the early 1980s, they began rebelling against the austerity of the Mao era.

local time as a matter of course; indeed, for most of them it is a matter of principle to do so, one of the few ways in which they may safely disobey the Chinese state and strike a small note of political dissent. As an anthropologist has remarked, in Xinjiang you may tell a person's race by the time on his watch.[17]

Officially, of course, there is no discrimination and no racial tension in Xinjiang. Outside the tomb of Khoja Apakh on the north-east side of Kashgar, one of the finest Islamic buildings in China, a noticeboard tells the story of Iparhan, the Fragrant Concubine, as an illustration of 'the good wish for unity and mutual love between different nationalities since ancient times . . . Love between this Uyghur maid and the emperor is evidence for great unity among different ethnic groups in China.'

That is a statement of hope, not fact. The differences between Han and Uighur are so many and so great that – even without the provocative style of the Han occupation and rule – it would be a miracle if social tensions did not exist. And they have a long history. The explorer Sven Hedin described how his servant Islam Bai was treated in the marketplace at Korla when a senior Chinese official passed him with an escort carrying the emblem of the Emperor. 'Everybody had to rise as a mark of respect to this symbol. But Islam, being a Russian subject, sat still. Thereupon the Chinese soldiers halted, seized him, bared his neck and flogged him till the blood flowed.'[18]

Muslim Chinese can be just as contemptuous of the Turkis. Peter Fleming, who travelled along the south road when it was under Dongan control in 1935, saw an old man grovelling at the feet of a Dongan general to seek redress for some domestic griev-ance. The soldiers laughed and shooed him off. This and other incidents reminded him, he said, of the Japanese behaviour in Manchuria. 'The Asiatic races can sometimes conquer,' he wrote, 'but never colonize.'[19] Other Western observers have witnessed Chinese youths standing insolently in front of Muslims while they pray, to make it look as if they are being honoured with a kowtow.

Every day produces its little provocations and humiliations. Travelling in a crowded bus on an empty stretch of desert road, fogbound after a dust storm, I watched an old Uighur couple struggling to find room for themselves and their bundles. They asked a young Chinese in a business suit who was sprawled across two seats if he would move up. His answer was to edge nearer to the aisle and stick out a leg, barring their way. In a society where respect is demanded and given as a matter of course, the discourtesy shown by many young Han is all too obvious. It looks like more than official carelessness, for instance, to provide a hot dog as the only available snack on a local Xinjiang Airlines flight, when everyone knows that pork is taboo for Muslims, whether they are religious or not.

Such things are in themselves trivial. But in the context of Xinjiang today, where officials pay lip service to racial harmony but routinely discriminate against the local inhabitants, they are incendiary.

The Han discriminate partly because their history has taught them to, partly because they live in fear of the people whom they are colonizing. They are afraid to travel on Uighur buses or to walk alone in Uighur areas. Many Chinese in the east are under the impression that Xinjiang is a no-go area, that some kind of war is being fought there. Fear leads the Han to take extreme measures. By clamping down on all expressions of difference or dissent, under the cloak of fighting 'splittism', 'nationalism', 'fundamentalism' or 'terrorism' – depending on the season – they have turned a minority of Uighurs to violence, and reduced the majority to an impotent and resentful silence.

Today the Uighurs are afraid to talk, not only to foreigners but to each other. A wrong remark can mean the loss of a job, or worse. People are arrested for things they have said at birthday parties. When they are at table with visitors, Uighurs warn each other under their breath to avoid any subject that might be deemed 'political'. Lawyers, journalists, teachers and schoolchildren are sent on indoctrination courses to remind them that they are part of China. 'It's as bad as during the Cultural Revolution,' a professional man told a visitor in 2002. Newspapers have been required to cull from their archives all articles written since 1990 which speak of Uighurs as having a separate history and identity. A lawyer who dutifully wrote a dozen pages on the evils of 'separatism' was told that that was not enough, and was sent back to write more. 'These are hard times for the Uighurs,' said a Uighur academic, one of the few who dared comment. 'Having been in control of our own affairs, it is hard to watch the Han taking over everything.' The native people of Xinjiang are no longer a majority. Outnumbered, subdued and marginalized, they find themselves foreigners in their own land.

POSTSCRIPT

The Dragon and the Wolf

A CCORDING TO ITS rulers, Xinjiang has been part of China since 60 BC. It would be more accurate to see it as an occupied country undergoing its sixth or seventh invasion from China in two millennia.

The first invasion, in 102 BC, was a military disaster; the second, under Ban Chao in the first century AD, was a temporary triumph. The Tang dynasty held brief sway in the first half of the seventh century and the Mongols regained the territory in the thirteenth. The Qing emperors conquered Xinjiang in the eighteenth, only to lose it to Yakub Beg in the nineteenth. General Zuo's reconquest did not survive the collapse of the imperial court at the beginning of the last century, and full control passed again to the Chinese capital only in 1949.

Like the cultural influences which have shaped it, government of the 'new frontier' has passed back and forth between east and west. China cannot be said to have been truly in control of Xinjiang for much more than 500 of the last 2,000 years. It was 250 years ago that the Emperor Qianlong took his bride from the west. She remained unsubdued until 50 years ago when another emperor, wearing a forage cap and a red star, tried to win her favour but ended by forcing her submission. Today she has been banished to the margins of society, and all pretence of a voluntary union has been dropped.

Mao applied the magic formulae of Marxist-Leninist thought to the ethnic problem. Not only did they fail, but his social engineering of the Turkis was highly destructive and led to the discrimination and segregation prevalent today. Determined to end the push and pull of centuries, his successors have set out, with their 'Great Leap West', to complete the sinicization of the region.

Nationalism can be driven underground but it still lies not far from the surface. If total assimilation is China's aim, the lesson of other countries which have been occupied or ruled from outside is not in her favour. After many hundreds of years of English rule, for example, the Welsh still feel Welsh and the Scots Scottish – while the Irish won their independence from a much stronger country. In the same way, Uighurs, Kazakhs and others may have found their way of life reduced and altered. But their sense of identity as an oppressed nation of Turkis is, if anything, greater than it ever was.

The cultural gap between Turki and Han could hardly be wider. Turkis look to a mythological past in which their ancestors were suckled by wolves, like Romulus and Remus, the founders of Rome. The Chinese look to the rain-making spirit represented by the dragon, with whom their emperors identified. Both are proud creatures who cannot inhabit the same domain.

To persuade people of different races to share a common space is not easy. Genocide and ethnic cleansing in Europe and Africa, religious gang warfare in Northern Ireland and suicide bombings in Israel are all modern manifestations of the fact. But building a nation out of different races or tribes, whether the United States, the United Kingdom or the People's Republic of China, cannot be done by forcing them into a single mould. Their differences have to be managed.

The present impasse in western China would be broken if one of two things happened: either Xinjiang's nationalists became much stronger, or the Chinese central government became much weaker.

Since Qianlong's conquest there have been major revolts inside Xinjiang in the 1820s, 1860s, 1930s, 1940s and 1990s. Today Uighur exiles repeatedly warn that serious ethnic conflict will break out if the repression inside 'Eastern Turkestan' continues. Beijing, for its part, is taking precautionary measures against what it fears could be another Kashmir or Kosovo. Is a general uprising inevitable, or even likely?

At present the Uighurs are too weak within their country, and too disorganized outside it, to present a credible threat. Even ardent separatists acknowledge that the Uighurs are in no position to confront the Han and their security apparatus: the army, the armed police, the *bingtuan* militia, their tanks and aircraft. The cost of insurrection would be enormous.

Historically, the oasis people have been passive, rising up only after long and serious provocation and usually under the leadership of outsiders like the Kokandi khojas, the adventurer Yakub Beg or the Chinese Muslim warlords. People may be obstinate – as the mandarin Aitchen Wu pointed out – in preferring self-government to good government, but the Uighurs' experience of Turki and Muslim rule has not been particularly encouraging either.

The context is very different now. Many Uighurs are urbanized, with education, experience and ambition. However much they may resent the Han occupation, and as much as they may envy the easily won freedom of their cousins in former Soviet central Asia, it is hard to see many of them joining a general mutiny. Older Uighurs especially, who have lived through the turbulence of the 1940s, cannot see how the Chinese could be driven out and are not prepared to live a life of constant resistance. However unpalatable, it is easier to take what opportunities may arise from the new market regime, and to hope for better times.

There are certainly Muslim fundamentalists at work in Xinjiang who would do their utmost to force a change of government. But the present troubles should be seen as the visible tip of a broad popular discontent which seeks an alternative future to the one on offer, a programme of modernization which takes Turki tradition and Islam into account. Discontent can express itself in two violent forms: spontaneous reaction to constant pressures and provocations, or planned terrorist acts designed to destabilize the region to the point where it becomes ungovernable. It is the former that we have mainly seen in Xinjiang so far.

Protest is bound to take on a religious character, because Islam is the great identifier – as Catholicism was in Communist Poland. But Islam itself is unlikely to be the cause of revolt, more the banner under which the rebels would fight for political and economic rights. Apart from the Khotan breakaway republic in the 1930s, no secessionist movement in the past has demanded a Muslim state – only better rulers.

Uighur freedom fighters are handicapped by the lack of a leader inside Xinjiang (as far as is known). Even if there were such a person, it is hard to see what a truly autonomous Xinjiang would look like, or how the different ethnic groups would combine in government.

Revolution could end in a messy stalemate, as in central Asia, with political power in the hands of former Communist cadres posing as nationalists, and Islamic-led rebels fighting from the mountains.

The same lack of leadership bedevils the exile communities. Someone has to resolve the arguments and answer the questions. How are the militants to be controlled? Is the campaign to be for democracy and human rights, or full independence? Does the former aim undermine the latter? Would the Chinese already in Xinjiang be included in a Republic of Eastern Turkestan?

The Uighurs do have new allies, however. Human rights campaigners, including many Western politicians, and the wider public are beginning to hear of their plight. A century ago, what China is doing in Xinjiang would not have raised an eyebrow: it would have been seen, like the elimination of the American Indians, as the regrettable but inevitable process by which a superior civilization displaces an inferior one. Leaving aside the question of whether Turki civilization is 'inferior', this view is no longer accepted. It is just China's bad luck that her internal colonization (as many observers call it) started so late and has collided with a changed perception – especially since NATO intervention in the Balkans – of what may legitimately be called 'internal affairs'. Western ideas of what constitutes commercial fair play will also intrude, now that China has joined the World Trade Organization and wants to encourage inward investment. Questions will be asked about labour camps.

If the Turkis are too weak to force a change, are the authorities in Beijing not strong enough to resist one?

Some commentators see in China's leadership not just a post-Communist pragmatism, but signs of a familiar cyclical crisis – what one might call end-of-dynasty syndrome. After years of strong central government and economic progress, corruption sets in, and underpaid officials begin milking the peasants. The consequence is peasant revolts. There have many such revolts in recent years, though few have been given much attention. Other systemic weaknesses include a shaky banking system, rising unemployment (which WTO membership will exacerbate) and a growing gap between rich and poor, and between the eastern and the western provinces, which will magnify centrifugal tendencies. The grip of

China's leadership is weaker than it has been for decades. The old idealism and the old certainties have gone, while economic liberalization has introduced new incentives: private greed in place of public service, for example. Communism is defunct, but the leaders cannot sign its death certificate without confessing to the illegitimacy of their rule.

Only too conscious of what happened in Soviet Russia, the Party will go to any lengths to maintain its control, and especially to control the natural resources of Xinjiang. One view inside China is that if the country were to disintegrate, the first province to secede would be Guangdong, being the richest, followed by Manchuria, Tibet and Inner Mongolia. Xinjiang would be the last to escape. Even then, it might fall into the hands not of native rulers but of Chinese supremos – dictators like Yang, Jin and Sheng who ran it in the early twentieth century.

Could Xinjiang expect a new dispensation from Beijing – offered voluntarily, or even negotiated? On the face of it there is not much for the Uighurs to hope for in the change of leaders confirmed at the beginning of 2003, least of all from President Hu Jintao, an apparatchik applauded in China for his ruthless treatment of separatist demonstrations in Tibet when he was in charge there. Yet there are straws in the wind.

The first concerns the environment. The new economic managers are worried by desertification, water shortages and pollution. Measures to prevent the dust storms that regularly engulf the northern cities of China could mean that a brake is put on the hectic development of Xinjiang, that futile 'reclamation' projects will be abandoned and plans for massive immigration deferred.

Second, there are suggestions that a review of the Party line on religion may be under way. The débâcle of the authorities' campaign against the Falun Gong movement, not to mention the perennial problem of Islam and other 'foreign' creeds, could lead to a redefinition of what an atheist state finds permissible. Some writers are arguing, for example, that Communists have misinterpreted Marx's dictum that religion is 'the opium of the masses'.

Third, a delegation of the National People's Congress was recently taken to the new Scottish parliament, to see devolution in action. A federal government for China is an old favourite with

Western academics, and has appealed to Taiwan as a means of returning to the fold without making a political surrender. Now, it seems, somebody inside China is looking at the possibilities. If so, Uighurs may be encouraged to hope for something better than the false autonomy that Xinjiang enjoys at present.

China is a more open place than it was. New thinking is no longer suppressed. In spite of the Muslim terrorist panic, Han intellectuals are said to be worried by the harsh treatment of the Uighurs and the simplistic view of them as potential terrorists. Perhaps the new men in the leaders' compound will come to feel, as their predecessors did after Mao's death, that things have been pushed too far; that they cannot keep the lid on ethnic grievances for ever without provoking the very reaction they fear.

Xinjiang remains a border region, and now the border is open to permit the expansion of China's trade and economic influence across central Asia. A constant theme of China's imperial history is that the people of the border must be kept pacified. One way of doing so is to cover the ground with soldiers and police, as at present. Another is to restore to the Turki citizens of China their cultural freedoms and give them equal civic status with the Han. A few, at least, of the so-called fourth generation of leaders must be wondering whether a climate of fear is really the best way to run the 'autonomous' region of Xinjiang.

The alternative prospect is that China will be allowed, in spite of everything, to bring her centuries-long dalliance with the Wild West to a final conclusion. Once kept at arm's length, Xinjiang has been repeatedly invaded, occasionally controlled, and finally annexed. Today its people and their way of life are being forcibly absorbed into a 'motherland' they do not recognize, and do not love.

Glossary

Place names in Xinjiang are confusing and are a subject of scholarly interest in themselves. Maps often don't agree. Names may be Uighur, Kazakh, Mongolian, Manchu or Chinese. With the rapid sinicization of the region, most towns and many villages have at least two names, often three or even four. On the other hand, many places (and rivers and mountains) have the same name.

Names used in the text are the most familiar, usually the older native name. This is the one which appears first here, followed by the new Chinese name. Variants, including *pinyin* versions of Turki names, are given in brackets.

Name in text (with variants)	*New Chinese name*
Altai (Altay)	
Altun Tagh (Astin Tagh, Altyn Shan)	
Andijan (Andizhan)	
Artosh (Artush, Artux)	
Endere	Andir
Barkol (Barkul)	Chensi
Beshbalik	Beiting
Bogda Ula (Bogdo Ula, Bogda Feng)	
Charklik (Qarkilik)	Ruoqiang
Cherchen (Charchan, Qarqan)	Qiemo
Chuguchak (Tarbagatai, Savan)	Tacheng
Dunhuang (Tunhuang)	
Dzungaria (Jungaria)	
Gulja (Kuldja)	Yining
Hami (Kumul)	
Niya	Minfeng
Kocho (Khocho, Karakhoja)	Gaocheng
Kargalik	Yecheng
Kashgar	Kashi
Keriya	Yutian
Khotan	Hetian
Korgas (Korgos)	
Korla (Kuerla)	

Glossary

Name in text (with variants)	New Chinese name
Kucha (Kuqa)	
Lop Nor (Lop Nur)	Yuli
Loulan (Kroran)	
Maralbashi (Maralwexi)	Bachu
Miran (Milan)	
Merket (Markit)	
Taklamakan (Taklimakan)	
Tashkurgan (Taxkorgan)	
Tian Shan (Tien Shan)	
Tongguzbasti	Daheyandadui
Turfan (Turpan)	
Urumchi (Urumqi, Wulumuchi, Tihwa)	
Uch Turfan (Uqturpan)	Wushi
Yangi Hissar (Yengisar)	
Yarkand	Shache
Yawatongguz (Yartongguz, Yatongguz)	

Notes

CHAPTER 1: IN THE WILDERNESS

1. A military satellite used for mapping by the US National Geophysical Data Center at Boulder, Colorado, in the late 1990s.
2. Le Coq, *Buried Treasures*, pp. 51–2.
3. Xiao, 'A Catastrophe in the Aqqikkol Basin'.
4. Quoted by T. Douglas Forsyth in Prejevalsky, *From Kulja*, pp. 25–6.
5. For a plausible statement of the case against Marco Polo see Wood, *Did Marco Polo Go to China?*
6. Hare, *The Lost Camels of Tartary*. A former British colonial administrator, the author joined three scientific expeditions to the wild camel's haunts in the western Gobi.
7. Hedin, *My Life as an Explorer*, pp. 163–4.
8. *T'ai-p'ing yü-lan*, 901.7b, quoted by Schafer, 'The Camel in China Down to the Mongol Dynasty'.
9. Maillart, *Forbidden Journey*, pp. 157–8.
10. Jarring, 'The Toponym Takla-makan', says the name did not reappear until the nineteenth century and suggests the Arabic *taq* with the Turki plural suffix *-lar*, to make 'ruined arches', and the Arabic *makan*, 'place' or 'habitation'.
11. Hedin, *My Life as an Explorer*, p. 118.
12. See, for example, Anderson, 'The Attraction of Sand Dunes', p. 4.
13. Le Coq, *Buried Treasures*, p. 36.
14. Results of a four-year survey of the desert's geology, fauna and flora can be found in the illustrated 1993 report of the Chinese Academy of Sciences, *Wondrous Taklimakan*.
15. Chinese Academy of Sciences, *Wondrous Taklimakan*, p. 99.

CHAPTER 2: KINGS, KHANS AND KHOJAS

1. Glob, *The Bog People*.
2. For a discussion of the textiles see Barber, *The Mummies of Urumchi*.

3. Mallory and Mair, *The Tarim Mummies*.
4. A theory advanced in 1933 by Wei Juxian, who later described how the Chinese had discovered America. From Dikötter, *The Discourse of Race*, p. 132.
5. Dikötter, *The Discourse of Race*, p. 134.
6. Dikötter, *The Discourse of Race*, pp. 6 ff.
7. Spence, *Treason*, p. 169.
8. Baumer, *Southern Silk Road*, p. 28.
9. Forsyth, 'Report of a Mission to Yarkund', p. 61.
10. Han, 'The Study of Ancient Human Skeletons from Xinjiang'.
11. Mallory and Mair, *The Tarim Mummies*, p. 251.
12. Sinor, 'The Türk Empire', says the idea that the Huns were descended from the Xiongnu is a widely accepted but unproven theory, put forward in the eighteenth century, which has little in its favour but for a 'fortunate consonance' of a Chinese transcription. If they were the same people, Sinor says, they went missing for two centuries.
13. Translations by Robert A. Rorex and Wen Fong, of the Metropolitan Museum, New York.
14. Eberhard, *A History of China*, pp. 85–100.
15. Schafer, 'The Camel in China Down to the Mongol Dynasty', p. 176, quotes *Shih chi*, 123.0268c. See also Mirsky, *Sir Aurel Stein*, p. 369.
16. Baumer, *Southern Silk Road*, p. 37.
17. Dubs, Professor of Chinese at Oxford University, presented his theory in a lecture to the China Society in 1955. He suggested that Lijian is a corruption of 'Alexandria' and that the Chinese got the name from Alexandrian jugglers presented to them by the Parthians. The jugglers came from inside the Roman Empire, but – like the rest of its subjects – they had no proper name for it.
18. Dubs, *A Roman City*, p. 15.
19. Smart, *The World's Religions*, p. 124.
20. Stein, *Sand-Buried Ruins of Khotan*, pp. 396–7.
21. Baumer, *Southern Silk Road*, pp. 3–4.
22. Tsering, *Spang rgyan me tog*.
23. Sinor, 'The Türk Empire', p. 285.
24. Quoted by Soucek, *A History of Inner Asia*, p. 91.
25. Quoted by Sinor, 'The Türk Empire', p. 297.
26. Quoted by Sinor, 'The Türk Empire', p. 307.
27. Quoted by Sinor, 'The Türk Empire', p. 310.
28. Soucek, *A History of Inner Asia*, p. 55.
29. For example, Peter B. Golden, 'The Karakhanids', *Cambridge History of Early Inner Asia*.
30. Gernet, *A History of Chinese Civilization*, pp. 132 ff.
31. Moriyasu, 'The Sha-chou [Dunhuang] Uighurs', p. 39.
32. Gladney, 'The Ethnogenesis of the Uighur', p. 7.

33. Mackerras, 'The Uighurs', pp. 330ff.
34. Mackerras, 'The Uighurs', p. 335.
35. For good accounts of Manichaeism and Nestorianism in China see Foltz, *Religions of the Silk Road*.
36. Mackerras, 'The Uighurs', pp. 319–20.
37. Mackerras, 'The Uighurs', p. 342.
38. Le Coq, *Buried Treasures*, p. 21.
39. Julien, 'Relation d'un voyage', pp. 50–66.
40. The story of Satuk is told by Takir Bughra Khan. It was translated from the Persian into Uighur, and into English by an English surgeon, Henry Walter Bellew, who travelled to Kashgaria in 1873.
41. Stein, *Sand-Buried Ruins of Khotan*, p. 195. The rats were probably marmots.
42. Bellew, *History of Kashgharia*, pp. 34–5, quotes the *Tabcati Nasiri*, whose author knew the witness.
43. Vambéry, *History of Bokhara*, p. 142.
44. Quoted by Bellew, *History of Kashgharia*, p. 63.
45. Bellew, *History of Kashgharia*, p. 59.
46. The hardships endured on the western frontiers are described by Spence in *Treason*, the story of a conspiracy against the Yongzheng emperor in the 1720s.
47. Gernet, in *A History of Chinese Civilization*, p. 482, estimates that the Sino-Manchu empire covered 13 million square kilometres compared with the 9.74 million square kilometres of the People's Republic of China.

CHAPTER 3: THE FRAGRANT CONCUBINE

1. Millward, 'A Uyghur Muslim in Qianlong's Court', pp. 427–58, analyses the intriguing legend. *Ipar* is the Turki name of a spice, and *xiang* is Chinese for 'fragrant'.
2. Cable and French, *The Gobi Desert*, pp. 67–8.
3. Arlington and Lewisohn, *In Search of Old Peking*, pp. 94–5.
4. Millward, 'A Uyghur Muslim in Qianlong's Court', p. 447.
5. Eberhard, *A History of China*, p. 303.
6. Millward, *Beyond the Pass*, pp. 18–19.
7. Millward, *Beyond the Pass*, pp. 197 and 201.
8. Gernet, *A History of Chinese Civilization*, p. 494.
9. Eberhard, *A History of China*, p. 300.
10. Waley-Cohen, *Exile in Mid-Qing China*, p. 172.
11. Bellew, *History of Kashgharia*, p. 77.
12. Bellew, *History of Kashgharia*, p. 78. Figures are from Turki accounts, which are prone to exaggeration. Fairbank, *China: A New History*, has 22,000 in the Manchu relief force.
13. Millward, *Beyond the Pass*, pp. 216ff.
14. Shaw, *Visits to High Tartary, Yarkand and Kashgar*, pp. 43ff.

15. 'Report of a Mission to Yarkund', p. 10. Forsyth had led an earlier mission in 1870 but Yakub Beg was absent.
16. Shaw, *Visits to High Tartary, Yarkand and Kashgar*, pp. 354ff.
17. Skrine and Nightingale, *Macartney at Kashgar*, p. 18.
18. Skrine, *Chinese Central Asia*, p. 115.
19. Kim, 'The Muslim Rebellion and the Kashgar Emirate', p. 50.
20. Kim, 'The Muslim Rebellion and the Kashgar Emirate', pp. 44–5, quotes from the *Tarikh-i-amniyya*.
21. Kim, 'The Muslim Rebellion and the Kashgar Emirate', p. 42, from A. Diakov.
22. Stein, *Sand-Buried Ruins of Khotan*, p. 418.
23. Bellew, *History of Kashgharia*, p. 97.
24. Cable and French, *The Gobi Desert*, p. 216.
25. Kim, 'The Muslim Rebellion and the Kashgar Emirate', p. 101.
26. Henze, 'The Great Game in Kashgaria', p. 71.
27. *The Times*, 31 August 1871. Forsyth himself had the impression that the peasants of the kingdom of Kashgar were the least oppressed in Asia. 'Report of a Mission to Yarkund', p. 13.
28. Meyer and Brysac, *Tournament of Shadows*, p. 233, quoting Donald Rayfield, *The Dream of Lhasa* (London, 1976).
29. Kim, 'The Muslim Rebellion and the Kashgar Emirate', p. 148, quotes the *Tarikh-i-amniya* (Pantusov edition), p. 233.
30. Forsyth, 'Report of a Mission to Yarkund', p. 41.
31. Kim, 'The Muslim Rebellion and the Kashgar Emirate', p. 222.
32. Forsyth, 'Report of a Mission to Yarkund', p. 36.
33. Tien, *Chinese Military Theory*, pp. 102–3.
34. Kim, 'The Muslim Rebellion and the Kashgar Emirate', p. 248.
35. Tien, *Chinese Military Theory*, p. 104.
36. King, *History of the Hongkong and Shanghai Banking Corporation*, pp. 536–48.
37. Public Record Office (PRO), Kew, FO17, 825–7.
38. PRO FO17, 825–7.
39. Kim, 'The Muslim Rebellion and the Kashgar Emirate', pp. 268–9.
40. Kim, 'The Muslim Rebellion and the Kashgar Emirate', p. 255.
41. PRO FO17, 825–7.
42. Kim, 'The Muslim Rebellion and the Kashgar Emirate', p. 269.

CHAPTER 4: THE BABY GENERAL

1. Wu, *Turkistan Tumult*, pp. 43–4.
2. Millward, *Beyond the Pass*, p. 232, says the song may have been a Han invention to encourage emigration.
3. Hamada, 'La transmission du mouvement nationaliste au Turkestan oriental', p. 30, quoting *Xinjiang tuzhi*, 1923.
4. East Turkestan Information Centre, March 2000.

5. Gernet, *A History of Chinese Civilization*, p. 617.
6. Cable and French, *The Gobi Desert*, p. 218.
7. Forbes, *Warlords and Muslims*, p. 37.
8. Wu, *Turkistan Tumult*, pp. 48–9.
9. Wu, *Turkistan Tumult*, p. 52.
10. Or so it was claimed by the explorer Nicholas Roerich. See Forbes, *Warlords and Muslims*, p. 37.
11. Vasel, *My Russian Jailers in China*, pp. 97–9.
12. Wu, *Turkistan Tumult*, p. 59.
13. Forbes, *Warlords and Muslims*, p. 43.
14. Le Coq, *Buried Treasures of Chinese Turkestan*, p. 104.
15. The engineer was Petro, whose account is quoted by Forbes, *Warlords and Muslims*, pp. 57–8.
16. Cable and French, *The Gobi Desert*, pp. 237–8.
17. Cable and French, *The Gobi Desert*, pp. 241–2.
18. Cable and French, *The Gobi Desert*, p. 241.
19. Cable and French, *The Gobi Desert*, p. 244.
20. Drew's introduction to Wu, *Turkistan Tumult*, reprint 1984, p. vi.
21. Wu, *Turkistan Tumult*, pp. 81–2.
22. Wu, *Turkistan Tumult*, p. 104.
23. Wu, *Turkistan Tumult*, p. 139.
24. Wu, *Turkistan Tumult*, p. 142.
25. Wu, *Turkistan Tumult*, p. 149.
26. Wu, *Turkistan Tumult*, p. 157.
27. Vasel, *My Russian Jailers in China*, pp. 56–7.
28. Fleming, *News from Tartary*, p. 291.
29. Vasel, *My Russian Jailers in China*, pp. 102–3 and 115.
30. Wu, *Turkistan Tumult*, pp. 179–83.
31. Wu, *Turkistan Tumult*, pp. 237–8.
32. Skrine, *Chinese Central Asia*, p. 86.
33. Or perhaps in the reverse order: Forbes, *Warlords and Muslims*, p. 28, n. 90.
34. The petition was issued at Karakash on 26 February: Forbes, *Warlords and Muslims*, p. 75.
35. N. Fitzmaurice, quoted in Forbes, *Warlords and Muslims*, p. 83.
36. Forbes, *Warlords and Muslims*, p. 114.
37. Fleming, *News from Tartary*, p. 301.
38. Vasel, in an anonymous article, quoted by Forbes, *Warlords and Muslims*, p. 126, n. 187.
39. Teichman, *Journey to Turkistan*, pp. 149–50.
40. Forbes, *Warlords and Muslims*, pp. 146ff.
41. Chen, *The Sinkiang Story*, p. 212.
42. G. Turral, quoted in Forbes, *Warlords and Muslims*, p. 182.
43. Forbes, *Warlords and Muslims*, p. 237, describes him as 'truly the great survivor of [Xinjiang] politics'.

44. *Far Eastern Economic Review*, 14 September 1979, quoted by Forbes, *Warlords and Muslims*, p. 222.

45. *Independent on Sunday*, 19 April 1992.

46. Erkin Ekrem, of Hacettepe University, in an interview for Eastern Turkistan Information Network, 'Freedom and Independence', p. 8.

CHAPTER 5: RED DAWN

1. The story is told by Godfrey Lias, *Kazak Exodus*, pp. 149–50; he interviewed Kazakh refugees in Turkey.

2. Millward, 'A Uyghur Muslim in Qianlong's Court', p. 446.

3. Dikötter, *The Discourse of Race*, pp. 75ff.

4. Forbes, *Warlords and Muslims*, p. 200, quotes the *Xinjiang Daily*, 14 August 1947.

5. Interview with the young man's son, 10 April 2001.

6. *Xinjiang Daily*, 29 April 1952.

7. Becker, *Hungry Ghosts*, pp. 48–9.

8. Wu, *Turkistan Tumult*, p. 201.

9. Gladney, 'The Ethnogenesis of the Uighur', p. 20.

10. Proclamation of 20 November 1917 by the Council of People's Commissars in Petrograd, quoted in Soucek, *A History of Inner Asia*, p. 211.

11. Soucek, *A History of Inner Asia*, p. 213.

12. Soucek, *A History of Inner Asia*, p. 225.

13. Lee, 'The Turkic-Moslem Problem in Sinkiang', p. 107.

14. Examples quoted by Lee, 'The Turkic-Moslem Problem in Sinkiang', p. 345.

15. Becquelin, 'Xinjiang in the Nineties', p. 86.

16. Moseley, 'China's Fresh Approach to the National Minority Question', pp. 20–2.

17. The speech was given by Zhou on 4 August 1957 and written up by him for *Hongqi*, the theoretical journal of the Party's Central Committee. But the editor-in-chief objected to it and it was not published until 1979, during the period of liberalization, when it appeared in all the major newspapers around New Year's Day. Quotations are from the *Beijing Review*, Nos. 9 and 10, 3 and 10 March 1980.

18. The phrase is Moseley's.

19. Both comments were made to the author.

20. McMillen, 'Chinese Communist Power', p. 91.

21. Lee, 'The Turkic-Moslem Problem in Sinkiang', pp. 352–67.

22. Zhou Enlai, *Beijing Review*, No. 9, 3 March 1980.

23. Zhou Enlai, *Beijing Review*, No. 10, 10 March 1980.

24. Becker, *Hungry Ghosts*, p. 158.

25. Lee, 'The Turkic-Moslem Problem in Sinkiang,' p. 321, quotes from Tieh Cheng, *Nationalities Unity*, No. 1, 1960, pp. 13–14 (author's retranslation). Lee

comments that this example shows that the Communists considered the local people unreliable, and sought 'to dissolve them in a sea of Chinese settlers'.

26. From an internal Party document, 'The Anti-Separatism Struggle and Its Historical Lessons since the Liberation of Xinjiang', August 1993.
27. McMillen, 'Chinese Communist Power', pp. 190ff.
28. Conversation with the author.
29. McMillen, 'Chinese Communist Power', p. 298.
30. Alptekin, 'Eastern Turkestan after 32 Years of Exile', p. 150.
31. Gore, 'Journey to China's Far West', p. 331.
32. Xinhua news agency, quoted by Dillon, 'Xinjiang: Ethnicity, Separatism and Control', p. 19.

CHAPTER 6: RIOTS AND REPRISALS

1. The notice is signed 'Kashgar Prefecture Cultural Relics Office'.
2. Tourist leaflet, Kashgar, 2002.
3. East Turkistan Information Centre (ETIC), 'A Special Report', p. 10.
4. According to the Keston Institute, an Oxford-based body which monitors religious freedom in Communist states. *Frontier*, No. 3, 2002.
5. ETIC, 'A Special Report', p. 12.
6. Keston Institute, *Frontier*, No. 3, 2002.
7. Some sources give his birthplace as Kyrgyzstan.
8. China News Service, 6 December 2000.
9. Radio Free Asia, 5 June 2002.
10. Telegram of 5 July 1988, reported in *Voice of Eastern Turkestan*, Vol. 5, No. 19, autumn 1988.
11. ETIC, 'A Special Report', pp. 13–14.
12. Amnesty International, 'Gross Violations of Human Rights', p. 52.
13. Amnesty International, 'Gross Violations of Human Rights', p. 78.
14. *Xinjiang Daily*, 17 July 1998.
15. *Newsweek*, 1 October 1990.
16. Becker, *The Chinese*, pp. 370–4, explains the failings of the system.
17. The incident, which took place in 1980, was recounted by Alptekin, 'Eastern Turkestan after 32 Years of Exile', p. 153.
18. ETIC, 'A Special Report', p. 7.
19. ETIC, 'A Special Report', p. 7. The case occurred that year.
20. Amnesty International, 'Secret Violence', pp. 4–5, and 'Gross Violations of Human Rights', p. 64.
21. Dillon, 'Xinjiang: Ethnicity, Separatism and Control', p. 21.
22. Chinese Communist Party, 'The Anti-Separatism Struggle', p. 7.
23. Chinese Communist Party, 'The Anti-Separatism Struggle', p. 7.
24. Interview with the author, 13 April 2000.
25. *Der Spiegel*, 13 September 1993, cited in Dillon, 'Xinjiang: Ethnicity, Separatism and Control', p. 25.

26. *Xingdao*, cited by the East Turkistan Information Centre, June 1993, in Dillon, 'Xinjiang: Ethnicity, Separatism and Control', p. 26.
27. Amnesty International, 'Gross Violations of Human Rights', p. 19.
28. General Riza Bekin in a speech to the Muslim League, Saudi Arabia, 1999.
29. Amnesty International, 'Gross Violations of Human Rights', p. 19.
30. In a comment on the incident, Amnesty said that it could not verify its report but that it knew of no official inquiry into these alleged extra-judicial killings nor of any charges against police officers.
31. *Xinjiang Daily*, 28 June 1997.
32. Letter from Jack Churchward to the *New York Times*, 31 October 2000.
33. Becquelin, 'Xinjiang in the Nineties', p. 87.
34. According to a Uighur merchant in Turkey who passed the news to the Eastern Turkestan National Centre in Istanbul.
35. *Inside China Mainland*, 1 June 1999, and Internet.
36. *El Mundo*, 10 September 2000, quoting Reuter from Beijing.
37. A former Amnesty researcher interviewed by the author, January 2002.
38. Lee, 'The Turkic-Moslem Problem in Sinkiang', p. 237.
39. Amnesty International, 'Gross Violations of Human Rights', p. 44.
40. No dissident in Tibet or Inner Mongolia was executed after 1990, according to the ETIC, 21 November 2000.
41. Marie Holzman, speaking at a seminar, 'The Situation in East Turkestan after Half a Century of Chinese Communist Occupation', Brussels, 17 October 2001.
42. Wu, *Turkistan Tumult*, pp. 255–6 and 57.
43. Wu, *Turkistan Tumult*, p. 258.
44. G. Turral, quoted in Forbes, *Warlords and Muslims*, p. 182. See Chapter 4, n. 42.
45. Chinese Communist Party, 'The Anti-Separatism Struggle'.
46. The document was apparently leaked, translated into English by Uighur exiles and broadcast on the Internet in August 1999. Its authenticity has not been challenged.
47. 'Research into Contradictions among the People under New Conditions', Beijing, Central Compilation and Translation Press, June 2001.

CHAPTER 7: SKELETONS IN THE SAND

1. Letter to Fred Andrews, 31 January 1907, quoted by Mirsky, *Sir Aurel Stein*, p. 249.
2. The Five Peaks are the holy mountains of China. Millward, *Beyond the Pass*, quotes from Wu, *Lidai Xiyu shichao*, p. 140.
3. Lee, 'The Turkic-Moslem Problem in Sinkiang'.
4. Gore, 'Journey to China's Far West'.
5. Zhang, *Grass Soup*, pp. 11–15.
6. Zhang, *Grass Soup*, pp. 210 and 101.

7. Pasqualini, *Prisoner of Mao*, p. 53.
8. From Wu's autobiography, *Bitter Winds*, p. 45.
9. Wu, *Troublemaker*, p. 166.
10. Jasper Becker's *Hungry Ghosts* is a definitive history of the Chinese famine. It was he who told me about the cannibalism in Ningxia when I met him in Beijing in 1985, following my own visit to the area.
11. Pasqualini, *Prisoner of Mao*, p. 11 n., guesses that over 30 million people might have been undergoing 'reform'. He spent seven years in the gulag.
12. The issue of 6 October 1990, quoted in Laogai Research Foundation, 'The World Bank and Forced Labour in China', p. 5.
13. Interview with the author, November 1995.
14. Blackmore, *The Worst Desert on Earth*, pp. 131–4.
15. Becker, *The Chinese*, quoting *South China Morning Post*, 30 May 1998.
16. Lee, 'The Turkic-Moslem Problem in Sinkiang', p. 232.
17. 'Stirring giant that says China means business', *Financial Times*, 3 August 1999.
18. Laogai Research Foundation, 'The World Bank and Forced Labour in China', p. 3.
19. Wu, *Troublemaker*, p. 302, quotes the Xinjiang magazine *Northwestern Militia*.
20. *Financial Times*, 3 August 1999.
21. Laogai Research Foundation, 'The World Bank and Forced Labour in China', p. 5. According to Becquelin, 'Xinjiang in the Nineties', the Corps was actually unprofitable in that decade and depended on subventions from Beijing, but the fact was kept secret by the authorities.
22. World Bank press release, 20 December 1995.
23. Interview with the author, 1995.
24. Anti-Slavery International, 'Can Prisoners Be Subjected to Forced Labour?'

CHAPTER 8: THE GREAT LEAP WEST

1. The title of this chapter I owe to the Tibet Information Network, whose booklet 'China's Great Leap West', November 2000, is a thorough analysis of the development campaign.
2. Becquelin, 'Xinjiang in the Nineties', pp. 75–6. In 1997, he reports, the Corps contributed 14 per cent of the province's GDP and a fifth of its foreign trade. The following year it accounted for 40 per cent of its textile output, 24 per cent of its agriculture and 40 per cent of its cotton production.
3. In 1714, the Russian governor of Siberia had proposed annexing Khotan for its gold fields.
4. *People's Daily*, 14 November 2000.
5. Tibet Information Network, 'China's Great Leap West'. The areas covered were Xinjiang, Tibet, Ningxia, Chongqing, Sichuan, Guizhou, Yunnan, Shaanxi, Gansu and Qinghai.

6. Norins, *Gateway to Asia: Sinkiang*, p. 34.

7. Norins, *Gateway to Asia: Sinkiang*, p. 34.

8. Millward, *Beyond the Pass*, p. 81. There was trade *through* the province, of course: with silk, china, medicines and silver going west, and jade, hides, furs – and also medicines and silver – going east.

9. Millward, *Beyond the Pass*, pp. 241–3.

10. Wei Yuan, *Sheng wu ji*, quoted in Millward, *Beyond the Pass*, p. 244.

11. Hamada, 'La transmission du mouvement nationaliste au Turkestan oriental'.

12. Wu, *Turkistan Tumult*, pp. 261–7.

13. Forbes, *Warlords and Muslims*, pp. 147–8.

14. *Selected Works of Mao Tse-tung*, Vol. V, Foreign Languages Press, 1977, quoted in a 1999 report by Amnesty International on Xinjiang.

15. *China Reconstructs*, February 1976.

16. Moseley, 'China's Fresh Approach to the National Minority Question', pp. 22–4.

17. Xinjiang was promised economic zones, like the coastal provinces, and 'open cities', with Urumchi acting as 'the head of the dragon'. In June 1992 it was given the tax sharing system enjoyed by coastal provinces. Also, as a minority region, it was allowed to keep 80 per cent of local taxes, instead of only half. Becquelin, 'Xinjiang in the Nineties', p. 71.

18. Becquelin, 'Xinjiang in the Nineties', p. 67, notes that between 1991 and 1994 infrastructure investment jumped from 7.3 billion yuan to 16.5 billion yuan and the province's GDP doubled from 7.5 billion yuan to 15.5 billion yuan, according to the *Xinjiang Statistical Yearbook 1998*. Between 1990 and 1997, the acreage under cotton doubled, whereas the area sown for grain decreased slightly.

19. In 1998, 82 per cent of industrial assets were still publicly owned, and Xinjiang was twenty-eighth out of the thirty-one provinces in terms of foreign direct investment. Budget revenue almost tripled between 1990 and 1998 to 6.54 billion yuan, but expenditure also tripled to 14.6 billion yuan. Becquelin, 'Xinjiang in the Nineties', pp. 72–3, says Beijing's 'cheating' over tax reimbursements was described to him by a researcher at the Xinjiang Finance Institute.

20. An observation which I owe to a regular visitor.

21. Mackerras, 'Some Observations on Xinjiang in the 1990s', p. 120.

22. *Newsweek International*, 2 July 2000, quoted in Tibet Information Network, 'China's Great Leap West', p. 7.

23. Writing in the Party's theoretical journal *Qiu Shi* on 1 June 2000, quoted in Tibet Information Network, 'China's Great Leap West', p. 8.

24. Report of Party conference on 'stability', 3–6 May 1996, by Xinjiang Television, via the BBC Monitoring Service, quoted by Mackerras, 'Some Observations on Xinjiang in the 1990s', p. 112.

25. Eastern Turkestan Dispatch, October 1993, quoted by Dillon, 'Xinjiang: Ethnicity, Separatism and Control', p. 25.

26. For example Per Gahrton, President of the European Parliamentary delegation to the PRC, speaking in October 2001.

27. Xinhua news agency, 28 February 2001.

28. Tibet Information Network website, 13 March 2001.

29. Tibet Information Network website, 13 March 2001.

30. Gladney, *International Herald Tribune*, 21 August 2001.

31. Gurevich, *China and the Peoples of Central Asia*, quoted by East Turkistan Information Network UK, March 2000.

32. Forsyth, *A History of the Peoples of Siberia*, p. 197.

33. Forsyth, *A History of the Peoples of Siberia*, p. 34.

34. Forsyth, *A History of the Peoples of Siberia*, pp. 110–11.

35. Forsyth, *A History of the Peoples of Siberia*, p. 398 n., quoting K. Mihalisko, 'Report on the USSR, 1989'.

36. *Cheyenne Daily Leader*, 3 March 1870, quoted in Brown, *Bury My Heart at Wounded Knee*, p. 180.

37. For example, see Zhou Enlai's Qingdao speech of 4 August 1957.

38. Quotations taken from Wallace, *Jefferson and the Indians*, pp. 273 and 278.

39. Ziegler, 'The Great Western Campaign', p. 5.

40. About 3 per cent of total direct foreign investment in China.

41. Dillon, 'China Goes West'.

42. Letter from Enver Can, East Turkestan National Congress, 13 May 2002.

43. The 1964 census, for example, was not published.

44. Forbes, *Warlords and Muslims*, p. 234.

45. Becquelin, 'Xinjiang in the Nineties', p. 69.

46. The so-called Yuan Mu plan, revealed by a Hong Kong journal in 1992.

47. Dillon, 'Xinjiang: Ethnicity, Separatism and Control,' p. 25.

48. Becquelin, 'Xinjiang in the Nineties', p. 76,who found the advertisement.

49. Barber, *The Mummies of Urumchi*, p. 171.

50. Report on Xinjiang of the Political-Legal Commission of the CCP Central Committee to a meeting of the Politburo, 19 March 1996.

51. Becquelin, 'Xinjiang in the Nineties', pp. 81–2.

52. Becquelin, 'Xinjiang in the Nineties', p. 84.

53. *Xinjiang Daily*, 5 June 1998, quoted by Becquelin, 'Xinjiang in the Nineties', p. 83.

54. Nathan and Gilley, 'China's New Rulers'.

55. Tong Yufen, *Xinjiang Society and Economy*, No. 4, quoted in Rahman, 'Western Development Strategy'.

56. Interview with the author.

57. Interviews with the author, Kashgar and London.

58. Interview with the author.

59. *Xinjiang Daily*, 5 June 1957, quoted by Lee, 'The Turkic-Moslem Problem in Sinkiang', p. 300.

60. Becquelin, 'Xinjiang in the Nineties', p. 85, n. 94.

Notes

CHAPTER 9: THE DIASPORA

1. Forbes, *Warlords and Muslims*, appendix 1, p. 254.
2. According to A. Doak Barnett, quoted in Forbes, *Warlords and Muslims*, p. 224.
3. Lias, *Kazak Exodus*, pp. 191ff.
4. Dolkun Yasin, Uyghur Information Agency, 20 November 2000.
5. Interviews with the author.
6. Besson, 'Les Ouigours hors du Turkestan oriental', pp. 3–4.
7. Besson, 'Les Ouigours hors du Turkestan oriental', p. 4.
8. Besson, 'Les Ouigours hors du Turkestan oriental', pp. 5–6.
9. Speech to the East Turkestan National Congress, 18 October 2001. It is noteworthy that Erkin Alptekin is not himself an official of the ETNC, but general secretary of a body called the Unrepresented Nations and Peoples' Organization.
10. Cao Chang-qing, 'Fighting to free another Chinese province', *Taipei Times*, 10 November 1999.
11. Speech to seminar, 'The Situation in East Turkestan after Half a Century of Chinese Communist Occupation', 17 October 2001.
12. Timothy Cooper, 'ambassador-at-large' of the China Democracy Party, 17 October 2001.
13. Conversation with the author, October 2001.
14. Comment to the author, 21 March 2002.
15. The latter was Emma Bonino, a leftwinger and former student radical from Italy. The noted Chinese dissident Wei Jingsheng is also a member of the Party.
16. Minutes of the Politburo meeting of the Chinese Communist Party, 19 March 1996.
17. Rashid, *Jihad*, p. 202.
18. *Financial Times*, 17 June 1998.
19. East Turkistan Information Centre, 'A Special Report', p. 8.
20. *Uighur Affairs Survey*, Vol. 1, No. 1, September 2001.
21. East Turkistan Information Centre, 'A Special Report', p. 8.
22. *International Herald Tribune*, 2 October 2001.
23. Quoted by the East Turkistan Information Centre, March 1992.
24. *People's Daily*, November 1992.
25. Reuter, 11 October 1999.
26. *Taipei Times*, 10 November 1999.
27. Besson, 'Les Ouigours hors du Turkestan oriental', p. 5.
28. *Sunday Times*, 25 August 2002, reporting on litigation in the US. American servicemen had been killed in terrorist attacks on Saudi bases in November 1995 and June 1996.
29. *Financial Times*, 18 October 2001; *International Herald Tribune*, 12 November 2001.

30. In a speech to the seminar 'The Situation in East Turkestan after Half a Century of Chinese Communist Occupation', Brussels, 17 October 2001.
31. Amnesty International, 22 March 2002; *International Herald Tribune*, 12 November 2001; Agence France Presse, 8 January 2002.
32. *Financial Times*, 22 January 2002.
33. Philip T. Reeker of the US State Department, *New York Times*, 13 September 2002.
34. Enver Can, president of the East Turkestan National Congress, in an appeal to Colin Powell, US Secretary of State, 7 October 2002.
35. Professor Dru Gladney, University of Hawaii, in *New York Times*, 19 November 2000.
36. Comments made to the author.

CHAPTER 10: SEPARATE TABLES

1. Interview with the author, 10 and 11 April 2001.
2. Bellér-Hann, 'Temperamental Neighbours', pp. 67–8. Her further research into Han–Uighur integration was cut short by a local uprising. The local media said nine Uighurs had been killed by 'criminal activity'. Her informants told her this meant peasants had killed corrupt Uighur officials for collaborating with the Han.
3. Wu, *Turkistan Tumult*, p. 93.
4. An incident recounted to me by a regular visitor to Xinjiang.
5. Bellér-Hann, 'Temperamental Neighbours', p. 65.
6. Bellér-Hann, 'Temperamental Neighbours', p. 76.
7. Bellér-Hann, 'Temperamental Neighbours', p. 75.
8. East Turkestan Information Network UK, 'Chinese Policy', p. 8.
9. Bellér-Hann, 'Temperamental Neighbours', pp. 65–6.
10. Transnational Radical Party, quoting Xinhua news agency, in a question to the European Commission, 13 August 2002.
11. According to the East Turkestan Information Network UK, however, 60 per cent of Turki adults were still illiterate; 'Chinese Policy', p. 10.
12. Enver Tohti Bugda to the author, 13 April 2000.
13. Bellér-Hann, 'Temperamental Neighbours', p. 70.
14. Uighur folk music may be famous, but Dr Rachel Harris, a British musicologist from the University of London, reported attending a conference in China on the traditional music of Uighur Xinjiang and finding not a single Uighur delegate in the room. *China Review*, Autumn/Winter 2000, p. 42.
15. Bellér-Hann, 'Temperamental Neighbours', p. 62.
16. Bellér-Hann, 'Temperamental Neighbours', p. 68.
17. Bellér-Hann, 'Temperamental Neighbours', p. 60.
18. Hedin, *My Life as an Explorer*, p. 167.
19. Fleming, *News from Tartary*, p. 308.

Bibliography

Alptekin, Erkin, 'Eastern Turkestan after 32 Years of Exile', *Central Asia Survey*, Vol. 1, No. 4, April 1983

Amnesty International, 'People's Republic of China: Gross Violations of Human Rights in the Xinjiang Uighur Autonomous Region', 21 April 1999

—— 'Women in China Imprisoned and Abused for Dissent', 28 June 1995

—— 'People's Republic of China. Secret Violence: Human Rights Violations in Xinjiang', November 1992

Anderson, Robert S., 'The Attraction of Sand Dunes', *Nature*, Vol. 379, January 1996

Anti-Slavery International, 'Can Prisoners Be Subjected to Forced Labour?', 1995

Arlington, L.C., and Lewisohn, William, *In Search of Old Peking* (Beijing, Henri Vetch, 1935)

Barber, Elizabeth Wayland, *The Mummies of Urumchi* (London, Macmillan, 1999)

Baumer, Christoph, *Southern Silk Road* (Bangkok, Orchid Press, 2000)

Becker, Jasper, *Hungry Ghosts: China's Secret Famine* (London, John Murray, 1996)

—— *The Chinese* (London, John Murray, 2000)

Becquelin, Nicolas, 'Xinjiang in the Nineties', *China Journal*, No. 44, July 2000

Bellér-Hann, Ildikó, 'Script Changes in Xinjiang', in Shirin Akiner (ed.), *Cultural Change and Continuity in Central Asia* (London and New York, Kegan Paul, 1991)

—— 'Work and Gender among Uighur Villagers in Southern Xinjiang', *Cahiers d'études sur la Méditerranée orientale et le monde turco-iranien*, No. 25, January–June 1998

—— 'Temperamental Neighbours: Uighur-Han Relations in Xinjiang, Northwest China', in Günther Schlee (ed.), *Market, Culture and Society: Vol. 5, Imagined Differences: Hatred and the Construction of Identity* (Hamburg, Lit Verlag, 2002)

Bellew, H.W., *History of Kashgharia* (Calcutta, 1875)

Besson, Frédérique-Jeanne, 'Les Ouigours hors du Turkestan oriental: de l'exil à la formation d'une diaspora', from 'Les Ouigours au vingtième siècle', *Cahiers d'études sur la Méditerranée orientale et le monde turco-iranien*, No. 25, January–June 1998

Bibliography

Blackmore, Charles, *The Worst Desert on Earth* (London, John Murray, 1995)

Brown, Dee, *Bury My Heart at Wounded Knee* (London, Barrie & Jenkins, 1971)

Cable, Mildred, and French, Francesca, *The Gobi Desert* (London, Hodder & Stoughton, 1942)

Chen, Jack, *The Sinkiang Story* (New York, Macmillan, 1977)

Chinese Academy of Sciences, *Wondrous Taklimakan* (Beijing and New York, Science Press, 1993)

Chinese Communist Party, Central Committee, 'Report on Xinjiang of the Political-Legal Commission', delivered to a meeting of the Politburo, 19 March 1996

Chinese Communist Party, Research Group Council, 'The Anti-Separatism Struggle and Its Historical Lessons since the Liberation of Xinjiang', August 1993

Davies, Robert H., *Prisoner 13498: A True Story of Love, Drugs and Jail in Modern China* (Edinburgh and London, Mainstream Publishing, 2002)

Debaine-Francfort, Corinne *et al.*, 'Premiers résultats de l'expédition franco-chinoise de la Keriya' (Paris, Académie des Inscriptions & Belles-Lettres, 1993)

Dikötter, Frank, *The Discourse of Race in Modern China* (London, Hurst & Co., 1994)

Dillon, Michael, 'China Goes West: Laudable Development? Ethnic Provocation?' *The Analyst*, 6 December 2000

——— 'Xinjiang: Ethnicity, Separatism and Control in Chinese Central Asia', *Durham East Asian Papers*, No. 1, 1995

Dubs, Homer H., *A Roman City in Ancient China* (London, China Society, 1957)

East Turkestan Information Centre, 'A Special Report about the Human Rights Situation in Eastern Turkestan for the Period of January–May 2002', Munich, 1 May 2002

——— 'A Special Report on Violations of Human Rights of Uighurs in East Turkistan by the Chinese Authorities', Munich, 10 September 2000

Eastern Turkistan Information Network UK, 'Freedom and Independence for East Turkistan', London, January 2000

——— 'Chinese Policy, Human Rights Abuses and the Consequences', London, March 2000

Eberhard, Wolfram, *A History of China*, trans. E.W. Dickes (London, Routledge, 1950)

Fairbank, John King, *China, A New History* (Cambridge, Mass., Belknap Press, 1992)

Fitzgerald, C.P., *China, A Short Cultural History* (London, Cresset Press, 1950)

Fleming, Peter, *News from Tartary* (London, Jonathan Cape, 1936)

Foltz, Richard C., *Religions of the Silk Road* (London, Macmillan, 1999)

Forbes, Andrew D.W., *Warlords and Muslims in Chinese Central Asia: A Political History of Republican Sinkiang, 1911–1949* (Cambridge, Cambridge University Press, 1986)

Bibliography

Forsyth, James, *A History of the Peoples of Siberia: Russia's North Asia Colony, 1581–1990* (Cambridge, Cambridge University Press, 1992)

Forsyth, T.D., 'Report of a Mission to Yarkund in 1873 under the Command of Sir T.D. Forsyth, KCSI, CB, Bengal Civil Service, with Historical and Geographical Information Regarding the Possessions of the Ameer of Yarkund' (Calcutta, 1875)

Franck, Irene M., and Brownstone, David, *The Silk Road: A History* (New York and Oxford, Facts on File, 1986)

Gernet, Jacques, *A History of Chinese Civilization*, trans J.R.Foster and Charles Hartman (Cambridge, Cambridge University Press, 1996, second edition)

Gladney, Dru C., 'The Ethnogenesis of the Uighur', *Central Asian Survey*, Vol. 9, No. 1, 1990

Glob, P.V., *The Bog People* (London, Faber, 1969)

Golden, Peter B., 'The Karakhanids', in Denis Sinor (ed.), *The Cambridge History of Early Inner Asia* (Cambridge, Cambridge University Press, 1990)

Gore, Rick, 'Journey to China's Far West', *National Geographic*, Vol. 157, No. 3, March 1980

Hamada Masami, 'La transmission du mouvement nationaliste au Turkestan oriental,' *Central Asia Survey*, Vol. 9, No. 1, 1990

Han Kangxin, 'The Study of Ancient Human Skeletons from Xinjiang, China', Institute of Archaeology, Chinese Academy of Social Sciences, Beijing, from *Sino-Platonic Papers*, No. 51, November 1944

Hare, John, *The Lost Camels of Tartary* (New York and London, Little, Brown, 1998)

Hedin, Sven, *My Life as an Explorer* (London, Cassell, 1926)

Henze, Paul B., 'The Great Game in Kashgaria', *Central Asian Survey*, Vol. 8, No. 2, 1989

Hopkirk, Kathleen, *A Traveller's Companion to Central Asia* (London, John Murray, 1993)

Hopkirk, Peter, *Foreign Devils on the Silk Road* (London, John Murray, 1980)

—— *The Great Game* (London, John Murray, 1990)

Jarring, Gunnar,'The Toponym Takla-makan,' *Turkic Languages*, Vol. 1, 1997, pp. 227–40

Julien, S., 'Relation d'un voyage officiel dans le pays des Ouighours (de 981 à 983) par Wang-yen-te,' *Journal Asiatique*, No. 4, 1847

Kim Ho-dong, 'The Muslim Rebellion and the Kashgar Emirate in Chinese Central Asia, 1864–1877', Ph.D thesis, Harvard University, 1986

King, Frank, *History of the Hongkong and Shanghai Banking Corporation: Vol. 1, The Hongkong Bank in Late Imperial China, 1864–1902, 'On an Even Keel'* (Cambridge, Cambridge University Press, 1987)

Laogai Research Foundation, 'The World Bank and Forced Labour in China', 23 October 1995

Lattimore, Owen, *High Tartary* (New York, Little, Brown, 1930)

Bibliography

Le Coq, Albert von, *Buried Treasures of Chinese Turkestan* (London, Allen & Unwin, 1928)

Lee Fu-hsiang, 'The Turkic-Moslem Problem in Sinkiang: A Case Study of the Chinese Communists' Nationality Policy', Ph.D thesis, Rutgers University, 1973

Lias, Godfrey, *Kazak Exodus* (London, Evans Brothers, 1956)

Lonely Planet, *Central Asia* (London, Lonely Planet, 2000, second edition)

Macartney, Catherine, *An English Lady in Chinese Turkestan* (Hong Kong, Oxford University Press, 1985, reprint)

Mackerras, Colin, 'The Uighurs', in Denis Sinor (ed.), *The Cambridge History of Early Inner Asia* (Cambridge, Cambridge University Press, 1990)

—— 'Some Observations on Xinjiang in the 1990s', *World of the Silk Roads: Ancient and Modern*, Proceedings of the Second Conference of the Australasian Society for Inner Asian Studies, Macquarie University, 21–22 September 1996

Maillart, Ella, *Forbidden Journey* (London, Heinemann, 1937)

Mallory, J.P., and Mair, Victor H., *The Tarim Mummies* (London, Thames & Hudson, 2000)

McMillen, Donald H., 'Chinese Communist Power and Policy in Xinjiang, 1949–1977' (Boulder, Co., Westview/ Dawson Replica Editions, Folkestone, 1979)

Meyer, Karl, and Brysac, Shareen, *Tournament of Shadows: The Great Game and the Race for Empire in Asia* (London, Little, Brown, 2001)

Millward, James A., *Beyond the Pass: Economy, Ethnicity & Empire in Qing Central Asia, 1759–1864* (Berkeley, Calif., Stanford University Press, 1998)

—— 'A Uyghur Muslim in Qianlong's Court: The Meanings of the Fragrant Concubine', *Journal of Asian Studies*, Vol. 53, No. 2, May 1994

Mirsky, Jeannette, *Sir Aurel Stein, Archaeological Explorer* (Chicago and London, University of Chicago Press, 1998)

Moriyasu Takao, 'The Sha-chou [Dunhuang] Uighurs and the West Uighur Kingdom', *Acta Asiatica: Bulletin of the Institute of Eastern Culture*, No. 78

Moseley, George, 'China's Fresh Approach to the National Minority Question', *China Quarterly*, No. 24, October–December 1965

Nathan, Andrew, and Gilley, Bruce, 'China's New Rulers', *New York Review of Books*, 26 September and 10 October 2002

Needham, Joseph, *The Shorter Science & Civilisation in China: Vol. 1*, an abridgement, by Colin A. Ronan (Cambridge, Cambridge University Press, 1978)

Norins, Martin R., *Gateway to Asia: Sinkiang* (New York, John Day, 1944)

Pasqualini, Jean, known as 'Bao Ruo-wang' (with Rudolph Chelminski), *Prisoner of Mao* (Harmondsworth, Penguin Books, 1976)

Polo, Marco, *The Travels*, trans. Ronald Latham (Harmondsworth, Penguin, 1958)

Prejevalsky, Nikolai, *From Kulja, across the Tian Shan to Lob-Nor*, trans. Morgan (London, Sampson Low, 1879)

Bibliography

Rashid, Ahmed, *Jihad: The Rise of Militant Islam in Central Asia* (New Haven and London, Yale University Press, 2002)

Rahman, Anwar, 'Western Development Strategy: Chinese Exploitation in Eastern Turkestan', *Uighur Affairs Survey*, Vol. 1, No. 1, September 2001

Renfrew, Colin, *Archaeology and Language: The Puzzle of Indo-European Origins* (London, Jonathan Cape, 1987)

Rorex, Robert A., and Wen Fong (eds.), *Eighteen Songs of a Nomad Flute: The Story of Lady Wen-chi* (New York, Metropolitan Museum of Art, 1974)

Rudelson, Justin Jon, *Oasis Identities: Uyghur Nationalism Along China's Silk Road* (New York, Columbia University Press, 1997)

Sadri, Roostam, 'The Islamic Republic of Eastern Turkestan: A Commemorative Review', *Voice of Eastern Turkestan*, Vol. 3, No. 9, April 1986

Salisbury, Harrison, *The New Emperors: Mao and Deng, A Dual Biography* (London, HarperCollins, 1993)

Schafer, Edward H., 'The Camel in China Down to the Mongol Dynasty', *Sinologica*, Vol. 2, 1950

Shaw, Robert B., *Visits to High Tartary, Yarkand and Kashgar* (London, John Murray, 1871)

Sinor, Denis, 'The Establishment and Dissolution of the Türk Empire', in Denis Sinor (ed.), *The Cambridge History of Early Inner Asia* (Cambridge, Cambridge University Press, 1990)

Skrine, C.P., *Chinese Central Asia* (London, Methuen, 1926)

Skrine, C.P., and Nightingale, Pamela, *Macartney at Kashgar: New Light on British, Chinese and Russian Activities in Sinkiang, 1890–1918* (Hong Kong, Oxford University Press, 1987, reprint)

Smart, Ninian, *The World's Religions* (Cambridge, Cambridge University Press, 1998, second edition)

Soucek, Svat, *A History of Inner Asia* (Cambridge, Cambridge University Press, 2000)

Spence, Jonathan, *God's Chinese Son: The Taiping Heavenly Kingdom of Hong Xiuquan* (London, HarperCollins, 1996)

—— *Treason by the Book* (London, Allen Lane, 2001)

Stein, M.A., *Sand-Buried Ruins of Khotan* (London, Mushussu Press, 2000, facsimile of the 1903 edition by T. Fisher Unwin)

Talbot Rice, Tamara, *Ancient Arts of Central Asia* (London, Thames and Hudson, 1965)

Teichman, Eric, *Journey to Turkistan* (London, Hodder & Stoughton, 1937)

Tibet Information Network, 'China's Great Leap West', London, November 2000

Tien, Chen-ya, *Chinese Military Theory* (Ontario, Mosaic Press, 1992)

Tsering Dhundup, *Spang rgyan me tog* (Beijing, Nationalities Publishing House, 1999)

Vambéry, Arminius, *History of Bokhara* (London, H.S. King, 1873)

Vasel, Georg, *My Russian Jailers in China*, trans. Gerald Griffin (London, Hurst & Blackett, 1937)

Bibliography

Waley-Cohen, Joanna, *Exile in Mid-Qing China: Banishment to Xinjiang, 1758–1820* (New Haven and London, Yale University Press, 1991)

Wallace, Antony F.C., *Jefferson and the Indians* (Cambridge, Mass., Harvard University Press, 1999)

War Office, General Staff, *Animal Management* (London, HMSO, 1908)

Whitfield, Susan, *Life Along the Silk Road* (London, John Murray, 1999)

Wood, Frances, *Did Marco Polo Go to China?* (London, Secker & Warburg, 1995)

Wu, Aitchen K., *Turkistan Tumult* (Hong Kong, Oxford University Press, 1984, reprint)

Wu, Harry (with Carolyn Wakeman), *Bitter Winds: A Memoir of My Years in China's Gulag* (New York, John Wiley, 1994)

Wu, Harry (with George Vecsey), *Troublemaker: One Man's Crusade against China's Cruelty* (London, Chatto & Windus, 1996)

Xiao Shi, 'A Catastrophe in the Aqqikkol Basin', *China Focus*, 1 January 1995

Zhang Xianliang, *Grass Soup: One Man's Survival in the Chinese Gulag*, trans. Martha Avery (London, Minerva, 1995)

Ziegler, Dominic, 'The Great Western Campaign', *China Review*, Autumn/ Winter 2000

Index

Index

Makhtum Azam, 53n
Maksud Shah, 97
Manchukuo, 112, 224
Manchuria, 54, 64, 272
Manchus
    empire: disintegration, 63–5, 68
    exiled to west, 185
    expansionism, 54–6, 60–1
    garrison: weakness (1960s), 75
    Han Chinese and, 61, 63
    master race, self-image, 61
    Muslims, treatment, 61–2
    as occupiers, 61–3, 70
    western empire, 130, 131
Mani (prophet), 45–6
Manichaeism, 45–6
Mansur, Khan, 53
Mao Zedong, 32, 59
    and chauvinism, 131, 136, 139,
        148
    collectivization, 134–5
    constructive criticism campaign,
        143–4
    death, 157
    and ethnic minorities, 138, 141–3
    and ETR, 119, 122–3
    Great Leap Forward (1958), 145–7,
        191–2, 200, 211, 227
    intellectuals, suspicion of, 189
    labour camps, 187
    social engineering, 268
    and Xinjiang, 132, 148–9, 204
    Xinjiang Production and
        Construction Corps, 135
Mao Zemin, 118
Maralbashi, 4
    cotton-packing plant, 247, 248
    redevelopment, 248–9
    segregation in, 247–8
Marco Polo, 12
marriage: inter-racial, 256, 258–9
Marx, Karl, 141, 272
Masud Sabri, 123
Mazartagh: Tibetans seize (790), 39

Mehmet Emin Bughra, Emir of
    Khotan, 114–15, 116, 123,
    223–5, 229
Mencius, 203
merchants: settle in west, 185–6
Merket village, 18, 193
meshrep, 168, 169
Ming dynasty, 52, 54
Mingdi, Emperor, 35
Miran, 12
    concentration camp, 181, 182–4,
        194
    Tibetan fort, 39
Mirza Hydar, 52–3
Mogao caves: Buddhist remains, 37
Mongolia, 40
Mongols, 40, 268
    assimilation into China, 130
    Chinese invasion, 49, 50–1
    Cultural Revolution, 151
    in ETR, 121
    literacy, 51
    prefecture, 139
    religious tolerance, 51
Mount Bogda, 9
Mount Karlik, 9
Mughol (descendant of Japhet), 40
Muhammad, Prophet, 42, 52
Muhammad Khan, 52
Muhammad Zahir, Shah of
    Afghanistan, 115
mullahs: re-education camps, 188
mummies: excavation, 24–6, 28, 181
Munich: Uighur exiles, 230
music: Uighur, 263–4
Muslims
    birth control, compulsory, 159–62
    hepatitis, 160
    insulting names for, forbidden, 62,
        136
    Manchu treatment, 61–2
    religious observance, 155–9
    rumoured extermination (1862),
        74

Index

Index

Index